Critical Political Studies
Edited by Jules Townshend

Analysing Public Policy

WITHDRAWN

Analysing Public Policy

Peter John

PINTER

London and New York

Pinter

a Cassell imprint

Wellington House, 125 Strand, London WC2R 0BB, England
370 Lexington Avenue, New York, NY 10017-6550
First published in Great Britain 1998

Reprinted 1999

British Library Cataloguing in Publication Data
A catalogue record for this book is available from the British Library.
ISBN 1-85567-586-2 (hardback)
1-85567-587-0 (paperback)

Library of Congress Cataloging-in-Publication Data
John, Peter, 1960–
    Analysing public policy/Peter John.
        p.   cm. — (Critical political studies)
    Includes bibliographical references and indexes.
    ISBN 0-7185-2294-X (hc). — ISBN 0-7185-2327-X (pbk.)
    1. Policy sciences.   I. Title.   II. Series
H97.J65 1998
320'.6—DC21
                                                            97-45752
                                                            CIP

Typeset by York House Typographic Ltd

Printed and bound in Great Britain by
Creative Print and Design (Wales), Ebbw Vale

Contents

Acknowledgements

I am very grateful to the series editor, Jules Townshend, and commissioning editors, Nicola Viinkka and her successor, Petra Recter, for their encouragement and support during the writing period. I am also grateful to Alan Harding for suggesting my name as an author in the series.

Chris Bailey, Alistair Cole, Keith Dowding, Dilys Hill, Bryan Jones, Helen Margetts, David Owen and Hugh Ward took the trouble to read and comment on some or all of the draft chapters. The book has improved markedly as a result.

I would like to thank the students in my public policy classes who responded both positively and sceptically to the ideas presented in the book. The best students attended my 'Policy-Making in British Government' course in 1993/94, which I taught at Keele University. This class showed me that teaching policy can be fun.

Finally, I would like to acknowledge my debt to Elizabeth Meehan, who introduced me to the study of public policy while I was an undergraduate at the University of Bath.

1

The Study of Public Policy

The Challenge of the Policy-orientated Approach

The study of politics is not just about elections, parties and the behaviour of governments, it concerns the whole process of public decision-making. In democratic politics, a multitude of public actions affect what governments do, and a host of public- and private-sector bodies seek to shape public decisions, much of which passes unnoticed by the media and the general public. Yet public policies are probably more salient for ordinary citizens than the effervescence of much political debate. While highly profiled subjects, such as stories of political corruption, the personalities of political leaders and changes in opinion polls, are important aspects of contemporary political life and deserve attention, citizens are more affected by such prosaic matters as the quality of education in schools, the performance of the economy and the efficiency of the public healthcare system. In the end, while elections and the activity of political leaders have meaning and significance in their own right, their importance rests on what they achieve for the public.

Research on policy seeks to understand how the machinery of the state and political actors interacts to produce public actions. The subject focuses on the decisions that create the outputs of a political system, such as transport policies, the management of a public health service, the administration of a system of schooling and the organization of a defence force. No less important is how these decisions produce changes outside the formal political system, like the effective use of transport, rising levels of health, good educational performance and an effective defence capacity – what are sometimes called policy outcomes. The main tasks of the subject are to explain how policy-making works and to explore the variety and complexity of the decision-making processes.

Public policy seeks to explain the operation of the political system as a whole. This is its main contribution to political science. The policy-orientated approach looks at public decision-making from the viewpoint of what comes out of the political process. Each element to policy-making is considered to cause a particular output and outcome. The political system is studied from the frame of reference of a policy sector, such as agriculture or energy, and from the differences between these activities. Each sector has all of the elements of the political system: interest-group representatives, bureaucrats, elected politicians and the general public, who operate within a complex institutional structure of voting systems, legislatures, courts, bureaucracies and public agencies. Thus one of the purposes of the policy-orientated approach is to sharpen up the analysis of politics by examining the links between decision-makers as they negotiate and seek influence in the governmental system.

Because of the breadth and depth of policy studies, the subject has the capability to transform both the topics and the methods of political science. The focus is less on discrete fields of political activity but more on the concrete actions that link them. Because public policy crosscuts many aspects of politics, the task of explaining decision-making requires theories which can connect such diverse activities. The same theory needs to cope with such contrasting activities as the salience of public opinion, the operation of legislatures and the detailed interpretation of public legislation. To capture the scope of the subject and the varying types of activity, analysts of public policy often adopt a more open and multidisciplinary approach to their subject than other political scientists. To theorize about policy-making, writers use insights from sociology, the study of organizations, management sciences, economics and psychology as well as using specialist knowledge from their policy sector, whether it is housing studies, criminology or educational research. Policy-orientated research uses methods that are attune to the highly variable relationships that occur within the decision-making process. For example, network analysis, the study of links between individuals and organizations (see Chapter 4), is uniquely placed to understand the complexity of policy-making. While there are many difficulties that arise from studying the complex and diffuse policy-making relationships, the potential is for a richer account of political life than that offered by more discrete research topics.

The Origins of the Sub-discipline

The neglect of policy in political science was partly due to the domination of the North American behaviouralist tradition. US and many European scholars examined readily observable phenomena, such as voting in legislatures and party strategies to win elections, usually the 'inputs' of the political system. With their concern to study just measurable behaviour, researchers isolated the sociological and cultural determinants of voting behaviour, party systems and the organization of political parties, and considered that these phenomena reflect the political traditions of each country, such as the experience of war or the progress of economic modernization. Behaviouralists sought to understand the particular constellations of social structures that produce the form of voting, interest-group interaction or type of party system under study. The political system was usually looked at as part of a chain of events leading from social change to political behaviour. With some notable exceptions (e.g. Lasswell 1951), policy appeared as a minor event occurring at the end of the process.

The belief that the discipline of political science left out the most significant aspects of public life created modern policy studies. It is true that the study of administration had been always been important. In the UK, for example, scholars had long examined the structure of the civil service and the means whereby parliament sought to scrutinize the executive (e.g. Chester and Bowring 1962; Walkland 1968). There was much research into the organization of local government (e.g. Robson 1948). In the USA too, there has been a long and productive tradition of studying public administration, particularly after the reform movement of the early years of the twentieth century proposed neutral administrative structures to overcome the excesses of party politics. Yet these studies tended to concentrate on the procedures of administration rather than on the practice of policy-making in sectors like agriculture or health. Traditional institutionalists investigated the detail of administrative decisions, but they were more concerned with the search for political accountability and the efficiency of the procedures of government than in explaining decision-making. Writers rarely mentioned the word 'policy'. There emerged a need for a sub-discipline to comprehend the totality of public decision-making and to investigate the complex links between inchoate public demands and the detailed implementation of policy choices.

It is no coincidence that the study of public policy emerged at the same time as most Western states expanded the scope of their responsibilities. While the twentieth century has seen a rapid expansion in the range of activities undertaken by governments and an acceleration of the proportion of national income taken up by taxes and government expenditure, the 1960s was the period when the rate of growth accelerated. In the late nineteenth century the state had taken responsibility for many 'public goods', such as sanitation and public health and, after the Second World War, had increased its reach to economic policy and to combating unemployment. But it was in the 1960s that public action extended to anti-poverty programmes, efforts to combat racial discrimination, policies to improve public healthcare and many other measures. The USA started to emulate Western European states by initiating some far-reaching social policies. Lyndon Johnson, after he was elected president in 1964, introduced the 'Great Society' programmes and the 'War on Poverty' as a drive toward a more socially interventionist state. Other Western states also increased public expenditure and strove to ameliorate public problems, such as urban deprivation and racial disadvantage.

For political scientists, fields of politics which hitherto had been understudied became more important. There was a plethora of new agencies and procedures administering the programmes, and thus novel processes and problems to study. Moreover, US electoral, presidential and legislative politics became, for a time, dominated by social policy issues. Even though the interest in the 'Great Society' programmes waned after the election of President Nixon in 1968, the association of politics with policy grew in the 1970s and 1980s. Now no aspect of politics occurs without the participation of policy analysts, academics, 'think-tanks' and consultants, all offering their preferred solutions to public problems.

The 1960s idea that public action could solve perennial social problems reflected the optimism and confidence of the decade. Just as US governments could put men in space, so they thought they could eliminate social problems. The optimism affected the social sciences and encouraged scholars to believe that research could contribute to success of public action. Part of the stimulus for the policy-orientated approach was the belief that all of the disciplines of the social sciences could be harnessed for the grand project of revolutionizing public intervention. The use of the social sciences in policy was encouraged by governments who were eager to deploy the insights of research when designing responses to public problems. As a result, in the USA, and later in Europe, policy-orientated research institutes sprang up and the employment of political scientists in government became fashionable. Research councils and professional associations sponsored conferences and publications on policy matters (Parsons 1995: 28). A new sub-discipline of public policy was announced.

If the optimism stimulated the involvement of political scientists in public policy studies, it was the perceived failure of many 1960s' programmes that fostered a more critical and analytical approach. The conventional wisdom of the policies of the 1960s was that, in spite of all the effort and money that went into them, they did not achieve their objectives. The programmes were even supposed to have adverse effects, often the opposite of their original intentions (Moynihan 1969). In response, public-policy researchers wanted to know why the policies failed, and to do that they had to devise models and theories of the policy process. Even though some of the self-confidence of policy studies waned in the 1970s and 1980s, interest in the subject grew largely because it is so hard to solve public problems.

Reflecting the importance of the sub-discipline, mainstream political science research itself has become more policy-orientated. For example, the study of elections has established that the public vote consistently on policy matters rather than just according to party affiliations and class loyalties (Heath *et al.* 1985). The policy role of parliament is examined in several studies (e.g. Judge 1990). The US Congress is the subject of many efforts to investigate its policy-making machinery and to understand the way it processes issues (see Chapter 3). The European Union, a topic that was formerly the purview of lawyers and institutionalists, is now becoming the target of the policy-orientated approach (Richardson 1996). The union rests on a highly sectorized and fragmented decision-making process which modern public-policy analysis is well placed to analyse. The interest in policy has grown in terms of new journals (e.g. the *European Journal of Public Policy*), the numbers of books with the word 'policy' in the title and textbooks with the mandatory chapter on the topic.

The Importance of Policy Sectors

The concept of policy weakens some of the certainties in the discipline of political science. The variability of policy-making challenges the unitary character of modern states, an assumption upon which much of political science rests, particularly in Europe with its strong national governing structures. Once the notion of a singular political system is abandoned, the variety of the political processes that surrounds each policy area can be observed in all its complexity. The issues, the pattern of bargains and structures of opportunities and constraints in each policy sector create a particular type of politics that may or may not resemble that suggested by national political traditions and constitutional norms. Thus the relative influence of politicians, bureaucrats and interest-group representatives differs according to whether the sector is say health, education or transport. Each policy sector varies by the extent actors cooperate to achieve their goals. The policy sectors are also different in the way decision-makers can achieve outcomes and whether success or failure of a policy feeds back into the rest of the political world. The policy-orientated approach shows that the practice of decision-making, the balance of power, the type of outputs, the likelihood of policy success and who benefits are often a function of the type of activity public action seeks to regulate. For example, health policy produces a certain type of relationship between professionals and politicians because of the specialized and technical nature of healthcare.

Policy sectors vary according to the instruments and resources available to decision-makers. Instruments can be either legal, that is laws that compel people and organizations to do things; financial, allocating funds to encourage or penalize organizations and people; organizational, by applying of bureaucratic power to solve problems; or personal, by persuading others to achieve goals. Tools to manage the environment are very different to those used for agriculture, for example. The environment is difficult to legislate for because it is harder to influence outcomes. Because of the size of the problem, the environment involves many more organizations and participants. There are contrasting local, national and supranational dimensions to environmental problems. In contrast, agriculture involves a smaller number of interest-group representatives, mainly farmers and representatives from the agricultural industry (although other groups, such as environmentalists and health professionals, are becoming more important in recent years). It is relatively easy to apply financial instruments to achieve limited policy goals, such as encouraging the cultivation of more land and protecting rural incomes (though farming problems are now less easy to solve with crises of overproduction, poor hygiene and the growing importance of the environment).

The breakthrough in the study of public policy was Theodore Lowi's 1964 and 1972 articles that distinguish between different types of policy-making. Lowi's schema is the idea in policy studies that has had the greatest effect on political science (Sabatier 1991: 149). Lowi distinguishes between distributive politics of subsidies and tariffs, which is characterized by logrolling (interest groups trading-off costs and benefits with each other) and a passive form of executive leadership; the constituency politics of boundary changes and electoral organization; regulatory politics, such as the control of competition; and redistributive politics, which is more ideological in character, producing policies like progressive income taxes. The type of activity affects how group and branches of government interact thus creating the four 'sub-systems'. Lowi's formulation challenges writers who argue that US policy-making changed with the evolution of its political system, such as from the unregulated politics before the 1930s to the federal intervention of the New Deal. Lowi argues that several types of politics, all involving different relationships between the different levels of government, co-exist at the same time.

Several writers doubt the distinctions Lowi proposes and detect a more messy reality. There is no empirical verification of his classification, partly because no one can agree on what counts as the various types of policy-making and the typology is difficult to apply (Heidenheimer 1985). Some writers believe Lowi's scheme better describes types of democratic system and forms of elite behaviour rather than explaining variation according to policy sector (Peters *et al.* 1977). Peters *et al.* find that consociational and depoliticized democracies (regimes characterized by long-term coalition politics) produce regulative and redistributive policies. More fragmented systems create distributive policies. Countries with homogenous political cultures and competitive elites, such as those with two-party systems, create regulatory policies. Lowi's scheme seems better able to describe differences across countries rather than within them.

However, it is not the exact application of Lowi's typology that is important but the idea that each policy sector should be studied in its own right and that it has a unique politics of its own. The change today is that instead of books about education, crime and the economy just being written by educationalists, criminologists and economists there are studies of the politics of education, crime and managing the economy. It is the characteristics of decision-making and the role of political action that is important rather than just the technical issues of, for example, educational performance, detecting crime and predicting economic growth. Each sector has a unique combination of technological attributes; problems to be solved; demands of managing the policy; and combinations of producer and consumer interest groups that conflict or cooperate to achieve common or group-based goals. There is also variation caused by the history of past decisions and programmes that affect current policy choices.

Instead of elaborate typologies, the Lowi schema has stimulated the policy subsystem approach where group interactions and the formation of coalitions are studied in each sector (see Chapter 4). Though always important, the concept of policy subsystems has now become central in the study of public policy in the USA. Instead of institutions, like the Presidency and the Congress, acting as one block, there are groups of decision-makers in each policy sector drawn from congressional committees, the executive, interest groups, analysts and political consultants.

The way in which decision-making differs according to policy sector can be summed up by the aphorism 'policy determines politics' instead of the more intuitive 'politics determines policy' (Lowi 1972). Party competition and constitutional traditions are not the only factors that affect policy, as relationships within the policy sector influence the type and degree of party competition and the extent to which bureaucrats or ministers have power. The direction of causation between policy and politics is thus two-way.

The Search for Causal Mechanisms

After the pronouncement of the importance of outputs at the end of the 1960s, analyses of policy multiplied. Researchers hoped that public policy would take off as an integrated study of politics by applying all the disciplines of the social sciences to explain public action and recommending improvements to the decision-making process. But, in spite of the expansion of the subject, no unified paradigm has emerged to organize research. Instead, there are now many approaches and a range of research methodologies. Trends and approaches often fall in and then out of favour with an endless succession of concepts and labels. A particular approach becomes the currency of the subject, only to be replaced by a new one a few years later.

The lack of unity to the study of public policy reflects the nature of the research topic. Public policy is hard to research as it is a composite of different processes that crosscut most branches of government and involve many decision-makers. The task of investigating decision-making in policy sectors is also highly complex. There are many types of policies. The same policy differs according to the different branches and levels of government where it is being decided. There are subsets of issues within policies and complex areas where policy fields intersect. Moreover, it is hard to explain the differences between policy outputs and outcomes.

Because of the difficulty of doing policy-orientated research, many studies are descriptive. It is often enough just to map all the relationships and the roles of the different organizations and to offer insights about the nature of, for example, health policy-making as opposed to urban policy. Much policy-orientated work, especially in Europe, tells the story of policy-making in particular sectors, such as health (e.g. Ham 1992) or housing (Malpass and Murie 1994). Researchers of policy tend to gain insights from secondary documents and interviews without using an explicit theoretical framework, and they often achieve this task admirably. The caution of much research is understandable, and is an indication of the difficulty of the overall project. There is the risk that complex theorizing could just turn into elaborate redescriptions of the intricacies of decision-making. Because human behaviour is multicausal and phenomena do not fall into neat categories, it is a hard task to specify the relationships between decision-makers and to acknowledge the complexity while at the same time offering parsimonious explanations. As Hill (1997: 2) writes in a despairing review of the state of the sub-discipline, 'such scepticism fosters uncertainty about whether ... phenomena are amenable to generalised explanation'.

To make sense of a complex and changeable world, metaphors have become an important tool in the study of public policy. Examples include seeing policy as a series of medical problems and solutions, such as disease, prevention and treatment (Hogwood and Peters 1985) or using the idea of dinosaurs and their habitat to explain policy reversals in economic policy (Hood 1994). Though often useful, metaphors sometimes disguise explanation and hide the complexity of the relationships rather than illuminate them. Researchers also use a bewildering array of labels to try to explain

policy-making that also tend to be descriptive rather than explanatory. Examples of technical terms which perhaps promise more than
they can deliver are issue networks, guidance mechanisms, policy
cycle, front-end policy-making, epistemic community, feedback, policy style and policy-action framework.

Further, much of public policy is concerned with evaluating
decision-making in governments and public bureaucracies. There is
a strong normative element to the study of public policy that
intertwines and often confuses the aim of explanation. The importance of policy analysis, the investigation of techniques that
explicitly aim to improve decision-making, is tribute to the mission of
public policy studies (see Chapter 2). The funding of much policy
research by practitioner bodies, such as government departments,
charities and local authorities, can also limit the search for causal
mechanisms. Effective policy analysis, however, needs to know how
policy works. If reformers do not understand causation in public
policy, they cannot know if their proposals for changes in decision-
making procedures will work or not. Often the inappropriateness of
new methods for making policy is due to the failure to understand
the context within which new decision-making procedures are
recommended to function.

The expansion of policy-orientated research has also compartmentalized the subject within political science, which is ironic given
the ambitious aims of the sub-discipline and the expansion of policy
research in mainstream political science. By conceiving a sphere of
action supposedly at the end of the decision-making process, and by
making it the province of public policy, the subject has tended to
neglect the central debates within political science and to develop a
language of its own. Public policy researchers have focused too much
on implementation and policy analysis as discrete forms of activity
(see Chapter 2), and researchers less often seek to explain precisely
the operation of the complex matrix of political relationships and to
understand the interactions and conflict within policy networks.
Well developed theories of political action and rigorous empirical
tests should be at the centre of policy studies. In political science, the
methodologically sophisticated academic work that has characterized the study of elections, electoral systems and party competition,
needs to be the normal form of analysis in the study of public policy.
For example, there is pioneering work comparing US state and
congressional policies, investigating policy outputs and in testing the
extent of bureaucratic power (e.g. Wood 1988; Wood and Waterman

1993). The precision of the theory and the sophistication of the methods need to be extended to the rest of policy studies.

There are signs that research in public policy is changing. There is some excellent research in the USA on ideas, agendas, policy analysis and coalition-formation (see Chapters 7 and 8). For example, Sabatier and Jenkins-Smith (1993) combine micro-analysis, complexity, interests and ideas in what they term as the policy advocacy coalition (PAC) framework. PACs are alliances of interests cemented by common forms of policy analysis and ideas within a policy sector. The framework tries to answer the big questions about policy change and stability as well those about policy variation (see Chapter 8). Their work, though not without its problems, echoes the theme of this book that the insights of political science need to be brought more to the centre of the study of policy.

Although the aim of explanation is laudable, it is often difficult to achieve in practice. The empirical world rarely arranges itself in a manner suitable for the testing of hypotheses. It is almost impossible to find experimental conditions to uncover the exact relationships between political variables, though there are some solutions to this problem. The other problem is that association and correlation between two variables are easy to find. They appear explanatory, but they can in fact be spurious because they are caused by some other factor not accounted for or impossible to measure. Many important causal processes are hard to observe because of the imperfection of research instruments. For example, much interview-based research only confirms the views of the participants and records how they justified the decisions in which they participated. Many social scientists believe the research process itself is 'theory-dependent' because researchers find the facts they are looking for. Investigators design research which embodies assumptions about the world and thus produces results with that frame of reference. Moreover, the subjects of research, individuals, are conscious and to an extent autonomous, so they can reinterpret and reimagine what might appear to be set patterns of behaviour. Political actors are capable of learning from events, which means it is very hard to replicate a piece of research. The contingency of the empirical world suggests that particularity and trendless variation are the norms, rather than regularity assumed in social science theory. Making generalizations is thus fraught with danger.

The difficulty of the research process does not mean social scientists should always fall back on description. The researcher has to make sense of complex chains of causation, appraise the other possible worlds of counterfactuals (Hawthorn 1991), weigh up the importance of pieces of information, and revise explanations in the light of new discoveries. Political scientists should not despair that they do not have all the conditions and methods of natural scientists. They can still theorize and test hypotheses providing they are careful about their research design and infer correctly from the results. By avoiding looking for explanations of a law-like nature, political scientists instead can look for mechanisms which show the links in a causal model: 'By concentrating on mechanisms, one captures the dynamic aspect of scientific explanation: the urge to produce explanations of ever finer grain' (Elster 1989: 7).

The Approach of the Book

Public-policy scholars need to be explicit about the aims of their research. This book suggests there are two main sets of phenomena students of public policy generally seek to explain: policy variation and policy change, each with two aspects. There are other questions public policy asks, such as which policy is more effective, what is the cause of policy success and failure and how democratic and accountable is public policy-making. However, the four questions here are the most basic and fundamental ones. Satisfactory answers to these can help answer the others.

Policy variation

Differences between policy sectors

Given the importance of spheres of activity, such as education, health or defence, it is essential to understand how and why policy-making differs between sectors. Is power concentrated in the hands of a few decision-makers or is it dispersed? Is it the case that some sectors are dominated by professional groups and trades unions whereas others have more input from elected politicians and lobbyists representing consumers? The implication is that policy in one sector may be driven by a few powerful interest groups whereas in another there may be more people involved and more innovation and change. The other question concerns the relative impact of the nature of the activity on the decision-making process. It may be the case that, irrespective of political culture and institutional history, policy-making takes the same form in a particular sector.

Differences between countries

Just as policy-making can be compared between sectors, so there are similarities and differences across countries. Often the way a sector is governed in two different nation-states is quite distinct. Education, for example, is administered centrally in France and less so, at least in the past, in the UK. The difference reflects particular state traditions and the principles underlying political systems, say between a centralized *étatist* or statist tradition in France and a parliamentary tradition in the UK. In the former case, decisions are made by central ministries and national groups partly in a 'top-down' approach; in the latter decisions were made by locally elected local authorities with the department of education taking a supervisory role. It can be argued that the pattern of policy-making depends on important political events occurring perhaps many centuries before. For example, the evolution of the state after the French Revolution created a particularly strong form of public intervention in France. In contrast, the gradual adaption of the British constitution from monarchy to constitutional monarchy to parliamentary democracy created an apparent practice of limited government and a balanced constitution. The policy researcher needs to know how important are these factors compared to contemporary demands, and to probe beyond the insights of the conventional wisdoms. The institutionalist and 'new' institutionalist approaches discussed in Chapter 3 explore the comparative dimension further.

Even if a researcher only investigates one country, it is important to know what is unique or generalizable about national policy-making so as not to assume uncritically the particular models of the world under investigation. Otherwise, it is easy to be ethnocentric and to make generalizations based on one case only. This charge is easy to levy against much US literature on public policy that often assumes that fragmented democratic government is the norm in all political systems.

Policy change

Policy stability

Policy-making in sectors like agriculture or foreign policy often changes relatively slowly. The same policy-makers dominate decision-making for long periods of time, whether it is the bureaucrats in a ministry or the representatives of powerful producer interest groups, such as doctors in health policy. Policy can thus reflect the long-term interests of an established elite. Public-policy theorists need to ask why is policy-making stable? Rather than accept a particular style of decision-making as the natural order of things, researchers need to find out what keeps certain decision-makers influential and why do participants in the policy-making process agree on what are the policy problems and the means for their solution?

Policy change

The obverse of policy stability is policy change. Why do policies emerge? Why does a stable period of decision-making sometimes give way to times of flux and unpredictability? For example, why is it the case that in one decade public pollution control hardly existed, but in the following one it became a major component of public policy (Sabatier and Jenkins-Smith 1993: 13)? Do the origins of change lie in human agency or socio-economic forces? Do political institutions allow policy-makers to adapt and to innovate?

To explain variation and change, social science seeks to understand the influence and interaction of social, economic and political processes, and the study of public policy explores the confluence of factors that shape public decision-making. This book argues that the way to explain how political systems make and implement policy is to specify the interests, resources, interrelationships, constraints and norms of the actors under study. Each policy space will have different constellations of these actors, and their relationships can change or be static over time.

To understand these relationships and thus causality in public policy, researchers have developed ways of understanding the world and guides to explaining action. Researchers can choose between three main types of explanation. The first is a *framework* or an *account* of behaviour which is a set of labels or a learning device that helps researchers understand the policy process. In this enterprise the task of social science is to invent a conceptual scheme or to create signposts, mainly to assist the investigator. Frameworks or accounts are simplifications of the complex real world which can illuminate what is happening. Although frameworks have their use, researchers need to be aware than they often tend to be descriptive rather than explanatory. The second, more parsimonious type of explanation is a *model* which explores sets of relationships under particular conditions, say between economic policy and voting behaviour (see Chapter 6). Though a model is an important tool for framing research problems, it does not adequately satisfy the aim of explanation, as a model is partial and only applies in limited sets of circumstances. Instead, the third and desired form of explanation is a *theory* which gives a generalized explanation of political behaviour. A theory contains assumptions about the individual, accounts of human action and explanations of the role of social and political structures, and it generates models of behaviour, and thus hypotheses, which can be tested.

In social science there are disagreements about what are the main causes of behaviour, and political science is no exception. Researchers usually locate their investigations within one type of understanding or theory. Although they may complement each other, sometimes they conflict. The argument of the central chapters of the book is that there are broadly five political science approaches or theories that can explain how policy is made and implemented. Each approach or theory claims to explain why policies differ between policy sectors and countries, and why some policies are stable and others change, though typically most researchers only address one of these problems at a time. Though the relevant chapter outlines and explains each approach or theory, the following is a brief summary.

1. *Institutional approaches*: political organizations, such as parliaments, legal systems and bureaucracies, structure policy decisions and outcomes.
2. *Group and network approaches*: associations and informal relationships, both within and outside political institutions, shape decisions and outcomes. At its most refined, the group approach turns into the idea that networks of relationships between actors determine policy outputs and outcomes.
3. *Socio-economic approaches*: socio-economic factors determine the decisions of public actors and affect policy outputs and outcomes.
4. *Rational choice theory*: preferences and bargaining of actors explain decisions and outcomes. These bargains take place as a series of games between the participants and where the structure of choices is determined by institutional and socio-economic constraints.

5.   *Ideas-based approaches*: ideas about solutions to policy problems
     have a life of their own. Ideas circulate and gain influence
     independently or prior to interests in the policy process.

The five main chapters of the book investigate each approach or
theory. All offer compelling accounts of the policy process. Institutional approaches examine the constraints actors face, and take
account of the norms and habits of policy-making in different
political systems and policy subsystems. Group accounts analyse
alliance building, networking and mobilization in public decision-
making. Macro socio-economic accounts focus on the importance of
socio-economic factors, both in terms of practical constraints on
action and as ideologies. Rational choice theory investigates the
preferences and choices of the actors themselves in the situations
they face. Ideas-based approaches appraise actors' beliefs and conceptions about policy.

In some ways these approaches or theories offer self-contained
'worlds' from which to view the policy process. Institutional approaches stress that rule-following within an institutional context is the
key feature of political systems and is the main explanation of policy
variation, stability and change. Institutions become all-embracing
because they carry norms embodied in constitutional rules and
conventions. Group approaches focus on the associational relationships which circumvent institutions and define the roles of
bureaucrats and other policy participants. In its most extreme sense,
every action is an expression of group dynamics whether operating
within or outside political institutions and bureaucracies. Macro
socio-economic approaches stress the primacy of the economic and
social systems, and explore the salience of ideologies that maintain
economic and social relationships. Power structures flow into politics because there is an unequal distribution of resources. In rational
choice theory the policy process is a bargaining game between
individuals. In some versions of rational choice, all phenomena,
such as social and economic forces and institutional arrangements,
result from games between actors, either over policy outcomes or
over the rules of the game themselves. In the ideas approach,
individual motivations, group dynamics and institutional frameworks flow from the intentions and beliefs of the participants in the
policy process.

Policy researchers can choose an approach or theory to situate
their analysis. It is possible to subordinate all political action to one

principle, and some writers do this, for example by thinking that all public policy is a reflection of socio-economic processes. But the more common approach is to assume one set of causal processes is dominant while the others assume a lesser role. Thus, for example, socio-economic approaches can include as part of their explanation the idea that bureaucrats have interests of their own that affect policy. The argument is that the interests of bureaucrats do not militate against economic forces in the long run.

Though the approaches usually co-exist in political science at the same time, they have also emerged in reaction to each other, and as responses to the failures of earlier accounts of policy change and variation. Thus the institutional approach was the traditional way in which political scientists understood decision-making in the first half of the twentieth century, which had the advantage that it corresponded with the formal arrangements in political systems. Group approaches, which became more prevalent during the 1950s and early 1960s, emerged in reaction to the limits of institutionalism. Associational political analysis was able to give a more realistic account of the everyday practice of decision-making than formal accounts. The network approach, which became popular in the 1980s and 1990s, continues the theme. Institutionalists in the 1980s, in the form of the 'new' institutionalism, countered by reasserting the importance of the state and the salience of routines in politics. Socio-economic approaches emerged as a reaction to the failure of political science to appreciate the context in which public policy is made, and were particularly in favour in the 1960s and 1970s. In turn, social scientists reacted against the neglect of politics in social and economic approaches, a feeling which in part fuelled the interest in individual level approaches in the 1980s. The interest in the influence of ideas in the policy process reflects the growing importance of debates about norms and discourse in the social sciences. In the 1990s, there is increasing criticism of the assumption of narrow self-interest which lies behind the group, socio-economic and rational choice approaches.

Though in dialogue with each other, the approaches or theories are also self-referential paradigms based on assumptions about the possibilities of human agency, the effect of structures, the meaning of power and the nature of the state. If these concepts are contested there can be no unifiable or agreed research programme that connects together approaches or theories in public policy. Indeed, the organization of the central parts of the book suggests a relativist epistemology. This, however, is not the case. Though it is possible to use the approaches as useful tools to investigate the policy process, especially if a particular set of relationships are prominent in one context, only an integrated framework, one that utilizes important insights from all of the approaches, can fully explain the variety and complexity of the practice of policy-making and implementation. The approaches or theories are not rivals; they can complement each other, and be part of an overall explanation.

However, policy-making and implementation is more than a varying amalgam of institutional, group, socio-economic, individual and ideas-based processes. While describing decision-making, such a multitheoretic framework would not explain it. The approach would be 'overdetermined', rather than parsimonious. It would always account for what occurred in any situation in terms of the inter-action between the five elements. Instead, the form of explanation needs to be a theory which integrates the five processes in such a way that the causal relationships between them are clear. The book suggests that rational choice theory has the potential to offer a better explanation of the policy process than the others, though it has many limitations. Its advantage is that it is a theory of action and motivation within a structural context. Some of the other approa-ches can be refined by the insights of rational choice theory, such as group approaches. Other accounts, when analysed carefully, are really constraints on rather than reasons for political action, such as the institutional and socio-economic approaches. The book argues that the rational choice theory is capable of linking action to structure by explaining how agents respond to a range of constraints and, more problematically, the theory seeks to understand how actors seek to shape those constraints. Rational choice provides a convincing account of causation because it has an explanation of human action but at the same time utilizes what is best from the other approaches. Thus a rational choice explanation can incorpo-rate the role of institutions, groups and political and socio-economic factors as well as look at individual choices.

But, as becomes apparent by the end of the book, the genie in the bottle is ideas. If ideas independently influence political action they do not just reflect prior individual interests or dissolve into con-straints. If argument and discourse shape the preferences of the actors, it is not possible to understand policy decisions simply as the consequence of interests. Once this line of argument is accepted, the project of founding an explanation of public policy in terms of individuals making choices within structures fails, because the nature of those individuals and the importance of the structures are shaped by ideas and discourse. The genie becomes all-present! Yet, while the book is sympathetic to the importance of ideas, the argument criticizes an ideational approach that does not adequately theorize about the importance of interests.

The solution the book offers is to specify the relationship between ideas and interests in an evolutionary theory. Evolutionary theory is relevant because ideas are continually emerging about how to solve public problems, such as crime, poor education performance and traffic congestion. These ideas, however, do not exist in a vacuum. To form and to be successful they need advocates, what are called 'policy entrepreneurs', who are people who invest time and energy in pushing for policy change and who can provide public goods. These entrepreneurs can be politicians, bureaucrats, experts or interest-group lobbyists who stand to advance their careers if the policy idea is successful. Similarly there are actors who defend the ideas of the established interests which are expressed in current policies. The entrepreneurs are again bureaucrats, experts and interest-group lobbyists with the difference that they stand to lose if their ideas do not find favour. The evolutionary approach neatly links ideas and interests because one cannot survive without the other.

The evolutionary approach does not imply beneficent progress or teleology. Instead, the rapid and contingent nature of change, the frequent obstacles to cooperation and the limits to human capability mean that contingency and chance play an important role in explaining policy choices and in accounting for the salience of certain ideas. In the policy process there is a continual debate and struggle for the success of ideas and their attendant interests. What causes policy variation and change is the way in which certain ideas are selected. Ideas emerge either from policy entrepreneurs' skill at advocacy, or from chance conjunctions of people and events or from a favourable environment. The various factors which affect the success of a policy are covered in the five approaches, but an evolutionary theory can synthesize them, and can give a plausible explanation of policy formulation and implementation. The attraction of the theory is that, while it gives prominence to ideas, interests are dominant because, out of the 'soup' of ideas, they are the ones that cohere with the pattern of interests and the structure of constraints that emerge at any one time and place.

The Plan of the Book

The task of the five main chapters of the book is to engage in an argument for and against each approach or theory. The chapters set up an approach or theory as clearly as possible. Then the discussions highlight the variations within each one, show how it has developed over time and then elaborate the main weaknesses. In the course of the argument, each chapter outlines and criticizes the use of the approaches by some of the key writers, concentrating on three main empirical applications.

After the five expositions and counterarguments, there follows a chapter discussing frameworks that synthesize the other five, including evolutionary theory. In the light of the five approaches and the different types of synthesis, the concluding chapter reviews the extent to which approaches to and theories of public policy can explain policy variation and change. It is hoped the argument shows that an approach based on just one perspective fails, and that explanations in public policy need the power of evolutionary theory to bring them together.

The text draws on policy-making in local authorities, in national governments and in the European Union, and selects examples from across a range of policy sectors, such as urban policy, education, the environment, tax and health. There is, however, no attempt to summarize comprehensively policy-making and implementation at these levels and in these sectors, as the book seeks to illustrate or advance arguments rather than to cover comprehensively the variety of decision-making. For more detail on the policy-making process, there are many other texts (e.g. Peters 1993; Savage et al. 1994; Mullard 1995).

The theory and examples draw from the policy-making environment in economically developed liberal democracies, particularly Britain, France and the United States of America, though there are examples from Sweden, Canada and the European Union as well. The implication of the book's argument is that the five approaches and their synthesis are applicable in any time or place as institutions, groups, socio-economic structures, rational actors and ideas are likely to be present in various combinations wherever policy is being made and implemented. The book, however, does not show this, and readers need to make their own judgement about the applicability of the framework to other contexts than the three economically developed liberal democracies mainly discussed here.

The book tries to avoid jargon, which is an impossible objective as the subject is laden with technical terms. These are often composed of ordinary words which writers render obscure by placing the term 'policy' in front (e.g. policy window, policy learning and policy mess). The book uses some of them because they are the common language of scholarly debate. But, when they appear, the text tries to give explanations of their meaning. As a fail-safe, there is a glossary of technical terms at the end of the book, although even here it is difficult to avoid using some technical terms to explain others.

Before the chapters on the approaches and theories, the next one summarizes and criticizes traditional models of the policy process. The book needs to cover them and to question the idea that policy proceeds in discrete stages. By abandoning the convention of dividing the policy into separate elements, researchers can more readily embrace frameworks which understand the policy process as a whole. Readers who do not need to be convinced may skip to Chapter 3.

2

'Stages' Models

The Failure of Simple Models

To illustrate some problems in the conventional study of public policy, this chapter discusses the weaknesses of four related and commonly used models. These usually appear in the introductions of textbooks on public policy, and are designed to help readers understand how policy-making works. They aim to simplify the vast array of decisions and forms of behaviour that characterize contemporary public decision-making. Because the policy process is complex and apparently chaotic, there is a need to impose some conceptual order on the policy process in order to comprehend it. If models tried to include the role of all the political actors who have some say in decision-making and tried to take account of the many disjunctures and contingencies, they might not be able to do any more than describe the complexity.

The four models summarized here are similar because they attempt to simplify decision-making by assuming that policy proceeds through distinct stages. They try to introduce some clarity and elegance into the process of explanation, and Sabatier and Jenkins-Smith gave them the catch-all term, 'the stages heuristic' (1993: 1), to indicate the pedagogic purpose. The straightforward idea is that policy emerges from the interrelationships between intentions and actions of political participants. Citizens elect politicians to carry out policy platforms. Politicians create programmes for bureaucrats to implement. Senior bureaucrats order lower-level officials to carry out policy decisions. Central governments tell local governments what to do, and so on. Thus, through many chains of cause and effect or commands and responses, policy emerges in stages. Through distinguishing between policy goals and outputs/outcomes, policy analysts are able to find out if policy intentions turn into reality, and when policies are successes or failures. The procedure allows the researcher to ask some pertinent questions about the effectiveness of the policy process, and to comment on how powerful are certain groups, parties or institutions by the extent they are able to get their policies on the agenda. The problem, however, is that the distinctions the traditional approaches outline are often misleading because the policy process does not operate at all in the manner hypothesized. At best, the traditional models offer a guide or a set of measures which can be the basis for further study and the generation of theories. Policy researchers should use the models summarized in this chapter as tools of research or a set of measuring rods, to lay alongside the complex sets of decisions, rather than as ways of understanding public policy. Moreover, the defects of these models suggest that in many cases researchers should explore more wide-ranging approaches or theories as substitutes rather than additions to stages models.

 ## The Inadequacy of the Sequential Model

The idea that policy follows a sequential process is the most popular characterization of public decision-making. Policy begins as a phase of policy initiation and formulation, is modified by negotiation and law-making and then is carried into practice by implementation decisions. The linear account of decision-making puts into concrete form the idea that the political system processes inputs and creates outputs. Policy derives from the interactions of public opinion, interests, elites and ideas which are then filtered and structured by the institutions that guide the measure through the political system. The attraction of the sequential idea is that it forces analysts to look at how political systems respond to policy problems. The idea neatly summarizes the political system for the student, and creates discrete chapters in the textbooks. The model allows analysts to make the links between institutions which otherwise would be studied in a formal legalistic manner. Because the heuristic or learning device corresponds to many human and natural processes, it is intuitively appealing. As these discrete events are easy to describe, they form the building blocks of research, and thus find their way as case studies in the textbooks.

It is possible to find examples of policies that are made sequentially. The Clean Air Act in the UK in 1956, for instance, originated from the growing public awareness of urban air pollution in the 1950s. Then the acute event of a large fog in London caused strong public concern. Followed by an effective lobbying campaign and the availability of a solution, public regulation in the form of legislation quickly ensued. Smoke control swiftly became a successfully implemented policy (Sanderson 1961). In this example there was a clear start, middle and end to the policy process which proceeded through the stages of democratic demands, the rational weighing-up of objectives. bargaining between interest groups and then the implementation of the measure.

The institutional structure of most political systems implies a linear model of policy formation and implementation. Elections vote into office leaders who promise to introduce distinctive policies. The structure of the legislative timetable and the practice of executive control ensures leaders have some opportunity to introduce and implement policies within a limited time period. Political control over the bureaucracy requires civil servants and public officials to implement policies. Regular elections are the opportunity for citizens to appraise these initiatives. Such are the claims of traditional democratic theory. Policy emerges from the will of the people, constitutional checks and balances modify political decisions, and groups and experts seek to have an influence at the formulation and implementation stages. Even though the institutions usually do not work in such a compartmentalized fashion, if decision-makers believe policy is made in a linear sequence then, to an extent, reality can sometimes reflect this collective exercise of will. Political expectations and institutional arrangements create, in semblance at least, a version of sequential decision-making. In addition, there have been many attempts to introduce rational decision-making procedures into government, such as rational budgeting exercises and policy-planning units, that were popular in Britain and elsewhere in the 1960s and 1970s. These procedures try to impose a structure and sequence upon decision-making (see the section later on policy analysis).

Journalists, bureaucrats and politicians also try to represent policy-making as an orderly process because of the attractiveness of clarity. The media need to categorize policy as an event, largely because of the conventions of what is news and how newspapers and television prioritize the more dramatic and easily observable phenomena. News routines dictate that policy stories have beginnings and ends. Journalists search for discrete events, and they simplify them for their audiences. Because of time constraints, both journalists and audiences have limited capacity to process information, and as a result they focus on one event at a time. Often a topic is only news until it is displaced by another event.

Bureaucrats also seek to impose order on decision-making in order to prevent too much participation, a practice which is often called 'gatekeeping'. Officials create time limits on the consultation process and invoke the need to progress to the next stage of decision-making to limit the extent to which interest groups and organizations participate in decisions. Thus bureaucrats favour a 'consultation phase'; they like the timing of the policy to be set out in government papers and for the implementation period to be negotiated and planned. Politicians also have an incentive to structure policies. To progress in a ministerial career they need to claim responsibility for successful initiatives in which they played a part, not least because their colleagues are quick to apportion blame if the policy fails. Finally, at an ideological level, the scientific rationalistic culture of Western societies encourages political participants to present their actions and those of others as part of simple casual stories. Because the dominant form of knowledge is based on means–end relationships, so people expect politics to be orderly and rationalistic. If they thought otherwise they would not be able to legitimize their decisions with critical audiences. They also need to deliver symbolic policies to satisfy popular demands and quiet troublesome publics (Edelman 1964). Given that governments invariably promise action that is hard to achieve in practice, the procedures for setting policy into place become as important as the concrete outcomes. Thus the paraphernalia of commissions of enquiry, statements of legislative intent and new initiatives can disguise the reality of governmental inaction. Governments must be doing something.

Just a casual experience of the messiness of policy-making, the twists and turns of decisions, the reverses, the quixotic failures and the surprises is enough to alert the researcher that, even as an ideal type, the sequential model has its problems. Governments often fail to introduce policies they promise, or they retreat in the face of opposition. On the other hand, sometimes radical changes occur suddenly, perhaps at the end of the legislative process, and are maybe little noticed by the public. In no way does the policy-process correspond to the linear model except in the minimal sense that a formal policy has to be proposed, legislated on and implemented. The more policy analysts acknowledge complexity in decision-making, the more the linear idea dissolves. The policy process becomes more about attempts to counteract the unanticipated effects of public decisions than about responses to the demands that caused the policy to be introduced in the first place. Thus there is no beginning and end to public policy; for the most part, there is only the middle.

Even though there are pressures for reform occurring at any point in the political system, policy change emerges from a pre-existing set of public decisions and regulations. Rose and Davies' (1994) analysis of the continuance of government programmes over many decades shows how policy-makers operate within a constrained context. Decision-makers have to acknowledge that the bulk of public decisions have already been made because of agreed programmes and expenditure commitments. Policy change is limited to minor variations in a pattern of continuity. Policies often continue by the force of their own longevity, and develop legitimacy in a political system. Interest groups become integrated into the decision-making process and increasingly depend on government expenditure and regulation. Bureaucrats develop interests in the perpetuation of certain types of policy because their career progression depends on policy success. When powerful political interests continually support a public measure, it becomes increasingly difficult to introduce new policies. Wildavsky (1979) neatly expressed the continuity and force of sectoral decision-making in his phrase 'policy as its own cause'. The policy itself becomes the reason for political action rather than resulting from interactions between public opinion and elite power.

To ensure the sequential model corresponds to reality, writers usually introduce complexity, but in a way that retains the concept of linearity. The idea is that the policy-making is characterized by a series of 'feedbacks' and 'loops' whereby events occurring later on in the sequence can influence decisions made at an earlier stage (Hogwood and Gunn 1984: 25). Hence policy formulation is affected by earlier attempts to solve similar problems. Implementation problems cause decision-makers to start again and to reformulate the policy. The question to ask is how much of policy is explicable by feedback. If feedback is a minor aspect of policy-making, the linear idea remains; if feedback is all present, then linearity extinguishes as policy is continuous and each aspect of it is happening simultaneously.

Participants must accept the rapidly changing, flexible and chaotic nature of decision-making if they are to be effective. Rather than guiding the policy through preordained stages, there is a premium to be excised from the qualities of adaptability, detachment, policy-learning, bargaining and the ability to recognize the diverse sources of policy change. Policy is by definition complex and changeable, and political actors who recognize its nature are likely to be more successful than those who uphold rational procedures. The linear model is more relevant for elucidating the presentation of policy than in detecting the reality of bargaining. It is the shell of policy presented for public and media consumption; it is a feature of the competition for rewards within governments and bureaucracies. The student of public policy must dig deeper to understand what is going on.

The Limits of Implementation Analysis

The emergence of policy sciences has seen the rise (and recently the decline) of implementation as a term to describe the post-legislative stages of decision-making. Rather than a simple enactment of political decisions, implementation analysis suggests the relationships within and between public agencies are highly complex and difficult to manage. What appears to be a neutral and straightforward mechanism to translate intentions into reality is in fact a complex matrix of public, quasi-public and private decision-making bodies, all of which are involved in the policy process but which have their own autonomy, interests and values.

Pressman and Wildavsky (1973), in their influential book *Implementation*, argue that the existence of joint decision-making between implementing agencies creates sequences to implementation. Each extra stage reduces the chance of a policy being carried out according to the objectives of the policy-maker. They apply a probabilistic theory to decision-making. The more decision-points there are, the greater the chance a policy fails. Thus if the probability of a policy failing at each stage in the sequence is one in ten then the chance of the policy succeeding falls very rapidly every time there is a new decision-point. The difficulty of implementation is because the probabilities are multiplied and quickly reduce. In this example, the probability of failure is $(1 - 0.1)^n$ where n is the number of stages in the sequences (which can be expressed as p^n where p is the probability).

In paying attention to the design of public policy, the model alerts researchers to the inbuilt mechanisms that cause policies, either intentionally or unintentionally, to fail. The model recognizes that lower-level bureaucrats have the requisite autonomy and desire to affect policies formulated at a higher level (Lipsky 1971). Even personnel who have mainly service-providing tasks have some discretion to affect whether a public measure is likely to be implemented successfully or not. The Pressman/Wildavsky model suggests that as the complexity of the decision-making environment increases, so too does the difficulty of effective policy implementation. Most politicians and commentators now accept this idea as common sense. In Britain, for example, urban policy has been described as fragmented because of the many central and local agencies that have been introduced or have taken on urban policy objectives, each with similar goals. The many organizations include local authorities which have companies, partnerships and development departments; private-sector bodies such as chambers of commerce and the regional organizations of the Confederation of British Industry, and the multitude of central government organizations providing economic support, the urban development corporations, training and enterprise agencies and city action teams (Atkinson and Moon 1994). In 1994 the British government tried to integrate some of the business support services into Business Links, a new organization. But this reform only succeeded in creating yet another body responsible for urban initiatives. In order to implement urban policies, government has to negotiate the maze of central government departments, their regional organizations, the numerous government agencies, and private-sector and local-authority bodies.

Traditional implementation analysis predicts it is very hard for policy to be implemented at all. It does not take many hurdles for the probability of successful implementation to drop below 50 per cent. Thus, to return to the example of a probability of 0.1 of failing at each stage of a given sequence, the probability of successful implementation drops below 50 per cent after seven stages. In reaction to this theoretical impossibility of governing, studies have tested Pressman and Wildavsky's model to find that implementation is not so difficult after all (Mazmanian and Sabatier 1981). In other words, the probablistic model is not quite right. In the light of the empirical deficiency, the predictions from the model can be altered according to the number of times policy-makers retry implementation. If the government tries introducing a policy a second and third time, there is more chance of successful implementation. Also, if the policy is successfully implemented at the beginning of the sequence, it is possible that there is more of a chance of a successful outcome at later stages, what is called the 'bandwagon' effect. The introduction into the model of some of the realities of implementation decisions shows that government policy does not fail quite as easily as the classic implementation model predicts (Bowen 1982).

Classic implementation theory can be criticized on similar grounds to the idea that policy is a sequential process. It is not often possible to specify a clear relationship between policy intentions and outcomes. There is no other clear sequence in decision-making as decision-makers continually reconsider policy problems and their solutions over long time periods. The basic flaw is that classic implementation theory is based on a 'top-down' perspective where the political system is seen from the viewpoint of policy formers rather than others involved with decision-making (Barrett and Fudge 1981). For example, Hood's (1976) model of 'perfect administration' is a clear example of the Olympian view. Perfect administration is the ideal outcome from the perspective of the policy-framers. The research task is to identify the obstacles, such as inadequate resources and unclear policy formulation, that limit perfect administration. But this presupposes that higher-level policy-makers ever thought of the policy clearly in the first place and that they wish to have such detailed control over decision-making. Politicians and senior bureaucrats are often happy to react to events, create symbolic policies and leave the harder and more controversial decisions to lower-level organizations and local authorities which can take the blame if a policy fails.

Rather than just frustrating implementation, lower levels of government, agencies, bureaucrats and interest groups have a role in deciding policy. Even though hierarchy is important, they are often jointly responsible for making policy. Policy decisions can move 'backwards' from implementing organizations, such as local authorities and government agencies, to the policy formulators, the politicians and top bureaucrats. The latter often make decisions just to legitimize policy choices that have already been made or to acknowledge the fact of administrative discretion. Implementation analysis assumes a static view of policy whereby leading bureaucrats and politicians formulate policy, then other bureaucrats implement it. But all the agencies and bodies in policy-making continuously learn from each other's experiences. As policy-makers grow to appreciate other decision-makers' reactions to their objectives, so too the original goals of a policy can change. Thus traditional implementation analysis is of limited use in understanding causation in policy except for the few policies where there is a distinct beginning and end, and for which policy-makers formulate clear objectives.

Subsequent implementation analysis offers more hope. Instead of looking on policy as a 'top-down' process, it is seen in the round. Policy does not just emerge from the intentions of ministers and senior bureaucrats because lower-level agencies and bodies have some input into decision-making. 'Policy drift', the way in which events gradually shift the aims of a policy, cannot just be explained by the obstruction of policy goals by bureaucrats, but is the natural evolution of policy by groups, agencies and expert bodies that advocate policy ideas and try to implement them. Instead of policy being a linear sequence of intended actions, that is followed by success or failure, decision-making is characterized by learning, adaptation and reformulation. Participants in decision-making respond to their environments and negotiate the pitfalls. Sabatier (1986) argues that policy-makers can learn from their mistakes, particularly in the long term. Successful implementation can happen over a 10–20-year period. In his argument, Sabatier integrates both 'bottom-up' and 'top-down' approaches to understand how policy-makers achieve long-term objectives by strategic adaptation. He adapts the study of implementation to reflect the multicausal and complex world of the policy-making process.

But the revisions to the classic model turns the analysis into an understanding of bargaining games and networked relationships within policy subsystems rather than the study of the discrete process of implementation. Sabatier is right to criticize the simplicity of 'top-down' models, because it is not possible to separate policy formulation and policy implementation. Decision-making is continuous. Yet, by challenging the intellectual framework of classic implementation analysis, Sabatier and other critics expand the subject into the study of policy-making as a whole. In order to understand how implementation words, the analyst needs to understand the policy-making process in the round. It is not possible to separate the stages of policy formulation and policy implementation. As a result the implementation analyst needs theories of public decision-making to understand what is happening. While the concept of implementation remains useful as a conceptual tool to understand the failure and success of policy, the project of creating implementation analysis as a separate field of study has largely failed.

The Changing Project of Policy Analysis

Policy analysis began as the study of rational techniques to improve the effectiveness of public decision-making. The subject draws on the belief, prevalent in the 1960s, that rational methods can improve public decision-making. The idea is that formal and well set out procedures for weighing-up the costs and benefits of courses of public action lead to more informed policy choices. Policy-makers decide policy goals based on their political values, but they follow specified decision-making procedures that identify the best course of action to realize these aims. The idea is again based on a stages model, because analysts assume policy-making systems can adopt procedures based on the recommended form of decision-making. Once individuals and organizations work well, decision-making transforms into neat stages.

Examples of rational techniques include cost–benefit analysis of government investment projects and zero-based budgeting systems that appraise annual public spending decisions from first principles. The former technique is a method of evaluating the economic and social costs of a public project in monetary values. Zero-based budgeting is a procedure to recalculate the annual budgets of organizations. Instead of accepting last year's budget as the basis for future changes, policy-makers discuss the whole budget from first principles. In the perspective of policy analysis, the study of public policy is about the ability of political systems to benefit from such techniques.

Early policy analysis recommended these techniques uncritically. An example is the recommendation of programme budgeting techniques in the UK to improve central government's annual budget-setting decisions. The idea was that the outputs could be measured and the knowledge would filter into central planning decisions. In the USA, policy analysis was applied to the War on Poverty, the Vietnam War in the 1960s and responses to the energy crisis in the 1970s. Policy analysis continued to be used to design polices under the Reagan presidency. An academic industry grew up. The initial popularity of policy analysis fitted into a period when governments believed they could modernize public administration.

These decision-making experiments, however, had a short shelf-life. Britain's crisis of public finances in the 1970s led to a moratorium on public spending. As a result, the budget-planning systems adopted in the 1960s fell into disuse. Most of all, political scientists found out that no matter how objectively reformers tried to specify the rational criteria, political factors affected how policy-makers selected and used policy analysis. In short, rational decision-making techniques are just as political as policy-making itself. Policy-makers often argue for and against techniques on the grounds that they produce a desired or non-desired outcome. With some techniques, like cost–benefit analysis, the procedures could not adequately calculate the social costs and benefits. In the end, policy-makers made judgements about the desirability of the projects, which was exactly the type of behaviour advocates of these techniques wished to avoid.

Failure has not proved the end of policy analysis. Realizing that rational decision-making procedures are intimately tied up with politics, contemporary thinkers argue that academics can create a new form of policy analysis. Believing that policy is essentially about deliberation and argument, Majone (1989) argues that analysis contributes to decision-making by criticizing conventional wisdom and by providing new ideas. By recognizing that ideas are intimately bound up with the recommendations for policy change, modern policy analysis is more flexible and adaptive. Hogwood and Gunn (1984) argue that, if done thoughtfully and responsively, policy analysis can help the policy-making by defining the relevant issues, setting out the options and evaluating what happened. Wildavsky (1979) also argues that policy analysis is not about prescription but about setting up mechanisms to ensure that debate and learning take place. In short, by watering down the scientific claims of policy analysis, something can be salvaged of its programme for change in government.

In the past academics and reformers thought policy analysis could revolutionize public decision-making. Now rational techniques do not offer so much. They can help the analyst understand why some ideas on how to improve public policy fail or succeed, but the rational techniques themselves become just one activity the political scientist investigates to understand policy-making. Policy analysis is part and parcel of the debate between policy-makers. The choices about how to make public decisions are politically informed acts which decision-makers deploy to win substantive arguments about policy. The decision to set up a committee or to use a procedure to allocate resources usually involves the application of political values to public decisions because the choice often rules out some courses of action and facilitates others.

Contemporary writers on policy analysis now see the subject within a 'post-positivist paradigm'. There is no inherent superiority of rational ideas. Instead interpretation and discourse underpin their use (see Chapter 7 for a more detailed account). Policy analysis belongs to the subjective world of politics rather than being above it (Stone, D. 1988). It is argued that policy analysis, the supposedly objective advice given to policy-makers, is just another form of rhetoric (Throgmorton 1991). Like implementation theory, policy analysis, by becoming a resource or an aspect of the interplay of interests, loses its distinctiveness as an approach to understanding policy. As this chapter argues with respect to the sequential and implementation models, the central problem in public policy is to develop a satisfactory account of causation. Understanding the role of policy analysis is just one part of this project. Just like the implementation theorist, the policy analyst needs theories of policy variation and change.

The False Debate between Rational and Incremental Models of Decision-making

Textbooks on public policy often set out the rational actor model, criticize it, and then conclude that incrementalism is a more accurate account of decision-making. Public-policy writers hope the contrast between the two models helps students understand how policy is made and implemented, even though it is common knowledge that the rational model does not work. The idea is that the two models generate insights into the policy process. However, rather than simplifying the analysis, the dichotomy obscures.

Put simply, the rational actor model conceives policy to be a logical, reasoned and neutral way organizations assess problems, propose solutions, then choose and carry out courses of action. The model has several assumptions (Downs 1957). As with the sequential model and classic implementation analysis, there are clear-cut stages to decision-making. Organizations can make decisions when they are faced with choices. They rank the decisions and one emerges as a clear winner. When organizations make their choices, the preference rankings between them are consistent. Every participant in the policy process gets what they want, subject to the constraints of resources. The model tries to explain how decision-makers deal with policy issues. Under the influence of the electorate, the media and pressure groups, political leaders become aware of public problems. Given these stimuli, political advisers and bureaucrats present options to political decision-makers for decision. Having weighed up the alternatives, politicians take the best possible decision to maximize their utility which is then carried out into law and implemented by the bureaucracy. This is, again, the stages model of the policy process.

There are, however, major difficulties with the rational model. In spite of the existence, in some countries, of a relatively unified executive and a reasonably compliant bureaucracy, there is no discrete organization aggregating all the elements of the political system. Instead there are myriad decision-making bodies across and within the executive, the legislature and bureaucracy as well as at the various levels of government. All these have to coordinate a response which may not be possible because they do not trust each other or there may be no easy compromise between their objectives. Conflicting interests exist within organizations and reflect the preferences of the individuals occupying various roles in them. Moreover, the preferences of decision-makers within organizations may be ordered in such a way that no rational outcome for the organization as a whole is possible. Organizations face high costs when collecting the information necessary to make a rational decision. In other words, because of the complexity of political or bureaucratic roles, organizations may not reach the most rational decision, and as a result public decision-making as a whole is not rational.

Some critics try to undermine the idea that decisions can be modelled using the techniques of rational choice. Simon (1957) argues that the pursuit of ends in public policy is better understood as an exercise in 'bounded rationality' as it is impossible for the decision-maker to gather all the information necessary to make a rational decision. Decision-makers satisfice. In the time available, they apply rules of thumb to approximately arrive at their decisions. The idea is to achieve a desirable outcome given limited information. Decision-makers are also constrained by their own values and those of the organizations they inhabit.

Writers such as Lindblom (1968) argue for a more limited model of decision-making in the policy-making process. Rather than the rational model, the policy process is best understood as incremental because decision-makers make little effort to follow procedurally rational decisions. Decisions are small adjustments from the existing state of affairs and are usually based on a low level of knowledge. Group negotiation within the organizations of the state is more important than the procedures for arriving at a rational decision. The policy process is an endless search for solutions. Decision-making is exploratory.

The power of incrementalism is that it undermines the stages model, and thus challenges the classic commentary on public policy. Rather than top decision-makers rationally making decisions and commanding lower-level bureaucrats and other public bodies to implement them, policy-makers interact and no one decision-maker dominates. Incrementalism neatly addresses the criticism of policy as a sequential process because it does not assume decision-making is linear. Lindblom's model rectifies the 'top-down' bias of implementation theories because it assumes that a wide variety of decision-makers interact to produce policy. Nor is there the assumption that policy-making improves as a result of human will or organizational efficiency. Instead of clear-cut issues, with beginnings, middles and ends, policy is continuous. Policy change consists of minor variations from what has gone before. Incrementalism has an explanation of the failure of rational policy analysis because decision-makers are likely to prefer marginal adjustments to the current state of affairs rather than to conceive policy in terms of all the costs and benefits.

Given what researchers know about the real world of policy-making, incrementalism corresponds well with how decisions are made. The approach fits the inheritance model proposed by Rose and Davies (1994) since political decision-makers generally accept the programmes they find when coming into office. Most national budgeting systems confirm the incremental decision-making model as ministers, bureaucracies and interest groups fight for a slice of the budget pie rather than rationally planning on the basis of clear objectives (Heclo and Wildavsky 1974; Wildavsky 1986). Incrementalism recognizes and celebrates the role of groups in policy (see Chapter 4).

The main problem with the rational–incrementalist debate is that both models capture elements of decision-making even though the textbooks present them as polar opposites. Aspects of each type of behaviour occur most of the time when political and bureaucratic actors make policy choices and carry out implementation decisions. Decision-making can be rational at certain stages; at other stages it is incremental. For example, at the beginning of a programme, policy-makers may rank their objectives to select the preferred option; once the programme is in place decisions may become incremental. Both models describe elements of decision-making; but they are silent about why decision-makers adopt policies at particular times and places. The study of public policy needs a theory which can explain why groups and individuals are powerful in one instance and not in another; and why change is sometimes rapid while at other times there is stasis. In other words, the character of decision-making differs widely in space and in time, and theorists of public policy are interested in understanding why.

Summing-up

The models and frameworks in this chapter are based on the idea that the policy analyst can neatly chop up the policy process into analytical pieces. These elements to policy-making are supposed to reflect the real world. Thus sequential models assume that every policy has a beginning, middle and end, and that the task of the policy analyst is to describe how policy moves from one stage to another. In implementation theory, the policy process divides into policy formulation and implementation, which creates the idea that the latter activity has special attributes and problems that need to be analysed and solved. Policy analysis creates the divide between the transforming power of analysis and the messier real world needing reform. Only incrementalism escapes from the rigidity of stages models and examines the continuity and circularity of the world of decision-making.

The stages model can still be used as a heuristic or learning device. Researchers can apply it because it imposes some order on the research process. By examining policy formulation, for example, researchers can examine how decision-makers select options. Also, most democratic political institutions are predicated upon the stages model. Thus, in formal terms, there are usually beginnings, middles and ends to public policy. Politicians often stress they are not involved with the implementation process. Policy is often justified in rational terms. The media and the public often expect the policy process to work in stages, because they need to make sense of the complexity of the policy process.

However, the stages idea confuses more than it illuminates. Policy is continuous. There are no neat divisions between different types of activities. There is too much change and messiness in public decision-making for the simplification to capture enough of reality. The analysis needs to penetrate the contingent and evolutionary world of changing interests, ideas and policy problems rather than accept the formal justifications. Most of all, the research needs a framework or a theory to make sense of the policy process as a whole.

3

Institutional Approaches

The Functions of Political Institutions

Institutions are the arena within which policy-making takes place. They include the political organizations, laws and rules that are central to every political system and they constrain how decision-makers behave. Institutions divide powers and responsibilities between the organizations of the state; they confer rights on individuals and groups; they impose obligations on state officials to consult and to deliberate; and they can include and exclude political actors, such as interest groups, in public decision-making (Schattschneider 1960). Not only do institutions affect the distribution of power, institutions make political life manageable by formalizing rules and norms of behaviour. While politics is possible without an institutional framework because decision-makers can bargain in a series of one-off interactions, political systems usually develop procedures to determine the manner in which decisions take place. Moreover, as a force of continuity, they express the values underpinning a political system.

Because institutions define how a political system operates, they have taken a central place in political science, particularly during the origins of the discipline. As Chapter 1 discusses, the founding scholars of political science treated institutions, such as legislatures and courts, as a key part of public life and worthy of study in their own right. Their importance was reinforced by the importance of institutions in classic works of political theory, such as in the works of de Tocqueville and in the *Federalist Papers* (Madison *et al.* 1788). For up until the behavioural revolution in political science, there were close links between empirical and normative scholarship. Thus, for example, the study of federalism used to be inseparable from the discussion of liberty and balanced government (Vile 1967).

Initially, public policy scholars tended to react against institutionalism, partly because of the arid and sterile character of institutional studies, particularly in the UK. Institutional research so often seemed to be descriptive, and obsessed with administrative details and formal procedures. In contrast, public policy researchers stressed the importance of rational planning or the role of groups. Institutions, however, continued to be important in mainstream political scientists' discussions of decision-making, for example, in the role of the US Presidency as a policy-maker (e.g. Fenno 1959; Neustadt 1960). Since the early 1980s, as this chapter shows, institutions have returned to their central place in the study of policy through the influence of 'new' institutionalism.

The Demise of Functionalism

Both theorists and researchers have often considered institutions, such as legislatures, executives, bureaucracies and judiciaries, to be manifestations of the functions of political life. These activities are, respectively, representation, policy formulation, implementation and adjudication. The idea is that there are distinct political tasks that need to be carried out by separate institutions, an insight that has been the staple of political analysis since Plato, Machiavelli and Montesquieu. Thus legislatures make laws, executives take decisions, bureaucracies implement them and courts resolve disputes. In terms of the development of political systems, the idea is that one individual or a ruling class or caste carries out these political functions in traditional societies, while modern democracies have differentiated institutions. Ideally each institution balances the other because the distribution of power and responsibilities within the state ensures government is both effective and legitimate. Institutions, when presented in this functionalist form, do not seem to count as an independent factor in policy-making. Institutions process demands from the political system and turn them into outputs (policies) (Easton 1965). They are a neutral transmission belt for political actions that begin in society, transmit to the executive and legislature, and are applied by bureaucracies to return to society again in the form of policy outcomes. Institutions form part of the mysterious 'black box', otherwise known as the state, that turns politics into policy. When thought of in this way, the functionalist analysis produces the stages models of policy-making described in Chapter 2.

Some defenders of particular institutional arrangements, such as the British parliamentary system of government, argue that a proper division of powers is a rational structure for the discussion, formulation and implementation of policy (Birch 1964). Institutions create a forum within which pressure groups can legitimately argue their point of view, and they are a means to reconcile the conflicting interests in society. But few contemporary institutionalists now commit themselves to such a strong functionalist logic except in obvious definitional terms. Instead, most institutionalists would claim only that political systems evolved democratic institutions to make government decisions legitimate and to respond to the political demands of newly enfranchised groups. Because the business of government expanded in the second half of the nineteenth century, political systems developed complex bureaucracies to implement policy. Functionalism anyway has ceased to be a coherent theory of politics, largely because there is no reason why political systems should automatically perform activities necessary for a democracy. In fact, rather than offer praise, experts and citizens often criticize their political systems for failing to deliver effective and legitimate policies.

State Traditions and Institutional Structures

While the structure of the modern state is similar in most economically developed countries, and complex industrial societies typically face comparable policy problems, the focus of the institutional approach is the uniqueness of institutions both in time and in place. Institutions embody cultures and past political decisions. Formal rules and structures, agreed or introduced long ago, influence how political actors exercise their current choices. It is the variety of traditions embodied in institutions that explains the complexity of political behaviour and unlocks the intricacies of the policy process.

History is important for the institutional account. For example, in the contemporary UK, the legacy of a medieval governing system that slowly turned into a democracy has implications for the practice of secrecy and closed decision-making. Although the UK has the institutions and procedures of a modern democracy, such as regular elections and executive accountability, it still retains older traditions and practices which limit democratic openness. Thus the existence of prerogative powers, formerly giving independence to the monarch, also can allow government ministers to exercise power without parliamentary authorization or even, at times, without control by the courts. Likewise, in the USA, the views of the 'founding fathers' of constitutional democracy created the divided government and the porous structure of the policy-making process which still operate today under the very different circumstances of the large state. Formalized in constitutions, the workings of organizations and political norms, past decisions and ideas structure how actors make and implement policy. Whereas political movements, parties and interest groups come and go with the cyclical fluctuation of issues, the institutional context that shapes policy agendas changes much more slowly. Bringing together the institutions into a coherent whole, each country has a state tradition which is an amalgam of a culture's ideas and institutions (Dyson 1980).

The approach to public policy is subtle because institutions are not static. They adapt to their political environment. Some writers believe institutions have an intelligence in the way they respond to fast-changing social and economic environments that is built up from their capacity to learn, to store collective experience and to create 'guidance mechanisms' to help decision-makers (Linder and Peters 1990). Others think of institutions as potentially dysfunctional because, when they are out of kilter with social and political change, they make incorrect adjustments.

Some institutionalists believe formal procedures define the policy process. Not only do institutions set constraints on action, they define the norms of the political system (Johnson 1975). Institutions routinize the values of a political system. Individuals who engage in conventional political behaviour find identity and meaning from following rules and conventions. Institutionalists commonly believe organizations have 'standard operating procedures' that process decisions. For example, not only is a parliamentary system defined by the supremacy of the legislature in law, the institutional framework affects how the decisions are processed. Even though the doctrine of parliamentary sovereignty in the UK appears to give unlimited power to the executive, norms or conventions constrain the exercise of that power, such as the accountability of ministers to parliament (Marshall 1984). Other norms, such as the legacy of the authority of the Crown, compete with democratic ones. Similarly, the power of the US Supreme Court to determine policy matters derives both from the US Constitution and from the way the court developed and enhanced its role through elite and public acceptance of its decisions in the nineteenth and twentieth centuries. If norms are included as part of institutional action, then the claims of institutionalism as an explanation of policy variation and change are more ambitious. Institutions become the defining feature of modern political systems.

Institutions in Comparative Perspective

Institutionalists believe that formal arrangements often affect policy through their capacity to influence the coordination of public decisions. Some institutional arrangements promote good coordination; others have negative effects. Institutionalists often make a distinction between systems with separated patterns of government and those with unified executives, in particular between the US and other political systems. Heidenheimer (1985) argues that European states, with their strong bureaucracies and weak legislatures, impose a more uniform pattern of decision-making across policy areas than the USA (see Chapter 3). The importance of national styles of policy-making, where decision-makers share the same values and habits of decision-making, suggests that national differences are as important as differences between policy sectors (Richardson 1982). Weaver and Rockman's (1993) survey of the effect of institutions on policy-making, *Do Institutions Matter?*, draws on the contrast between parliamentary systems (strong parties, strong executive) and presidential systems (weak parties, weak executive). Institutions have a direct effect on political behaviour by creating veto points in a political system. Institutional rules, which may vary greatly across political systems, allow interest groups to block and to modify policy decisions.

The complexity of the research problem, however, makes Weaver and Rockman careful to qualify their argument. There are substantial variations across the different types of parliamentary or presidential systems; there are also many other factors that mediate the effect of institutions, such as political culture and economic development; and there are also variations within a country between regions and between policy sectors. Policy-makers' goals, past policy choices, levels of cohesion between governing elites and types of access of interest groups are different depending what policy is being examined. The conclusion of Feigenbaum, Samuels and Weaver's (1993) comparison of energy policies between the USA, Canada, France, Germany and Japan is that the separation or fusion of executive and legislative power does not make much difference to policy-making. On the other hand, the presence of federalism, the type of bureaucracy and the power of constitutional courts do have an impact.

Research on the impact of the structure of US government on policy-making reaches similar equivocal conclusions. The argument is that if different parties control the Presidency and Congress, the result is deadlock or 'gridlock'. The two institutions are likely to have leaderships with different objectives. The system of checks and balances means the administration will find it hard to get its legislation through. Such a characterization of policy neatly seems to apply to the Clinton presidency after the Democrats lost control of Congress in 1994. Mayhew (1991), however, challenges the impact of institutions in his comparison of the passage of legislation between when there is divided government and when there is not. The system seems to operate just as well when presidents have their party in control in Congress as not. Not that a particular president does not make a difference or that legislation varies in type, but that the system coordinates as effectively in situations when different parties control the branches of the state as when they are the same. Similarly, C. Jones (1994) argues that the process of government works just as well when the government is divided as when there is unity, mainly because of the vast amounts of administrative, executive and legislative interaction which occurs with little presidential oversight. On the other hand, to confound what seems a nice revision of conventional wisdom, Edwards *et al.* (1997) conclude that divided government does stop legislation getting through Congress. They find that presidents oppose legislation more often, and that much more important legislation fails to pass, under divided government than undivided government. On the other hand, divided government does not affect the amount of legislation the administration supports or that passes. It seems that nothing is simple when assessing the impact of institutional structures.

A plausible line of argument is that institutions are important in so far as they show how actors try to cooperate in a policy sector. Instead of being an object of study in themselves, institutions and elite values structure the constraints and opportunities of decision-makers and affect, but do not determine, how a policy sector operates. In this way it is only possible to understand decisions in their institutional context when policies are examined comparatively, because the politics of decision-making in a policy sector interacts with the culture and institutional framework of each country to produce policy variation and change (Freeman 1985). Likewise in the divided government example, the importance of institutions is that they affect policy when different parties control the two main branches of government, not that institutions have an impact on their own.

The Bureaucratic Politics Model

Bureaucracy is the focus for much institutional analysis because of the importance of the state and the weakness of legislatures in many European countries. The bureaucracy represents the state and implements its decisions. Officials are often permanent appointees so they have the expertise and knowledge to participate in and to shape policy. In France, for example, until the founding of the Fifth Republic in 1958, governments were weak and unstable, and the legislature was ineffective. So it was the bureaucrats who provided continuity and stability to policy-making. Their power was reinforced by a tradition of the strong state and the practice of elite training in the *grands écoles* (elite training schools).

The bureaucratic politics model claims that interactions within bureaucracies explain policy-making as much as the intentions of politicians. The idea is one of the models of decision-making in Allison's seminal *Essence of Decision* (1971), a study of how the United States responded to the Cuban missile crisis of 1962. He argues that bureaucracies are not integrated hierarchical bodies which operate according to a chain of command. Instead, they are fragmented into bureaus which compete with each other for resources and influence on policy. The way in which bureaucracies are sectorized, and the manner in which policy issues cut across different departments of state, explains policy outputs and outcomes, a point noted in many other analyses of American executive policy-making (e.g. Neustadt 1960). Policy often arrives as the outcome of an uncoordinated fight between government bureaus.

Following Allison, political scientists commonly apply the model to foreign policy-making to challenge the idea that nation states are unitary actors when they negotiate with other states. For example, Rosati (1981) examines bargaining within the US foreign policy bureaucracy before and during the Strategic Arms Limitation Talks (SALT) in the 1960s and 1970s. Bargainers included the State Department, the Defense Department, the Arms Control and Disarmament Agency and the Central Intelligence Agency. The last two of these bodies were more interested in verification and were more hardline than the others; the rest were more concerned with arms limitation. Rosati argues that the bureaucratic politics model applies best when the executive is weak; but intra-bureaucratic conflict and cooperation is less relevant if the executive takes a prominent role. When the president gives clear leadership, bureaus do not have much opportunity to fight each other and tend not to suggest alternative courses of action. Rosati argues that bureaucratic politics varies according to presidential style and to the extent an issue is critical for the political system.

The attraction of the bureaucratic politics model is its simplicity. The divisions of the state create different bargains and coalitions. The difficulty is that the model describes an everyday feature of public decision-making. Bureaucracies are inevitably complex, and the state is always fragmented. What the perspective does not explain is why coordination is possible at some times and in some sectors but not in others. Nor does bureaucratic politics account for when executive power prevails and when it does not. Rosati's simple account based on the power of the executive does not solve the problem. Bendor and Hammond (1992) note that the bureaucratic politics model includes too many phenomena to deduce how policy is shaped. The model tends to neglect the role of hierarchy in the bureaucracy which can overcome factional conflicts and enhance the role of the executive. What is needed is a theory of bargaining, based on the opportunities and constraints open to bureaucrats and to political leaders rather than just the assumption of bureaucratic fragmentation. But this adaption to the pattern of interests and strategic interaction would make the bureaucratic politics model more an application of institutional rational choice theory than of institutionalism (see Chapter 6).

An alternative critique suggests that decision-making between the different bureaus should take account of the role of ideas. E. Rhodes' (1994) analysis of US naval expenditure tests the bureaucratic politics model. He finds the careers origins of chief naval officers are not a guide to the level of expenditure on the three types of vessels, the surface vessels, submarines or aircraft carriers. There is no evidence that a fight between the bureaus leads to the appointment of chief naval officers who favour their own group. Instead, it is trends in naval fashion, favouring certain types of weapon, and foreign policy influences that determine expenditure. Policy-makers have to respond to external factors rather than just defend their bureaus' interests. The research rejects the narrow conception of bargaining in the bureaucratic politics model and adopts a more complex understanding of policy-making.

The Core Executive in Britain

Given the importance of the executive in the UK, the bureaucratic politics model has been used as part of a new approach to researching central government policy-making, the core executive perspective (Dunleavy 1990; Dunleavy and Rhodes 1990; Rhodes and Dunleavy 1995; Rhodes 1995). Rather than understanding power relations within the British state as a tussle between the prime minister and the cabinet, the core executive approach suggests the fragmentation of the state is the main cause of different types of public decisions. The core executive 'refers to all those organizations and procedures that coordinate central government policies, and act as final arbiters of conflict between different parts of the government machine' (Rhodes 1995). The account sets out the possible relationships and alliances that can form in different policy sectors and issues. The advantage of this term is that it combines the politics of both the executive and the bureaucracy, and can encompass many different types of relationships.

Dunleavy (1990) uses the core executive framework to understand the Westland affair in the UK in 1985 and 1986. The episode was a dispute within the executive between two plans to rescue the failing military helicopter firm, Westland. It was a conflict of interests between the alliance of defence company executives, bureaucrats and ministers, who supported the US bid, and a similar group of actors who advocated the European consortium. The conflict turned into a public battle between Michael Heseltine, Secretary of State for Defence, and Leon Brittan, Secretary of State for Trade and Industry. The outcome was the resignation of the former minister and then the latter. The event was bureaucratic wrangle because the departments of state split on the issue as they faced different costs depending on which scheme the government approved. They also did not agree whether there should be an American or a European controlled defence industry. The unplanned and unpredictable nature of the dispute suggests there was intense bureaucratic infighting which extended into the executive itself. But Dunleavy argues that the bureaucratic politics model does not take account of the important power relationships operating behind the conflict. The two factions of industry represented in the two bids had their respective allies in the Conservative Party and in the central state. The bureaucratic politics model concentrates heavily on the minutiae of policy decisions at the centre to the exclusion of the factors shaping the bigger picture.

The verdict on core executive studies is that it is a valid attempt to shift the focus of research away from the analysis of the formal working of institutions. The approach includes the behaviour of the larger structures and actors at the heart of the state. As is shown by Dunleavy's study, the perspective is far more likely to capture how decisions are made and how policy is coordinated than conventional approaches to the role of the executive. The core executive approach leaves to one side the sterile debate about the extent to which prime ministers have gained power over their cabinet colleagues. Instead there are complex processes and alliances within the central state. The approach itself, however, does not explain policy variation and change. It merely helps students of policy-making understand what there is to be explained. For explanatory purposes, other approaches or theories are needed, which can apply the insights of core executive studies.

Complex Legislatures

Researchers who study legislatures attack the idea that groups rather than institutions shape policy. In the UK, some writers consider institutions to be unimportant because power has been transferred away from Parliament toward policy communities of actors who make agreements behind the scenes (see Richardson and Jordan 1979 and other references in Chapter 4). The institutional framework is not important because the formal institutions for scrutinizing decisions do not have a great impact on policy outputs and outcomes. Groups, the executive and bureaucrats get their way through control of the legislature. Institutionalists, such as Judge (1993), counter by arguing that the parliamentary framework sets the context of politics. Judge argues that Parliament legitimates a particular form of interest intermediation which can be delegated to policy communities. Thus it only appears that Parliament does not have a role when interest groups and bureaucrats decide most routine matters. Parliament shows its importance when the consensus breaks down. In time of crisis the policy community dissolves and direct parliamentary control re-emerges.

For example, the 1980s' neo-liberal governments in the UK, led by Mrs Thatcher, used Parliament to break up or to neglect established policy communities, such as introducing legislation to privatize the water industry. Yet it is hard to say that this example shows that institutions have been responsible for the policy changes because the changes in group politics may have resulted from changes in public attitudes and the outcome of factional politics within the parties. Parliament is only important because these discontents are partly expressed through it. The institution is the means of change rather than the reason for it. It is not sufficient to argue that because politicians debate issues in Parliament and governments use parliamentary procedures to introduce policies, institutions affect the policy process. What needs to be shown is that the structure of parliamentary institutions has an effect on policy deliberation and outcomes independent of the origins of the issue. However, this line of argument creates an almost impossible research project as it is very hard to know if a different type of legislature would have discouraged neo-liberal policies.

However, some empirical studies can reveal the effect of political institutions, particularly well focused comparisons. For example, Freeman's (1979) study of French and British immigration policies shows that, because legislation had to be introduced through Parliament, the process of policy-making was open and controversial, as opposed to the French style, where decisions were made behind closed doors with little legislative scrutiny. While the executive is powerful in Britain, it has to announce policies in Parliament and debate them, a practice which opens up policies to public scrutiny. Though the executive often has its way in Britain, it can be unstabilized by debates and pressure in Parliament.

The impact of the legislature in the USA is easier to detect because the structure of the institution varies by policy sector. The similarities and contrasts between Congressional committees and subcommittees, particularly in the way they process policy, makes it possible to deduce institutional effects. Institutional rational choice theorists (see Chapter 6) argue that the structure of Congress produces equilibria in the bargaining between interests. Otherwise there would be endless cycles and perpetual instability (Shepsle 1979; Shepsle and Weingast 1981). Browne's (1995) study of agricultural interests in Congress from a network perspective (see Chapter 4) also argues that institutions set and limit policy choices: 'Institutionalised structures, or established procedural and policy rules, and the complementary need for internal order obviously makes some agricultural policy vehicles more prominent than others' (1995: 42). Browne shows how legislative procedures and powers of agency oversight mean that constituency agricultural groups easily advance their interests. The complex portmanteau legislative framework allows legislators to adjust the benefits they receive from programmes. Other policies, such as food stamps, are not so easily advanced because they cannot be so readily manipulated. In addition, even though much of the policy-making proceeds by logrolling, whereby legislators do something in exchange for somebody doing something for them, the institutional framework governs the extent to which legislators can carry out these exchanges.

Critiques of Institutionalism

The first limitation of the institutional approach is that actors and groups often circumvent institutions in the pursuit of their interests. Institutions are the 'dignified' aspect to political life that disguise the conflicts between interests. For example, farmers' interests tend to dominate agricultural policy-making no matter whether the country is parliamentary (UK), presidential (USA), bicephalous or twin-headed (France) or federal (Germany). The idea is that any institution becomes weak if powerful groups gain access to public decision-making. Interest groups have the resources to ensure politicians and bureaucrats respond to their interests no matter what legal and constitutional weapons there are. In Britain, for example, even though there appears to be a unitary structure to government departments operating under a powerful executive and a subservient legislature, the way in which policy is determined has much to do with the character of interest groups. Thus the operation of the Department of Health is very different to the Department of the Environment, Transport and Regions. Even though the two organizations have a similar constitutional structure, are headed by ministers responsible to Parliament and are staffed by permanent civil servants, they differ. In the former, powerful doctors' groups, such as the British Medical Association, ensure that, to an extent, policy reflects their interests. In the Department of the Environment, Transport and Regions, on the other hand, the civil servants and ministers are able to stand back from the politically weak subnational authorities.

An example of an institutional process whose salience is thought to depend on group power is the changing role of the US Supreme Court. The institutional argument is that the court has an impact on policy as a result of its embedded power and the values it embodies. The Supreme Court, when interpreting the US Constitution, has the power to strike down unconstitutional legislative and executive actions and has the freedom to promote the values of liberty and justice. It is very hard for political and bureaucratic decision-makers to argue against such a legitimate institution even when they think the court's decisions are overtly political. While operating in a social and political context, Supreme Court justices have freedom of manoeuvre which allows them to bargain and play games with other actors, such as legislators and bureaucrats, who anticipate their decisions. As a recent study examining the separation of powers and the Supreme Court concludes, 'The federal judiciary was designed to be independent, so we should not be surprised that in fact it is' (Segal 1997: 42). The other argument is that the court's role as a policy-maker does not depend so much on formal powers, which are anyway unclear, as on the publics and coalitions that mobilize and lobby it (Shapiro 1978). The political process, the practice of agenda-setting and the extent to which, at a given point in time, other institutions and political actors obey Supreme Court judgements shape the decisions of the court. The Supreme Court is a political body like any other, and fuses into the dominant pattern of group and electoral politics.

The celebrated example of Supreme Court policy-making was the ending of school desegregation by race in *Brown* v. *The Board of Education* in 1954. The case appears as an example of institutional power and of the salience of constitutional values. It was an example of both the power of a political body to override the powers of another and the role of a constitutional court in initiating policy change. The opposing argument is that Supreme Court activism did not come about as the result of an institutional logic, but derived from the power of the civil rights coalition that used the court to advance its interests before it influenced the executive and overcame the entrenched power of southern Democrats in Congress. Without the legitimacy and role of the Supreme Court in US political culture, no change could have been achieved, but it was also the wider political forces that were responsible for introducing the change and transformed the role of the institution itself. The Supreme Court acted in response to the political coalition which had become dominant in the 1930s. Since President Roosevelt threatened to pack the court with his nominees to ensure the judges acceded to the New Deal programme, the court accepted Congressional legislation extending federal intervention in economic life and social affairs. In time, the court became so imbued with the values of the dominant electoral coalition that policy in civil rights was often initiated by judicial decisions. The liberalism of the Supreme Court was partly a function of presidential nomination and partly derived from the contemporary elite liberal culture. If the Democrats lacked a long-term electoral majority the court would probably not have become such an activist for social and political rights. While the court can, to an extent, create values, wider social and political forces structure how the institution works. In this way there is a complex interaction between institutional and other processes, such as between political action and social change.

Another example of the complex effects of institutions are in central–local politics. It is often argued that unitary states are highly centralized because the central government control of law-making institutions makes local government a creature of the central state (Sharpe 1985). In the UK, such writers can usually cite examples of central government legislation designed to stamp out practices that central politicians do not like being carried out by local government. However, examples of policy formation, such as urban policy in the 1970s, show that formal powers count for less than the constitutional framework implies. Instead, policy communities of actors stretching across institutions exercise influence. There is a circulation of ideas and influence from the different bodies which have an input into policy by virtue of their role in the implementation of decisions (Rhodes, R. 1986; 1988).

A similar story can be told about central–local systems in other countries, such as France before 1983. France appears highly centralized. Representatives of the central state, the prefects and field administrators, have extensive powers originating from the Napoleonic regime at the beginning of the nineteenth century. Local government had few functions, and the prefects could exercise strict legal control. But, because of close relationships between prefects and elected mayors, central state actors could not get their own way (Worms 1966). Local mayors, and even central state bureaucrats, often adapted central government schemes to reflect local interests. Powerful mayors used their contacts in Paris to override central dictats. The decentralization reforms introduced by the Mitterrand presidency in 1982 and 1983, which gave new freedoms to local authorities and created new tiers of sub-national government, reflected and consolidated the power of local elites (Mabileau 1991).

The examples of central–local politics in both nations, however, do not just show how informal communities of decision-makers override the unitary stamp of national decision-making. While it is true that policy-making is sometimes 'bottom-up' in both countries, the extent of local influence on decision-making often varies from period to period and between policy-making sectors. Thus, in Britain in the 1980s, central government managed to centralize policy-making in some sectors, such as housing and transport, but could or would not do so in other policy sectors like community care or the environment. France decentralized urban policy decisions in the 1980s but centralized them again through a system of state-run planning contracts in the 1990s. These contrary examples show that the pattern of policy-making is sometimes based on institutional processes while at other times it is not. The researcher needs a form of explanation or a theory that sets out why and when institutional factors are sometimes important.

A second limitation of the institutional approach is that the social context shapes and mediates formal arrangements. The political environment of a country causes policy variation just as much as the operation of political institutions. Institutional effects may themselves be the result of wider changes. An example is the argument that certain forms of institutional arrangement promote policy stability. The classic case is the idea that the British two-party system fosters the oscillation of policies through the additive power of the electoral system. The idea is that the institutional rule of the plurality electoral system produces clear majorities for one party, and four or five years later another party takes over with a similarly powerful mandate. This appears to give the government of the day a free hand to introduce ideological policies, a latitude that does not seem to exist in countries with more proportional electoral systems and frequent coalition governments. The claim is that the power of parties to control policy in a two-party system explains unnecessary policy reversals, such as why the steel industry was nationalized, privatized, renationalized and reprivatized in the post-war years (Finer 1975). In fact, the two-party system had no such simple effect, and the bi-partisan consensus on many issues ensured that much policy-making carried on unchanged whatever government was in power (Rose 1980). Though recent research shows the parties were more ideological in the post-war period than is commonly supposed (Glennerster 1995), they tended not to let their preferences interfere with policy content except on a few narrow partisan issues. The consensus was either sociological or institutional. It was sociological because economic growth and the decline of social conflict in the post-war period encouraged the parties to follow similar political ideas. It was institutional because organizations, such as the civil service, cabinet government and the constitutional monarchy, constrained the decisions of political parties and created an elite 'rules of the game' which neutralized the centripetal tendencies of parliamentary and party politics.

The third limitation is that the institutional approach presents a static view of the policy process. Institutions can explain how political systems structure policy, but they tend not to account for why policies change. In other words, institutionalism lacks a theory of human action as it tends to consider that the rules and norms that constrain behaviour are reasons for action in themselves. This criticism is not too damaging if researchers accept that institutions do not offer a complete explanation of public decision-making, but it presents difficulties if researchers call themselves institutionalists.

On the other hand, it is possible to argue that institutions can play a role in pushing for change because formal rules dynamically interact with the power of interest groups and politicians. For example, the structure and powers of institutions can allow radical change to be pursued with greater speed than otherwise would have been the case. For example, the policies of the Johnson administration in the USA in the 1960s set up radical bureaucracies, such as the Office for Economic Opportunity, which sought to empower local communities, often against state and municipal governments. The idea to promote the interests of the poor derives in part from the intentions of Democrat policy-makers and their awareness of the institutional obstacles in a federal political system. The reason for the institutional dynamism was the organizational form, though it could only survive within a supportive political context. Alternatively, institutions can slow down change by allowing conservatives to block reforms. For example, the slow progress of policies on civil rights in the USA can be explained by the institutional power of conservative southern Democrats. They were able to use their power as chairs of Congressional committees to obstruct progressive legislation.

Institutions can also change their role over time. An example is the development of the power and scope of the European Court of Justice (ECJ). The ECJ used to play a minor role in European Union policy, but, through a series of decisions since the late 1970s, it became more influential. In an institutional perspective, the change in role is an example of institutional capacity-building, showing a dynamic role for institutions; in another perspective, the power of the ECJ is a consequence of the growing number of EU directives and the greater legitimacy of the European institutions, particularly after the Single European Act of 1986. In one explanation, the growth in institutional power derives from an institutional dynamic; in the other, social and political forces drive institutional power. It is difficult to disentangle the relative impacts.

The fourth limitation is that institutions themselves are not an independent influence in the policy process, but that institutional rules and their operation depend on political choices made by individuals, such as bureaucrats and politicians. Political actors can change how institutions function. In countries which have an entrenched constitutional document, change occurs through amendment and judicial review. In other systems constitutions can evolve through the reform of political institutions, such as the internal structure of public bureaucracies and changes in the rules of parliamentary scrutiny. New political actors often try to reform institutions to accrue more power. In addition, changes within political practice alter the operation of institutions. For example, the growing factionalism within the UK Conservative Party in the 1990s undermined the practice of collective cabinet responsibility.

Institutional approaches tend to downplay the importance of conflict, interests and thus of politics in the study of policy. As a result these accounts tend to neglect the obvious reasons for policy change, largely because it is often argued that institutions structure actors' responses more than ideas and interests. For example, Thatcher (1994) offers a highly detailed account of why policy change in the telecommunications sector was similar and different between Britain and France, and he looks at why the extension of competition was more pronounced in the former country. Although he argues that European policy pressures, particularly European Union policy, were responsible for policy change in both countries, he also contends that the institutional presence of OFTEL, the regulatory agency, was responsible for the form and pace of policy change in the UK, and this factors shows the importance of institutions. However, his argument seems to neglect the vital difference between the two countries, because since 1979 Britain was headed by a government whose main successful and repeated policy aim was privatization and competition. It was the policy aims that led to the setting up OFTEL. Political choices explain both the difference in approach and the institutional framework the two countries adopted.

What often happens is that discontent about the workings of an institution causes it to change, a non-institutional process. An example is the reform of the US House of Representatives' committee system in the 1970s, which lessened the power of committee chairs. Rather than institutions being the source of change, it is the adaption of the US party system, in particular the electoral decay of southern Democrats, who had had a stranglehold on the committee system and thus on policy-making, and challenges by young Democrats to their power, that explains the change rather than an autonomous institutional development.

The argument that institutions count rests on the difficulty of changing constitutional arrangements. Even though the preferences and balance of power of certain groups is the reason for a particular arrangement, their preferences and strength are only salient in special circumstances. Institutions make it easy for decision-makers to follow established procedures and to uphold the principles of government. It is often costly to reinvent those procedures. Institutionalists also argue that institutions shape policy by affecting the context of debate and the power of the actors wishing to reform policy-making. For example, March and Olsen (1989) argue that, though there have been a large number of administrative reforms of US federal government, their lack of success in changing the practice of decision-making is witness to the power of routines that carry on in spite of attempts to change them. Institutions change much more slowly than policies. Their argument, however, shows the weakness of institutional forms of explanation, as in time the balance of political interests subsumes any institutional arrangement.

Fifth, and finally, institutionalism tends not to emphasize the distinctiveness of each policy sector. Given that institutions are generally uniform in European states, the particular dynamics of policy-making in a policy sector are more due to the role of interest groups and characteristics of public activity than whether, for example, there is a prime minister, president or a legislative committee. This argument returns the discussion to a key point discussed in Chapter 1. The reason why policy became an important aspect of political science is that public decision-making is more complex than the standard (institutional) approaches assume.

On the other hand, institutionalists are able to make their accounts more complex because the formal and organizational context for each policy sectors differs, even within a unitary European state, and especially in the USA. Congressional committees have very different procedures and rules, such as the powers allocated to chairs and vice-chairs (Fenno 1973). In other countries the legal framework differs between the sectors, which means that policy-makers introduce public measures in a different fashion. For example, the institutional framework of local economic development and local education policies in the UK differs because the legal framework governing schools was based on the landmark 1944 Education Act which set up a partnership between central and local government. The Department for Education and Employment and local education authorities were given complementary roles. The institutional providers, schools, were in a formal relationship with local education authorities set down in statute and convention. The reform of education policy during the 1980s, which took powers away from local education authorities and gave them to schools, had to proceed from the formal powers already allocated to the various public bodies. In local economic development policy the powers are distributed among a variety of agencies such as local authorities and training agencies, and various central departments take an interest such as the Department of the Environment, Transport and Regions, the Department of Trade and Industry and the Department for Education and Employment. Thus strategies supporting local economies must proceed according to the balance of institutions at the central level and the variety of local providers.

The question to ask is whether these frameworks derive from the 'technology' of the sector or from unique institutional processes. To what extent does the nature of policy-making, such as education, drive the legal and formal framework of governing or does the regulatory framework and the culture of political organizations drive policy-making? Rather than national cultures and political traditions, institutional structures could depend on the character of education policy-making itself. Thus policy-making in a sector may be the same in a variety of country contexts. On the other hand, the particular role a policy sector played in a country's history can be a good explanation too. Chance or the length of time since a previous reform could be the explaining factor as institutions gain their own legitimacy. Thus in France, for example, the reason why national institutions play such a strong role in education is the republican tradition which placed an emphasis on state schooling. In Britain, the tradition of localism and local innovation in the nineteenth century created a more decentralized system. Once set in motion, the contrast between the historical foundations of British and French education means that policy-making, characterized by incremental change, takes on a different course because of greater centralization in France, even though the two countries face similar pressures to increase standards, to obtain value for money and to make education relevant for employment (Ambler 1987). These arguments show how complex are the interactions between institutions and the decision-making process.

New Institutionalism

During the 1980s there was a revival of academic interest in the role of institutions in politics, an academic industry called the 'new institutionalism'. Within the field of comparative politics, researchers became disillusioned with approaches that assume that policy results from socio-economic factors (see Chapter 5). Instead, new institutionalists place the state at the centre of their analysis. As institutions are the manifestation of the state, they count in explaining outputs and outcomes, and they show how countries with broadly the same pressures on government follow different policies (March and Olsen 1989; Steinmo *et al.* 1992). New institutionalism has several types of adherent: historically orientated political scientists, rational choice theorists and organizational theorists (Kato 1996). This section discusses the first version; Chapter 6 examines the second.

Rather than reassert traditional institutionalism against an over-confident behaviouralism, new institutionalists set out a fresh approach. Unlike the old version, the new one accepts that there are a variety of influences on policy, in particular those that derive from the economy. They prefer to integrate societal and state-orientated perspectives to understand better how policy is made. Casting their net rather wider than old institutionalists, the new ones consider that institutions affect the power of groups, shape the way ideas circulate to influence policy, and influence the coordination of public decisions. The profound and subtle influence of institutions is because they comprise the norms and conventions of behaviour as well as being the formal apparatus of government. Institutions are habits of decision-making and belief systems. These routines process policies in accordance with accepted practices; they are embedded within the institutional framework, which in turn affects the power of groups in the policy process. Because institutions are more stable and resistant to change, they are an independent factor affecting political behaviour.

New institutionalists put their case with subtlety. Rather than just being descriptive, the approach aims to analyse the varying impacts on public policy. New institutionalists recognize the complexity of decision-making, and they seek to place the contribution of institutions in a prominent place alongside the many other causes of political action. Nevertheless, new institutionalists search for factors that cause institutions to have a life of their own. They use to great effect the methods of comparative analysis to examine the role of different institutions in the same policy sector.

Some Applications

Hall's analysis of state intervention

P. Hall (1992) wishes to explain how Western countries reacted to the economic crisis of the 1970s, in particular he wants to know why policy-makers radically changed their ideas about economic policy. He argues that the shift in the UK from Keynesian economic management, based on the control of the aggregates of consumption and investment, to monetarism, founded on the measurement and regulation of the money supply, requires an understanding of the role of institutions. Institutions structured policy by influencing how new ideas came to the surface and the manner in which they were expressed in government decisions. In the early 1970s, Keynesian ideas were dominant in the Treasury and other governing institutions. In the mid-1970s the economic crisis of inflation and unemployment meant that the Labour governments of 1974–79 were unable to use fiscal measures to bring the economy out of recession. By the time Margaret Thatcher became prime minister in 1979, there had been a change in the balance of power. New centres of decision-making emerged, such as the financial markets. An oppositional media promoted new think-tanks. The institution of the competitive party system ensured the opposition party, the Conservatives, rapidly adopted and advocated the new set of ideas. These institutional factors allowed the prime minister to wield a new coalition to unseat the old orthodoxy and to build on the shifts in policy that had already occurred. She was helped in her task by the independence and power of the executive in the British system of government which allowed her to push the policies through.

Hall's analysis is important because he uses institutions to explain policy change. Most analysts tend to deploy institutions to account for policy stability because they tend to constrain behaviour and to promote continuity and stability. In this economic policy case institutions allowed some decision-makers to propose radical changes. Monetarism appeared in the UK because of the pattern of institutions, in particular the competitive party system. However, the problem with Hall's argument is that institutions play different roles at the various stages in the story depending on what needs to be explained. At the beginning of the tale, institutions were powerful drags on innovation and held up the influence of ideas, but by the 1980s they had became innovative. Hall seems to use the same process to explain both stability and change.

Rather than institutions, it is the realignment of political forces that explains the new policies. A faction of the Conservative Party promoted these new ideas and then one of their number became party leader, winning partly through the unpredictability of the party's selection process. The charismatic leadership of Margaret Thatcher, the dominance of the new right in the Conservative Party, and then electoral success in 1979 were more important than institutions. Likewise, the emergence of the centres which promoted the ideas was not caused by institutional factors, but by the failure of the old way of thinking to solve policy problems. The problem with new institutional analysis is not that the institutional structure of government does not have an effect on policy. Indubitably the roles of the Treasury, the Bank of England and the party system influenced policy outcomes. But they label as institutional too many aspects of the decision-making process. Hall includes as institutions electoral constraints, forecasting centres and institutes, the media, trades unions and attitudes of civil servants (1992: 106–9). The analysis is circular, tracing causes from institution to institution. Though Hall recognizes the interplay between institutions, interests and ideas, and he understands that institutional explanations are only part of the story, he needs an account of political conflict and strategic interaction to offer a full explanation of the change from Keynesian to monetarist economic management.

Steinmo's comparative explanation of tax policies

Steinmo (1989; 1993) wishes to explain why tax policy varies between the USA, Sweden and Britain. Counterintuitively, taking the period of the 1970s and 1980s, he finds that Sweden had a less progressive tax system than the United States; and Britain had rapid shifts in policy. He argues that institutions explain these differences. In the USA the fragmented institutional structure helped the representation of a multiplicity of interests which ensured that a regressive national sales tax was never introduced. In Sweden, in contrast, Steinmo finds that the centralized state structure and the system of proportional representation led to a light level of corporate taxation and a low redistribution of income. The power of the state allowed the ruling Social Democrats to structure the relationship between interest groups and to accommodate business with the state. The idea was that economic growth would be fostered by a favourable tax regime, and this would in turn fund a generous social welfare system. Thus the government introduced a sales tax in the face of much public opposition. The proportional representation electoral system ensured that one party dominated the political system so that these policies could be introduced over a number of years. In Britain, the first-past-the-post electoral system led to frequent changes of party control of government, and thus to instability in tax policy. The system of adversary politics caused the twists, turns and irrationality in decision-making. The absence of checks on the executive excluded the opposition and thus any means of stabilizing policy-making.

Though Steinmo's critique is interesting, there are a number of problems. The crucial difficulty is that he does not fully explain why the corporate sector is taxed heavily in the USA. If there are institutional blocks to policy innovation, why did not the corporate sector mobilize against high corporate taxes? After all, it is easier to resist a policy than to introduce one. Perhaps business was not able to wield an effective electoral coalition in Congress because of the way in which constituencies have such a strong hold on their representatives? But how does that factor explain the success of various lobbies in US politics, such as the defence industry? After all, cannot business mobilize a coalition to argue that jobs depend on the level of corporate taxation? The results also fly in the face of the conventional wisdom about the power of business in US politics (Lindblom 1977; Stone, C. 1989). In Sweden, Steinmo almost argues that the formalized pattern of state–interest group relationships – the corporatist system – causes the pattern of public decisions. Even with the power of the state, the secret of the corporatist framework is that the intermediation of groups depends on the social milieu of the country in question. The only way the proportional representation system can cause stable government rather than that other possible result of proportional representation, political instability and policy change, is through the effect of consistent voting patterns. For corporatism to work thus there must be compromise and agreement based on a supportive political culture, which feeds into voting behaviour, rather than simply the effect of the pattern of political institutions on policy decisions.

The contrast with tax policy-making in the UK shows some of the limitations of Steinmo's approach. In the twentieth century Britain had the experience of long periods of Conservative rule (1951–64; 1970–74; and 1979–97) which coincided with periods of classic corporatism and also of 'one-sided' corporatism which describes the close alliance between government and business in the 1980s and 1990s. Rather than changes in tax policy across governments as suggested by the adversary politics model, there were changes within the period in office, such as Steinmo's example of the 1984 overhaul of corporation tax. The adversary model misses the way in which policy is formed within the bureaucracy and from pressure of interest groups outside the arena of Parliament (Richardson and Jordan 1979; Rose and Davies 1994). The adversary politics model can only explain the style of British politics. The substance has more to do with bureaucratic politics and the drive for consensus in the party system.

There is also less difference of institutional patterns between Sweden and Britain than Steinmo allows. Instead, interests played a role, such as the Swedish economic elites which influenced the policies of the Social Democrats at an early stage of their electoral dominance (Steinmo 1993: 88–89). Within the text of Steinmo's analysis are the other determinants of policy. In the UK case he cites Heclo and Wildavsky's (1974) work on the influence of Treasury elites. The changes in tax policy can be seen in the context of a pragmatic culture that ensured that there were no fundamental governing principles behind the tax system. The elites tended to respond to short-term pressures under the influence of Parliament and the media. Nevertheless, even with these criticisms, Steinmo's study is an interesting test of the new institutionalist framework, and he uses the comparative method to great effect.

Health policy in Sweden, France and Switzerland

A third example of the new institutionalism is Immergut's (1992) account of health policy in Sweden, France and Switzerland, examining insurance. She claims that institutional analysis is able to explain both policy stability and change. She argues that, even though each country started from a similar initial position in terms of the power of its doctors' interest groups and government proposals for health insurance, the ways in which such proposals were implemented were different. In Switzerland, a compulsory national healthcare programme was rejected, and the government only provides subsidies to private insurance; in France, the government managed to introduce national health insurance as a compulsory programme; and the Swedish government established a national health system. Immergut argues that, rather than reflecting ideas or the power of interest groups, the rules of the game, in particular the number of veto points in the political system, determined when and how the government introduced the policy. In Sweden the constitution limited the number of veto points, in France there were more points of access. In Switzerland institutional rules of direct democracy ensured the debate moved into the public arena. A series of rules limited the freedom of the national government. The sharing of decision-making between the cantons slowed policy-making down even further; and the referendum transferred power to the interest groups which dominated the petitions and the campaigns.

One of the problems with Immergut's analysis is that the difference between the politics of France and Sweden is left to one side. In Sweden the Social Democrats had a stable electoral base in a context where other political parties accepted the broad objectives of social insurance, a point accepted by Immergut. Such a strong political impetus for reform never existed in France. Although the executive is strong in Sweden, Immergut does not confront the variable power of the French state, which can be very powerful in certain contexts but weak in others. Even though governments back down to powerful producer groups in times of crisis, public pliancy owes more to traditions of protest and the symbolic aspects of bargaining than to veto points governed by institutions. The links of doctors into the political parties and parliament also cannot be categorized as an institutional veto point: they reflect elite networks. The analysis is much more convincing when she examines the effect of the Fifth Republic in France, which gave more power to the executive. As a result the government was able to introduce reforms against the wishes of doctors. The danger, however, of relying on the institutional differences between the Fourth and Fifth Republics is that the argument neglects the political factors affecting institutional change between those periods. The failure of the Fourth Republic and the success of the Fifth owed as much to the role of personalities and parties which created the new institutions and made them work. First, President de Gaulle and his successors created a new governing system; then Mitterrand consolidated and extended the legitimacy and efficiency of the Fifth Republic.

Does the New Institutionalism Offer a Convincing Account of Policy-making?

Good institutional analysis recognizes that institutions are constraints and that they vary across space and time. Some institutionalists accept that there are many causes of public policy. As Weaver and Rockman write (1993: 39–40), 'institutional arrangements that create opportunities for effective governance in one country may heighten risks of governmental failure in another because the latter government faces different facilitating and limiting conditions ... it makes little sense to speak of one set of institutional arrangements as inherently more effective than another ... a government's capabilities involves finding the best fit among three factors: the nature of its policy challenges, its institutional arrangements, and the conditions that facilitate and limit institutional effects'. Though institutions matter, policies emerge from a complex environment. An example they cite is France's adoption of nuclear power as a solution to the energy crisis, a policy choice that contrasts to those made by other nation states. They argue that the scarcity of alternative sources of power generation was as much a reason as the traditional strong state. Comparing five nations' policy responses, they conclude that policy and the availability of resources are more important than institutional arrangements and government capacities. Nevertheless, one of the salient institutional factors is the number of veto points in a political system.

As well as having many of the problems of the old institutionalism, the new version has some of its own. The first weakness is the frequent assumption that countries and policy sectors emerge from a similar starting-point. For example, with national responses to economic crisis, it is very hard to disentangle institutional effects from others because each economy reacts differently to external shocks. Because policy-makers receive such contrasting signals, even similar institutions work uniquely. For example, the impact of the international economy drives economic policy-making in the UK. The high proportion of British national income that is traded internationally makes the country vulnerable to international economic events, such as the oil price hike in the 1970s. The importance of the City of London in the English economy is also considerable; it shapes economic policy because politicians fear currency speculation and drops in stock market prices if public decisions do not find favour.

The second limitation is that new institutionalists rely too much on comparing one policy sector across countries. It is fairly likely that policy-making differs between countries (though it is almost impossible to disentangle the effects of institutions, political ideologies, cultures and interests), but it is harder to know the extent to which policy-making differs between sectors and across countries, and almost impossible to conclude which factor is more important. The research design of the new institutionalists encourages a perspective based on country differences without acknowledging the extent to which policy-making varies according to sector in the same institutional context.

The main problem with the new institutionalist approach is its definition of what counts as institutional. By incorporating values and norms as part of institutions, they include too many aspects of political life under one category. The resulting amalgam of processes appears to explain change under the rubric of institutions, but in reality it disguises the variety of interactions and causal mechanisms that occur between the contrasting elements of the political system. Explanations in political science need to separate out constraints from the motivations and interests of the actors or else it becomes impossible to identify what causes variation and change. What is needed is a less all-encompassing definition of institutions which is more limited in scope, but has more cogent explanatory power. Institutions limit the choices of actors without determining them.

Summing-up

This chapter reviews the idea that institutions shape policy. It criticizes the institutionalist approach to policy formulation and implementation without undermining the important role political institutions play in the decision-making process. Institutions constrain the choices open to decision-makers rather than shaping the preferences of those actors. This chapter resists the idea, prevalent in the new institutionalist literature, that decision-makers internalize the norms of institutions, though institutions do, to an extent, embody political values. The chapter also rejects the broad definition of institutions offered by the new institutionalists because it makes the argument too circular. By including ideas, norms and interests as institutions, the new institutionalism turns too much of politics into a set of formal processes. Such an expansion robs institutions of their explanatory power.

The institutional approach works best when comparing policy-making and implementation between nation-states. It highlights the unique character of each country's formal rules and stresses the values shaping a state tradition. In a policy sector, like education, it is likely the institutional framework has a major impact on how policy is made and implemented. The approach is less able to explain policy-making within nation-states, particularly between policy sectors, and while the approach can account for policy stability, it has less to say about policy change. Attempts by Hall and others to use institutions to explain policy innovation often end up disguising the political processes that drive such changes. On the other hand, the institutional approach can understand how change gathers momentum once it becomes unstoppable. Thus once nation-states start reformulating their macro-economic policies in an economic crisis, the institutional approach gives an indication of the varying ways in which they go about it.

The chapter suggests it is easy to overestimate the role of institutions. Institutional approaches tend to neglect the political and social context that affects how formal rules and norms operate. In satisfying the criteria for a theory of public policy outlined in Chapter 1, institutions fail because they are a process not fine-grained enough to explain the variation in the politics between sectors, over time and in space. In truth there is no institutional approach, institutions are just one factor constraining public policy choices.

4

Group and Network Approaches

Introduction

Group and network approaches stress the importance of interactions between the participants in the policy process. Whereas traditional accounts of politics tended to concentrate on procedures and constitutions, many studies since the 1950s directed their attention to groups and their influence on policy, and reacted against the limitations of the institutional approach. When narrowly conceived, institutions do not seem to explain the variety and changes in political relationships. It is not just the cabinet or the President and Congress that make decisions; policy emerges as a result of informal patterns of association. Groups formulate policy and set the agenda; they try to influence the legislative and executive decisions; they usually participate in the decisions about implementation; and they often implement policies themselves.

Governments and bureaucracies need groups because they are sources of policy ideas. Groups are repositories of expertise; they can help make a policy legitimate; and their cooperation can ensure the successful implementation of a policy. The importance of group politics reflects the weakness of political institutions and their separation from social and economic life. Whereas governments can come into office with grand ideas and proposals for change, and legislatures and bureaucracies can swiftly enact policy measures, formal office holders need groups to formulate and implement those policies in a manner which reflects the complexity of the real world. Reflecting their importance, there are many studies examining the role of groups in policy and the dependence of governments upon group politics (e.g. Richardson and Jordan 1979; Wilson 1980; Lembruch and Schmitter 1982; Petracca 1992).

The Group Approach

The classic works of American political science, in particular A. F. Bentley's *The Process of Government* (1908), which greatly influenced D. Truman's *The Governmental Process* (1962), formulated the group approach to politics. These writers argue that groups are not just important, but that they define the policy process. Thus Truman (1962: 502) could write that 'the behaviours that constitute the process of government cannot be understood apart from the groups, especially the organised and potential interest groups, that are operative at any one point in time'. Still more explicit is Latham's *The Group Basis of Politics* (1953), whose theme can be deduced from the title. Group accounts do not simply update institutional accounts of the political process with the idea that groups are an aspect of policy-making that can be studied alongside legislatures, parties and bureaucracies. Group approaches say that politics is about associational relationships because the formal office holders are as much part of interest-based politics as are groups themselves. Thus political parties are composed of groups; legislatures are constituted by group action; and different branches of public bureaucracies behave as groups in their own right.

The inclusive conception of association makes group approaches different from the others discussed in this book. The behaviour of all political actors needs to be understood in the group context. The presupposition leads to the idea that the state itself is composed of groups rather than being an autonomous entity. In particular, government bureaus articulate their interests rather than neutrally supervise the implementation process. The idea has something in common with the 'bureaucratic politics' model outlined in the preceding chapter. But the group approach regards the fragmentation of the state as only one element to the story. The patterns of the alliances that build up between outsider groups and the bureaucrats themselves structure policy rather than the institutions of the state. The group approach abandons the idea of a strict public/private or a state/non-state distinction. In practice, a maze of official and quasi-legitimate groups share the exercise of authority and jointly make most public decisions. Group politics reflects the increasing complexity and specialization of economic and social life.

The group approach, in its original formulation, is synonymous with pluralism, the idea that there is an equal balance of power between interests. Writers such as Truman (1962: 14–44) drew upon contemporary sociological work that rejected the idea that society was becoming individualized, and argued that it was composed of groups. The increasing differentiation of social relations has its reflection in political life. Naturally, writers on associational politics have moved on. They now recognize the inequality of groups and acknowledge the active role of the state. But the idea of complexity as a force in politics remains as an organizing principle of group-based policy research. Pressure-group studies, by taking the variation in public policy as given, understand the intricacies of policy-making far more than institutional accounts.

Lindblom's Incrementalist Model (again)

The group approach is apparently captured by the incrementalist model of policy-making discussed in Chapter 2. Lindblom (1960; 1968) argues that decision-making is not rational, but is unplanned, disjointed and incremental. There is a process of 'partisan mutual adjustment' between the actors involved. Decision-makers make 'selective limited comparisons' when weighing-up policy choices. Incrementalism is often taken to be a justification of the pluralist model of decision-making as it implies that policy results from the slow-moving bargaining between groups (Richardson and Jordan 1979: 22–4). Characterizations such as this precipitate the standard critiques of pluralism. It is often argued that incrementalism does not recognize the inequality of power in the policy-making process and justifies a conservative approach to politics. Nor does incrementalism recognize the autonomy of the state and give enough salience to the influence of political institutions.

However, Lindblom in his later work (1977), in response to the criticisms, does not subscribe to the pluralist model. He is really a neopluralist who believes that groups are unequal participants in the policy process. This is because incrementalism is compatible with the idea that powerful interests block change rather than that policy results from an equal balance between the groups. Lindblom also includes actors other than groups in decision-making. In *The Policy-Making Process* there are three types: citizens, group representatives and proximate policy-makers (mainly office-holders) who interact to make policy. He largely discounts citizens for the usual reason that they do not participate much in political life. Even groups have a limited role because proximate policy-makers need not accept their demands, interest-group pressures often cancel each other out, and the internal functions of interest groups, such as providing a service to members, sap their influence. Thus Lindblom is less of a pluralist and group theorist than is commonly supposed. Rather than groups, it is partisan mutual adjustment between the proximate policy-makers that accounts for policy in the incrementalist model. Even the classic 1960 article, 'The science of muddling through', does not mention groups much as it is more an account of decision-making and the limits to knowledge than a study of group interaction. The only reference to groups is one paragraph arguing that incrementalism usually incorporates a wide range of interests and 'fits in the multiple pressure pattern' (1960: 86). Thus Lindblom is much more a complex thinker than the tag of the incremental model suggests.

Nevertheless, incrementalism influenced group accounts of policy-making. As Chapter 2 argues, the incremental model offers an account of policy that is universal to most political systems. Slow adjustment is the reality of much policy-making, and there is usually much interaction between the people who are involved in policy-making, both pressure groups and other policy-makers. The model helps analysts break down the conventional monolith of the state. However, because incrementalism is a general characterization, it does not offer an account of different types of group interaction and thereby an explanation of policy change or stability and variation. It has almost nothing to say about the varying influence of interests, ideas and economic change in each policy sector. Yet, when Lindblom is read carefully, he anticipates much of the new policy analysis, in particular ideas about policy adaption, the 'intelligence of democracy' and policy learning (see Chapters 7 and 8).

Some Applications of the Group Approach

Beer's account of British policy-making

Because policies affect different collections of groups, an important insight of the group approach is that the nature of policy-making differs according to the type of group involved with decisions, such as whether policy-making is secretive and operates behind closed doors or is open and involves a large number of participants. One early study of the varying role of pressure groups in the policy process is Samuel Beer's *Modern British Politics* (1965). He distinguishes between producer and consumer groups. Producer groups, having a direct role in providing goods and services, include such as trades unions and business associations. They have an influence over policy because they help implement public decisions and provide expert advice. An example is the British Medical Association, which exerts a powerful influence over policy because of its role as a producer of medicine and healthcare (Eckstein 1960). Consumer groups, on the other hand, seeking to represent issues affecting society as a whole or broad sections of it, are less powerful because they are less able to block policy and are not so valuable to policy-makers.

Naturally, it is possible to undermine Beer's simple distinction. As the 1979–83 and 1983–7 UK Conservative administrations show, the executive can sideline producer groups, such as trades unions, by confronting them and excluding them from consultation. Policy can be made by a small number of ministers and civil servants using the advice of privately organized research institutes, the 'think-tanks'. Consumer groups, by virtue of their ability to manipulate public opinion, to influence the media, to penetrate political parties and to become experts in their own right, have become more important. State institutions seek to integrate these high-profile lobbyists into policy-making. Bureaucrats and politicians seek to co-opt and manage them. With government grants, these groups have even become part of the implementation process. An example is UK environmental groups, which have increased their public salience and are invited into consultations. Thus, in agri-environmental policy, radical groups, like Friends of the Earth, are consulted alongside the producer groups, such as the National Farmers Union. The explosion of the number and activism of pressure groups undermines the cosy understanding of public policy captured by the corporatist approach. Rather than stable relationships among producer groups, there is now a vast number of relationships between groups of all kinds. The growth of protest and political activism have fractured the traditional boundaries of public policy.

Nevertheless, Beer's distinction remains important in alerting the researcher to the different character of groups. Groups in different policy sectors have different sources of power and the variation in type of groups can explain cross-national and cross-sectoral differences in decision-making. In the study of comparative public policy, the group approach leads to the generalization that because group structures and power differ in each country, decision-making and policy outcomes vary as well.

Governing under pressure

The seminal British work in group politics tradition is Richardson and Jordan's *Governing Under Pressure* (1979). This account begins with a statement of the value of groups as set out in Bentley (1908), Truman (1962) and Latham (1953). While the book carefully qualifies the view that all political life amounts to group interaction, Richardson and Jordan consider groups to be essential to the process of government. They are the real forces at work. Richardson and Jordan apply the group idea to British policy-making. Instead of policy being mainly determined by institutions, in particular by Parliament and the political parties, it is group politics within the executive and civil service, as well as the traditionally defined interest groups, that shapes policy. Richardson and Jordan study the pressure groups that are proximate to central government departments in decentralized policy subsystems like transport, energy and education. The integration of bureaucratic and group politics is captured by the metaphor of a policy community. Policy often emerges from within these systems and is not much influenced by party and parliament. The British policy-making style is consensual and accommodatory to group demands. Applying Hayward's (1974) idea that British politics is 'humdrum', Richardson and Jordan argue that the policy process resembles the incrementalist model. Attempts at radical change and planning are bound to fail because of the group process of policy-making.

Richardson and Jordan's study is a critique of institutional approaches of British politics. It pays dividends to examine decision-making behind the closed doors of Whitehall and to realize that the transitory issues that dominate the media and debates in the House of Commons usually have less impact on important decisions than the pressure applied by groups, both within and without the central government bureaucracy. The text of *Governing Under Pressure* has many examples of seemingly dull decisions that have a major impact on the everyday life of citizens.

But, of course, there are problems with the account. The main one is that it is descriptive rather than explanatory as is so often the case with approaches to public policy. It is a better version of how policy emerges in the UK than the adversarial politics model and other institutional accounts. But there is not much attention to why decisions emerge at some times and not at others. It is also not clear why policies are different between sectors. Although Richardson and

Jordan recognize diversity, they generally assume the political system is homogenous, an idea captured by the term 'policy style'
which can be contrasted to other national styles (Richardson 1982).
They assume there is little change or change that is very heavily
processed by the group system and is moderated by the values of
consensus and accommodation.

Even the description has its problems. Richardson and Jordan's
book was finished in 1978, but in 1979 Thatcher's Conservative
administration come into a power with a policy programme and
style of governing intended to disrupt existing consensual decision-
making patterns. She promoted activist ('can do') civil servants who
pushed through policy decisions. Conservative governments lifted
policies from new right groups and think-tanks rather than balanced
interests. Policy was announced away from established practices of
consultation in committees and deliberation by royal commissions
and other bodies. In the long term the Conservatives succeeded in
reducing the power of some established groups. The apotheosis of
this form of policy-making was the introduction of the poll tax, the
single person adult local tax, in 1990 (1989 in Scotland), which was
formulated by activist ministers and civil servants against the wishes
of the pressure groups and institutional interests (Butler *et al.* 1994).
Thus Richardson and Jordan did not predict the emergence of
ideological party government.

It is no doubt unfair to criticize the book for its failure to account
for events that occurred after publication. If the framework works up
until 1979, then that is enough. No political system remains based
on the same political principles for all time. It is also the case that
some policy sectors were not greatly affected by the Thatcher
governments as many interest groups were able, at least at first, to
resist change, such as in agriculture (Marsh and Rhodes 1992b). It
may be the case that the Thatcher governments were a diversion
rather than a revolution in the British policy-making style. After
Thatcher's fall from power in 1990, political life became more
consensual again in some policy sectors, such as education, with a
slow-down in reform and growth in the power of the groups in policy
formulation. The other view is that the neo-liberal revolution was a
fundamental change in British politics, which is so powerful that the
marketization of education and the privatization of government
continued under the Labour government elected in 1997.

Political scientists, however, prefer to apply models to most cases,
and *Governing Under Pressure* gives examples of the loss of consensus

and the importance of political conflict within the group approach. The book considers the example of the 1973 Water Act. Richardson and Jordan use the policy to show the importance of 'negotiated order', which is the idea that policy-making takes place within norms of agreement and the avoidance of conflict. The parties to a dispute try to avoid damaging ideological feuds by bargaining and concentrating on technical matters upon which all can agree. The water bill proposed taking away the powers of local government as water authorities. This naturally met with intense opposition from the local authorities, which did not wish to lose their functions. They lobbied decision-makers both before and while Parliament considered the measure. Richardson and Jordan argue that the Department of the Environment tried its best to retain consensus in the face of the intense opposition, which included a local government boycott of the proceedings. The department managed to bring the local representatives back to the decision-making process after offering them incentives, and indeed they did return. Instead of showing the breakdown of the norms of cooperation, Richardson and Jordan argue that the events demonstrate that, even when intensely opposed to government policy, the parties still come back to the negotiation table.

In a liberal democracy political actors do not usually refuse to communicate with a legitimate and democratically elected government, so it will be possible to find examples of cooperation in most cases. Even with such a controversial measure as the poll tax, which was highly unpopular, officers of the local government associations cooperated with the Scottish Office and the Department of the Environment to ensure the implementation of revenue collection and recovery systems to try to make the impossible tax work. This reflected the 'Bridge On the River Kwai' mentality of professionals. They were able to keep up standards even in the face of the destruction of the traditional local government tax and the principles of local government finance they believed in. But the experience also reflected the way in which local authorities, most of them controlled by the opposition parties and lobbied by a discontented citizenry, still, albeit reluctantly, accepted the right of the elected government to implement an unpopular and even illegitimate policy. When cooperation is described so broadly, it is hard to find any example of conflict that would undermine the idea of 'negotiated order' because everything fits into the concept except the actions of protesters. Again this is another example of a definition covering too much ground and thereby losing its explanatory power. For a consensual model to work, there must be instances where consensus and the influence of groups breaks down, covering cases when the government keeps formal negotiations open and where interest groups, preferring to accept a few palliatives or symbols to deliver to their followers, continue to sit on formal consultative committees. Thus the poll tax episode cannot be described as group politics because normal procedures and routines of decision-making had come to a halt (Butler *et al.* 1994; also see application in Chapter 8). There needs to be another explanation of why it happened. In other words stable group politics might be a good explanation of why policies stay the same, but it is not very good at explaining why the change comes about, particularly when reformers seek to circumvent the normal routines of decision-making.

Policy-making in the water industry

An attempt to see if the group approach can survive in the turbulent politics of the 1980s is the study by Richardson *et al.* (1992) of the role of the groups involved in decision-making before the water industry was privatized in 1989. Here the proposal for privatization had not come from government departments or from the water industry, which opposed privatization, but from the executive and other groups. Richardson *et al.*, however, do not see the marginal role for groups in policy formulation as evidence against the group approach because lobbying from the producer groups shaped the implementation of the policy. The government decided to privatize the industry rapidly so it did not have a clear idea of how to implement the policy. In the early phase of the policy process new groups influenced decisions, but once the issues had become more technical and practical, there re-emerged the close relationship between government departments and the water industry. Though the norms of policy-making can be disrupted by radical proposals, before long policy-making settles back into an established policy style and includes the familiar set of participants, partly because of the practical issues that need to be solved. However, the reader is left wondering what the approach explains. Rather than explain why policy-making returned to its previous pattern, the more interesting questions are why the government introduced such a radical measure and how were the central departments able to forge policy against opposition. The criterion for an effective theory of the policy process is not whether it can explain that 'high' politics often returns to questions of detail and implementation or that rapid policy change results from adversarial politics or economic crisis. An effective theory should be able to account for both policy change and negotiated stability, and show how decision-making moves from slow to rapid policy change and back again.

Criticisms of Group Approaches

Group approaches sensibly qualify institutionalism. They offer a description of the 'real' process of politics that coincides with most people's experience of how decisions are made within organizations. Generally, policy changes slowly and groups are usually involved in decision-making. A group-based approach does not commit the researcher to the idea that interests have equal access to policy, merely that associational interactions are important. The approach addresses the complexity of policy-making because it appreciates the large number of actors operating from within and outwith the state. Bureaucracies and other governing institutions are themselves fragmented and form alliances with groups. With the group lens, the researcher is better able to appreciate the circularity of policy and the difficulties of bringing about change. However, the recognition of the importance of interests in the decision-making process does not amount to the group approach to policy. The group approach's claim that politics reduces to or is mainly about associational relationships cannot be supported either in theory or in practice. Moreover, the existence of group politics is consistent with other approaches or theories within which group politics plays a role.

There are three other limitations to the group approach. The first is that it has limits as an explanation of decision-making because it does not have much to say about what issues are processed and why they are different between sectors and countries. It predicts that groups participate in decision-making, but is silent on how interests interact to produce policies. The group approach does not explain why interest groups are strong in one sector but not in another. It is not a precise tool for understanding policy change and variation. The questions that need to be asked are what incentives there are in a policy sector for groups to form, such as from the distribution of selective incentives to members, and what is the link between collection action and policy outcomes? The study of groups in the policy process needs to be complemented by a theory of rational action by the political actors within associations and organizations rather than being based on the role of groups on their own.

The second problem is the circularity to the argument. If the approach explains everything in terms of group processes, the account leaves little to be explained because it makes no distinction between cause and effect. The whole of politics becomes refracted into groups, so that the mapping and labelling of group politics appears as explanation rather than the description it really is. The group account filters out the more interesting questions that a more restrictive definition of the role of groups would consider important. If researchers conceive groups to be important actors in the policy process, that have incentives for organization and mobilization, and which constrain bureaucratic and political decision-makers, then studies could find out under what conditions groups are powerful, when groups cooperate or conflict and what is the effect of group interaction on policy. It would seem that the group approach applies a similar broad-brush approach to understanding policy as does institutionalism.

The third problem is that institutions and the state are underplayed. This criticism might seem rather ironic given that the last chapter takes so much space to criticize the institutional approach for not considering the informal aspect of politics. However, the argument there is not that institutions are not important, but that they are only part of the story. It is true that institutions appear in group approaches. For the classic pluralists, such as Dahl (1991), the structure of democratic government, polyarchy, accounts for multiple group access and the distribution of power. For critics of pluralism, powerful groups use the institutions of the state as a way of consolidating their power either to exclude other groups from the decision-making process or to control the agenda so issues of importance to weaker groups do not get discussed and considered (Schattschneider 1960). Such arguments follow on from the authors' perspectives: institutions buttress the poor or the rich depending on views of the political world. More difficult for group thinkers is the idea that institutions shape group interactions rather than reinforce them. This was the argument of Steinmo and others who apply new institutionalist insights to understanding the variation in policy outputs across countries (see Chapter 3). Different arrangements for arriving at decisions lead to different policies. Moreover, political parties, rather than just being aggregations of interests, are institutional entities as well and seek to fuse their actions with branches of the state. Likewise, bureaucracies are sites for group politics; but they are also organizations or institutions which have rules and practices that are separate from the actions and projects of the groups inside them.

A more interesting idea is that the state has an interest of its own in its relationships to interest groups, and this may differ from time to time and from place to place. In Nordlinger's (1981) formulation the state is weakly autonomous from interests because the state seeks freedom of manoeuvre to follow, for example, a coherent foreign policy. In general, this idea has been applied to problems of comparative public policy, but there is an interesting sectoral example of it. Christiansen and Dowding (1994) argue that the influence of the same group, Amnesty International, was different between two UK departments of state, the Home Office and the Foreign and Commonwealth Office. The Home Office excluded the lobbying group from the decision-making process because it criticized British policy on human rights; in the latter case, the Foreign Office included Amnesty in its deliberations because its public stand against the abuse of human rights in other countries, such as China, could be used to put pressure on those governments. It would seem that a state's interest varies depending on the policy sector. This suggests the group analysts' strategy of treating sections of the bureaucracy as just another group needs to be qualified by the political environment institutions inhabit. Factions of the bureaucracy behave exactly like groups in some kinds of decisions, as, for example, in public expenditure decisions where bureaus become lobbyists for more cash. But, when carrying out government policy or performing a regulative function, bureaucracies take on other roles.

Corporatism

The argument that the state pursues its own interest and structures the influence of groups is pushed to its fullest extent in the corporatist literature (Winkler 1976; Lembruch and Schmitter 1982). Corporatism is an account of group politics in the context of powerful states in Western European democracies, particularly in the post-Second World War period. Because of the centrality of the economy to politics, the state institutionalizes producer groups' relationships to the state and to each other, particularly the relationship between the leaders of the private sector and the trades unions. This can apply differentially to each country. Germany, Austria and have long-established corporatist styles; France and Britain have more unstable state–interest-group relationships, and corporatism only periodically existed. As the last chapter indicates, the problem of using descriptive research tools means that other forms of explanation need to be used to explain how arrangements, such as corporatism, function. Corporatists need to explain why groups cooperate and how traditions of accommodation and state traditions emerged. The other problem with corporatism is that national experience is so variable and changeable that it is hard to account for a typical pattern of interaction. Sometimes a corporatist arrangement is stable, lasting for 30 years or more; then the governing regime dissolves or changes. The approach does not explain change. It is a case, yet again, of big concepts collapsing under the weight of complexity. The decline in currency of the concept reflects its inability to generate testable hypotheses.

Corporatist theory also could not cope with the executive dominant politics of the 1980s and 1990s, particularly in the UK. The demise of Keynesian macro-economic strategies removes the obvious need for tripartite relationships to control inflationary pressures in Western economies. In the 1980s, the decline and change in character of the unions and the emergence of new management strategies broke down many traditional accommodatory arrangements. The fluidity of the new interest-group politics, particularly at the European Union level, undermines the more stable decision-making routines that are necessary for corporatism to work (Streek and Schmitter 1991). On the other hand, the approach still has some applicability to the long-term consensual relationships between the state, industry and trades unions in several north European states and in Scandinavia.

The Network Approach

The network approach has largely replaced the group perspective in the study of public policy, largely because of the limitations of approaches like corporatism. Researchers now use the network metaphor and research technique to describe and try to explain relationships between the decision-makers as they operate in various policy sectors. The claim of the approach is that the different types of relationships between group representatives, bureaucrats, politicians and other participants in decision-making account for the various ways in which political systems process policy. The network approach is different from group politics because the relationships between decision-makers matter, rather than the effect of the presence an organization in the policy process. The network approach is similar to the group account because it focuses on the informal and associative aspects of decision-making rather than just on formal arrangements.

The network approach originates from the changing way in which US analysts came to understand the politics of subgovernments. In studying the actors involved in a policy sector, like agriculture or foreign policy, US researchers used the metaphor of the 'iron triangle' to describe relationships between congressional committees, executive agencies and producer groups. The three sets of actors had key roles in the decision-making process and they maintained strong relationships with each other. Other decision-makers, even from inside Congress and the executive, were usually not involved. These policy subsystems were stable, and only a few decision-makers dominated policy-making. Other actors did not participate, either through the lack of interest of other actors or because they were excluded from decision-making.

The conventional wisdom about policy-making in the USA emerged from case studies carried out in the 1950s and 1960s. Examples include the sectors of water, agriculture and public works (e.g. Maass 1951). As is usually the case with familiar concepts, it is hard to find writers who actually use the term 'iron triangle' before the 1970s when the term became commonplace. What was usually discussed were sub-governments or policy 'whirlpools' of close relationships usually involving a small number of participants. However, even if the name was not common, the other terms to describe relationships were similar and, as many critics note, these ideas were too simple to be able to capture the reality of policy-making. As Heclo writes, 'the iron triangle is not so much wrong as disastrously incomplete' (1978: 88). There are too many participants in the policy process to support the metaphor.

The changes in US politics since the late 1960s disrupted the stable politics of policy subsystems. The emergence of post-material values (the politics of issues, such as the environment, rather than mainly economic interests), the prevalence of protest, the questioning of authority and the loss of certainty and optimism in solving policy problems fractured the consensus behind the power of producer groups and the practice of bureaucratic government. Instead of iron triangles, there are now issue networks or 'webs of influence'.

If there ever had been a closed world of policy-making, it was disrupted by the expansion of the number of lobbyists, experts, policy analysts and executive administrators who are connected by loose and open relationships. Echoing the prevalent idea of the late 1970s that government had become 'overloaded' by the number of demands and high expectations placed upon it, Heclo argues that the extended role of the state creates a greater number of interests affected by the policy and multiplies the number of demands placed on decision-makers. Policy-making became less predictable and more changeable as a result.

Heclo's (1978) article, now frequently cited, heralded the arrival of the network concept in policy studies. Partly as a result, the literature on policy subsystems became more sophisticated as writers sought to show that the iron triangle was not a realistic account. Gais *et al.* (1984) argue that new tactics of interest groups affect the structure of US policy-making and break down the iron triangles. Similarly, C. Jones's (1979) study of energy policy-making in the USA shows that the cosy policy circles in energy policy-making fractured under pressure from the Arab oil embargo. Browne's (1995) account of agricultural policy-making in Congress argues that the looser idea of a network rather than an iron triangle better accounts for relationships because of the large number of actors and the shifting relationships between them, particularly in the post-reform Congress. There are more opportunities for members of Congress to influence policy, and constituents increasingly pressure members to represent their interests because the reforms of the committee structure in the 1970s weakened the control over policy exercised by committee chairs. Policy networks exist between members of Congress and extend into their electoral districts, rather than just between the 'nodes' of the triangle. He also argues that the network concept describes the reality of conflict within policy 'domains' and between networks rather than the consensus implied by the iron triangle metaphor. Participants put some effort into 'networking' to build relationships for mutual advantage. Because of the complexity of policy-making, networks need to be 'open, responsive, opportunity laden, and permeable to wide-ranging demands from Congress' (1995: 28) if they are to work. Rather than following Heclo's presage of the chaos of interest-group liberalism, Browne regards networks as an essentially coordinative device whose permeability enables the policy domain to respond to change and to resist or co-opt destabilizing demands. This does not mean a return to a stable policy environment of the iron triangle. In the USA, constituency interests mainly explain policy change and content. But some order and common understandings are needed to counter policy instability and the large number of interests. It is important to stress that networks only form part of Browne's explanation. Policy outcomes arise from a complex balance of shifting interests, institutional constraints and networking.

Formal Network Analysis

More methodologically complex is the application of formal network analysis to the study of policy sectors. The sociometric mapping technique applies concepts used in sociology and anthropology to political relationships. The idea is that the relationships within a network can be measured by finding out how dense it is (to what extent are the actors linked to each other), where is the centre of the network (who is the person people contact in order to reach each other), what is the structural equivalence of the network (how close are the actors to each other in terms of the structure of their relationship) and how many cliques are there (clusters of relationships). These formal network approaches test more rigorously some of the ideas conveyed by the more impressionistic accounts. But, as Dowding (1995) points out, the results of the tremendous effort in data analysis are often not much more than could be deduced from common sense even though it is useful to have the intuition backed up by figures.

For example, Robert Salisbury, Ed Laumann, John Heinz and Robert Nelson have applied the technique to understand policy-making in the USA. One of their studies examines the elites involved in policy-making in agriculture, energy, health and labour (Heinz *et al.* 1990). The Lowi idea that policy subsystems have a different form of politics does not seem to be confirmed by the network analysis as each one had the same structure. There is a 'hollow core' or no centre to the policy-making systems, and each one has the similar lack of clear structure.

Finding contrasting results in a more sophisticated event and network analysis is the Laumann *et al.* (1985) study of US health and energy policy. Instead of similarities between the networks, they discover the energy network to be highly unstable with all actors participating, whereas health policy has a more restrictive set of relationships including only those actors with resources. Laumann and Knoke's *The Organisational State* (1987) is the most developed application of network analysis to policy change, using the cases of US health and energy policy, again finding important differences between the policy sectors. Recently there have been studies of policy-making across nations (Knoke *et al.* 1996). As with the descriptive approaches, network modelling shows that the coalition politics of networks is unstable, with few long-term alliances and a large number of private organizations participating in policy-making. It is difficult to find straightforward cleavages in policy networks, confirming the idea that policy-making is highly complex.

Policy Networks

More prolific than the US literature is research from the UK policy network approach. Initially, UK thinkers took much of their inspiration from US studies (Jordan 1990). For example, Richardson and Jordan's *Governing Under Pressure* (1979) applies the term 'sub-government'. The classic study of the UK budgeting process, *The Private Government of Public Money* (1974), was carried out by two Americans, Heclo and Wildavsky, who were steeped in the sub-government literature. Although budgeting is less amenable to the policy sector approach than, for example, the study of agriculture, because it encompasses the whole of policy (every policy sector needs public money), Heclo and Wildavsky use the concept of a community to describe the close interactions between policy-makers, especially between Treasury civil servants and their allies across Whitehall. They argue that policy can be explained by the values and ideas of this small group rather than the principle of accountability to democratic institutions. Policy emerges through the roles and values of the participants rather than through debate in the wider democratic process. Contrasting with Heclo's (1977) description of the many individuals involved in the American policy process, the 'government of strangers', the authors conclude the small numbers involved and the closeness of the policy community explains the distinctiveness of the British policy style and the type of decisions that emerge.

A more explicit UK network approach was pioneered by R. Rhodes (1986; 1988), extended by Marsh and Rhodes (1992a; b) and reiterated and refined in many research monographs and commentaries (e.g. Wilks and Wright 1987; Wright 1988; Smith 1993).

Rhodes' idea is that contemporary policy-making involves a large number of institutions in each policy sector, especially when there are several tiers of government and there are elected and non-elected bodies. Rhodes takes from Benson (1982) the idea that organizations exchange resources. Although decision-making bodies have some room for manoeuvre, they usually depend on each other, and thus form close dependent relationships within a policy sector. Out of resource dependencies form policy networks. Rhodes identifies different types of networks. He distinguishes between issue networks of the Heclo (1978) variety that have loose, open and shifting constellations of actors, and policy communities of the Heclo and Wildavsky variety, characterized by stable and restricted membership, shared responsibilities for delivering services and a high level of integration. It is the policy community idea which seems to fit the practices of European governments which have stronger bureaucracies and executives than the USA. The Rhodes model argues that most decision-making takes place in these limited, closed communities.

Researchers often use the policy community model as a descriptive device. By deploying the metaphors to understand complexity, the investigator is able to comprehend how policy is made. The word 'community' captures the idea of a small number of participants who know each other well and who share the same values and policy goals. More ambitiously, researchers use the idea to explain policy variation and change. In the original formulation Rhodes argues that the presence of networks of actors is one of the reasons why policy is often so hard to implement. Rhodes gives the example of British central–local relationships, particularly over local government finance, to demonstrate the idea that the executive's attempts to sideline policy communities usually leads to policy failure or a 'policy mess'. For example, in the early 1980s, UK central governments were unable to realize their intention of reducing the level of local-government expenditure in spite of many attempts to legally regulate relationships. Local authorities were able to avoid or evade the new rules by creative accounting. The policy failure apparently shows the power of policy communities to resist unwanted policies.

Marsh and Rhodes (1992b) use the network idea to examine the relative success and failure of policy intentions in sectors of housing, agriculture, European policy and industrial relations during the British Conservative administration led by Mrs Thatcher. They argue that the inability of governments to recognize policy communities was one of the causes for the policy failures (though there were successes). It is not clear, however, that Marsh and Rhodes really need the policy community idea to solve this problem. Accounts of policy failure are all contained within conventional implementation analysis, the importance of which Marsh and Rhodes acknowledge. Implementation analysis, with its focus on the reasons for implementation success and failure, would examine the importance of the number of implementation jumps in the process, the clarity of the policy design and the resources which policy-makers bring to bear, and all these factors have an impact on the structure of the networks. The network is the result rather than the cause of implementation success and failure.

More ambitious is Marsh and Rhodes' *Policy Networks in British Government* (1992). They argue that the character of the network explains policy outcomes and policy change. Policy networks constrain the policy agenda because they are regularized relationships which exclude some groups from exercising power. The classic case is agriculture, where network writers believe the closed nature of relationships causes policy stability and incremental change. The variation in the characteristics of policy communities, in particular the strength and exclusiveness of relationships, is the reason why policy-making in one sector may be different to that in another. Thus, in the examples in *Policy Networks in British Government*, the closed world of agriculture contrasts with sea defence policy. The reason why the professionals in sea defence were not able to advance their interests was because of the more fractured nature of the network. Although engineers dominated the decision-making process, there were other interests which exercised power.

Marsh and Rhodes argue that it is possible to observe how networks change under the influence of outside events, such as economic change, ideology, knowledge and supranational policy-making. Examples are the introduction of programmes by newly elected governments, such as to introduce more training or to provide education through quasi-markets. Economic changes can also precipitate public expenditure cutbacks and thereby influence the structure and functioning of a policy network. They argue, however, that these changes are not completely independent of policy networks, but are mediated by them. The actors within networks choose how to respond to external events. The networks shape how decision-makers exercise policy choices. In healthcare policy, for example, many changes originate from outside the network in the form of rising demands on healthcare and limited budgets, but the way in which decision-makers allocate limited resources depends on the relationships within the network and their norms. The authors qualify the claims of the importance of networks because patterns of relationships are only an element of policy change and are not even the crucial part.

Smith (1993) makes the strongest defence for an autonomous influence of networks. He seeks to broaden the concept by including aspects of the state, and he also gives a detailed exposition of the social and economic changes that affect networks. Smith stresses that policy communities are institutionalized relationships that exclude other groups; and he even goes so far as to argue that they are 'to some extent the structuring institutions' (1993: 70). Networks are a means whereby state actors can increase their autonomy; they are a mechanism for coordination and for controlling actions; and they provide the link between state and society. Communities of decision-makers enhance the freedom of manoeuvre of state officials and hence affect policy outcomes. As with Marsh and Rhodes' account, networks mediate vast social and economic changes. By linking networks to the needs of public officials and complex social processes, Smith tries to meet the criticism that the network approach does not have an account of the state and cannot explain policy change.

Criticisms of the Network Approach

Criticisms of the network approach abound. The network idea finds both wide application and intense criticism. Because the metaphor is easy to adopt as an organizing framework, it becomes the subject of research. Most aspects of politics are about relationships. But if researchers wish to describe political relationships as networks, they often end up describing most of politics. While such inclusivity is important, as a concept must not relate to too narrow a range of phenomena, the all-encompassing nature of networks creates a problem. They are both everything and nothing, and they occur in all aspects of policy-making. But the concept is hard to use as the foundation for an explanation unless the investigator incorporates other factors, such as the interests, ideas and institutions which determine how networks function. The result is an endless circle of argument whereby the network idea is extended to breaking-point to try to explain something it really only describes. As always in social science, the secret is parsimony. A theory needs to be able to account for an aspect of social or political phenomena with as few explanatory variables as possible.

Lack of parsimony is the main problem with Smith's work. He describes networks as institutions that are fully integrated with all aspects of the state and social change. The results of the integration make it is hard to follow the exact claims the account seeks to make. But networks are not institutions in the familiar sense of that term. Instead, they are patterns of relatively informal and personal relationships that have a relationship to institutional structures, but do not merge with those structures. When networks are defined tightly, they, or certain aspects of networks, such as network structure, may be thought to have a causal effect.

Dowding argues that the policy network approach fails as a model 'because the driving force of explanation, the independent variables, are not network characteristics *per se* but rather characteristics of components within networks. These components explain both the nature of the network *and* the nature of the policy process' (1995: 137). Network researchers consider networks to be an independent variable when an important aspect of network acts is really what policy research seeks to explain. Dowding argues that the fact the networks are open or closed explains nothing. Their structure and operation merely reflect other changes affecting the policy sector. The issue network and policy community are merely labels. Dowding examines some of Marsh and Rhodes' case studies, and he argues that it is the resources and bargaining strategies of the actors that count, and that Rhodes' formulation of the power-dependence model is the motor that drives networks. He suggests that Marsh and Rhodes abandon this idea to the detriment of their analysis.

The implication of Dowding's argument is that the network idea is not needed when bargaining games explain what happens. Indeed, several of the case studies in the Marsh and Rhodes volumes do not often mention the network idea except by way of introduction and conclusion. Thus Wistow's (1992) description of the policy community of health examines the interests of the different participants in health policy, which include doctors' and nurses' bodies, managers, and the bureaucrats operating at various levels; but it also explores the shifting conflicts of interest. The sea defences example, as Dowding comments, shows that the drainage engineers in the local and regional Land Drainage committees wished to have full sea protection and were opposed to the officials in the agriculture ministry and the Regional Water Board. The course of decision-making is determined not by networks, but by the bargaining strategies and the various interests at play.

The other criticisms of policy network approach are not so damaging. The main charge is that the approach does not have an account of institutions and the state. This is largely because networks circumvent the more formal aspects of politics. It is relationships that are important as they generate values and norms of behaviour. This point returns the debate to the arguments posed in Chapter 3 and the counter-attack of the new institutionalists against network approaches (Kassim 1994). Here policy network advocates have been defensive. Marsh and Rhodes claim that policy networks is a 'meso' theory linking the macro level of analysis (the state) with the micro level. Policy network research can be used with different understandings of the state. Possibly network writers have been too sensitive. Clearly networks operate in a different context in either a particular country or a different state tradition. Different sectors may have particular arrangements of regulating bodies and special interests of state officials. It is possible to acknowledge the role of institutions in the network approach (Peterson 1995) as institutional strategies are the basis of the relationships within networks. As with the other approaches discussed in this book, an approach that focuses on only an aspect of making policy cannot be extended to explain everything. The question is how much it does explain and whether network analysts can answer Dowding's criticisms.

A further criticism, Kassim (1994) argues, is the boundary problem, particularly in complex policy spaces, such as the European Union. Critics argue that it is not clear where networks begin and end. Nor is it is specified who is in the network and who is not. Definition and identification issues, however, are familiar problems in social science as it is hard to know exactly when any process begins and ends. Chapter 3 argues that institutions are hard to define, especially when they are considered to cover not just bodies like legislatures, courts and bureaucracies, but norms and standard operating procedures. It would seem that both approaches suffer from the definitional problem. Social scientists have to realize that the phenomena they examine are highly differentiated and complex, and the best research strategy finds ways of coping with the fuzziness rather than ditching its concepts. It is possible, however, that networks are particularly vulnerable to the boundary problem because they are relationships that change almost as rapidly as the issues which affect a policy sector. The argument leads to Kassim's other criticism that networks are too flexible a concept to apply. Because network analysis is sensitive to changing relationships, it is so flexible that it merely describes rather than explains the variation. The point elaborates Dowding's critique that networks are the object rather than the subject of explanation. This criticism seems to apply particularly strongly in the European Union context, where stable policy communities do not exist, so that the main claim of the policy network analysts, the ability to explain policy stability, applies much less.

The penultimate problem of the approach is that is does not have an account of the exercise of power. Network writers tend not to use Rhodes' power-dependence model to explain bargaining relationships. The assumption of most network accounts is that actors cooperate and agree. Even the Rhodes model implies that policy evolves consensually because the participants share conceptions of their interests. Network analysts do not have a theory to explain how policy is made in the shifting, more diffuse, issue networks except to say that it contrasts with that made in policy communities. The practice of policy-making, whether carried out with a large number of actors or in a small selection, usually involves conflict, bargaining and coalition-formation. Even though actors agree on the 'rules of the game', there is usually room for manoeuvre on what those rules mean. This criticism is damaging to network advocates, because it undermines the one causal claim in their approach, the idea that there is a difference between networks that include actors and those that exclude them. It is, however, possible to rescue the model from this criticism, as Chapter 8 shows.

The final criticism is not so destructive. This is the idea that policy networks are designed to operate at the sectoral level and not below that. While early analyses examine whole policy sectors, for example agriculture (e.g. Smith 1990), it is just as possible to research networks nested within sectoral communities or communities that exist between the sectors. Agriculture is an example, particularly when the stable policy community is under pressure, as in the UK in the 1980s. There are now new participants, such as environmentalists and food-consumer lobbyists, and new policy areas, such as agri-environmental policy. Agriculture provides natural examples of sub-sectors, like poultry or food-labelling (Jordan *et al.* 1994). The difficulty here is that the network account becomes too specialized and differentiated to answer the big questions. There is a need to rise above the minutiae of who is in which network to ask why policy changes and varies.

It is possible that the critics expect too much from the policy network approach. Rather than explaining policy formation and change, networks only explain policy in the context of other factors. This restatement is wise, as the policy network approach can never be a theory of public policy. Nevertheless, policy network advocates still need to give their account some explanatory power and to address Dowding's critique head-on. There are two ways to do this. The first is to argue that Dowding, while rightly criticizing policy network typologies for not distinguishing dependent and independent variables (1995: 141), has adopted a too-simple account of cause and effect as he assumes a model must always have fixed dependent and independent variables. Instead, it can be argued that researchers specify variables depending on the model being tested. Policy network structures can be the dependent variable if the researcher examines the effects of institutions, group structure and resources, and ideas on networks. In another model, the dependent variable can be policy outcome, where all the variables are included in the analysis, and one of these may be network structure. Where the difficulty comes in, and where sociologists have developed complex procedures to analyse causal effects, is to determine the relative influence between the variables. In addition, the direction of causation can be in both directions at same time, as in structural equation models. The problems of such a research design are immense, but it formalizes the common-sense notion that everything affects everything else. Thus network structures can affect how institutions work and the way political actors make choices; but institutions in turn structure how networks function, and political choices affect the long-term relationships political actors have with each other, and both paths of causation occur at the same time. The task of the political scientist is to unpack these relationships and to derive and test a multicausal model. Nevertheless, Dowding's criticism of Rhodes and Marsh stands, as they have not thought carefully about these issues; nor have they tested the importance of network structures in a rigorous manner.

The second way to rescue networks is to argue that network properties have an effect independent of other factors, like group resources. From the network literature, there are several ways in which this could be achieved. As networks specify a particular structure of linkages, the way in which that structure influences communication between actors can affect the way in which issues are processed. An example is whether a network has one or several centres. Also, a fairly dense network processes issues faster than a loose one. As well as having structure, networks are based on the development of knowledge and trust, which can affect how decision-makers engage in bargaining games. Over time participants of the network get to know each other, their relationships change as a result of bargaining, and networks become more dense. Relationships of trust facilitate the exchange of ideas within networks and show that strong networks promote policy change and learning. As rational choice theorists argue, trust and learning can be explained within a theory of bargaining. Thus the conclusion to draw is that bargaining theory and network analysis converge rather than conflict.

The other aspect of networks which is important in explaining policy is their multidimensional nature. Relationships on policy matters are often an amalgam of professional, propinquitous and friendship associations. Policy-makers relate to each other in different ways, and the network idea captures how different aspects of relationships reinforce each other. This idea was explored in Heclo and Wildavsky's (1974) famous account of 'village' life in Whitehall. Relationships across policy spaces are more than just the direct exchange of resources, but result from relationships built up over time and occurring in previous time-periods. Thus the personal character of networks is important, especially when the organizational focus of the policy-network school is replaced by individuals as the building blocks of analysis, as in the sociometric method. The participants in networks invest in relationships with each other. They network to seek cooperation and information. These consciously evolved relationships impact on policy choices because decision-makers value their contacts with each other when they make decisions.

This defence of networks is necessarily modest. The idea of making policy networks a theory of public policy is doomed to failure. This point is accepted by the policy network theorists themselves by their more cautious claims (Rhodes and Marsh 1994). Networks are a research tool for identifying relationships whose structure is mainly determined elsewhere. But that does not mean they have no effect. The research strategy must identify the structure of networks first, then ascertain the reasons why those structures function in the manner observed. Then it may be possible to deduce network effects after researchers have explored the main power relationships.

Summing-up

Associational approaches take the analysis far. Both the group and the network approach examine complex relationships as they shift and change. Group and network interactions correspond to the fluid and changeable reality of policy-making much more than the institutional approach. Most of all, when developed into the sub-government approach, they start to examine the particularities of policies in each sector. While institutions are usually similar in a nation-state, relationships between the participants in a policy sector often differ. The approach is particularly useful in understanding how policy is often processed by small groups of organizations and individuals in a policy sector. These actors usually have close and trusting relationships with each other. Group and network politics seems to be an explanation of stability in policy-making. The dependencies between groups and state officials seem to account for why policies are not adopted and the form implementation takes. The idea that networks are a space within which trust and policy-learning takes place is also useful for the explanation of policy-making. When actors learn to trust each other and exchange policy ideas, there is a potential for policy innovation.

As with the institutional approach, the main problem is the extent to which groups or networks offer a sufficient explanation of policy variation and change. The network approach, by focusing on relationships and applying labels to describe those relationships, whether policy communities, issue networks, whirlpools or triangles, does not account for how those relationships form and why they change. Various extensions try to rescue the model, but they do not seem to work. The idea that policy communities are a form of exclusion does not really say much about why some policy sectors are able to exclude groups and others to include them. Similarly, Smith's argument about institutionalization can be similarly criticized as it is not really an explanation. The lesser criticism of boundary problems, lack of consideration of institutions, the problem of power within networks and the lack of a sub-sectoral analysis are also damaging, though not fatal. So yet again an account of the policy process fails. Group and network approaches offer an incomplete and partial explanation of policy change and variation.

5

Socio-economic Approaches

Introduction

One of the most persistent themes in the study of politics is the idea that social and economic factors explain behaviour. Many scholars believe that society and the economy present 'objective' conditions that structure factors such as voting behaviour, group access to political resources, regime stability and democratic accountability. The classic treatises on social science by Marx, Weber and Durkheim can, if treated simply, be labelled as a social determinist or a sociological approach to politics whereby collective decision-making can be 'read' off from the most powerful forces at work in the economy and society. In public policy, this type of explanation is at the heart of the sociological approach to policy formation popular in the 1960s, extends to Marxist theorizing in the 1970s and, after a retreat in the 1980s, resurfaces in regulationist political economy and in studies of the globalization of political life.

The simple idea is that the policy process, far from being a rational weighing-up of alternatives, is driven by powerful socio-economic forces that set the agenda, structure decision-makers' choices, constrain implementation and ensure that the interests of the most powerful (or of the system as a whole) determine the outputs and outcomes of the political system. Public policy flows from the structure of economic and social power in nation-states. Sets of power relations and the measures needed to regulate society and the economy explain the balance of power and the arrangements for making policy in different sectors and in various countries. When examining policy change, research assumes that changes in the socio-economic conditions propel shifts in policy choices. Socio-economic approaches usually criticize mainstream political science for giving undue weight to the autonomy of politics and for neglecting the wider context of policy-making.

This chapter claims that the socio-economic approach provides a powerful family of explanations about the formulation and implementation of public policies which can tell part of the story of how public policy emerges and is implemented. The problem starts, as in previous chapters, when policy analysts believe socio-economic factors explain public policy or at least are the dominant influence. For the purpose of completeness, the socio-economic approach usually subsumes into its framework other explanations to confirm the overriding importance of structural factors. The approach considers institutions, group dynamics and ideas to be epiphenomenal in that they are an expression of socio-economic forces. However, if structuralists err in oversimplifying politics and institutions, they also fail when they try to cope with the complexity and multidimensional nature of policy. Moreover, the chapter argues that the ingenious attempts to introduce political autonomy and to recognize the role of institutions often weakens or undermines the claim for an integrated framework based on social and economic structures.

Marxist Accounts

The Marxist account of the policy process follows clearly from its analysis of politics. Politics reflects the mode of capitalist production and the power of the capitalist class. Given a certain substructure (capitalism), there is a corresponding superstructure or political organization (the capitalist state). Marxists think 'the executive of modern state is but a committee for managing the common affairs of the whole bourgeoisie' (Marx and Engels 1848), so it follows that what is produced by the state, policy, reflects the interests of the bourgeois class and the dominant economic system. Marxists seek to explain policy in terms of the power of the capitalist class and/or the political logic created by the capitalist mode of production. These powerful factors structure the policy process. Even if subordinate classes express their political power and some class compromise is possible, there are limits to the extent to which movements of labour and other dominated groups can gain access to decision-making, particularly if they aim to control the regulation of capital and wish to affect its productivity. Given that the state provides a regulatory apparatus within which capital accumulation can take place, it follows that capitalism constrains policy-making.

The Marxist approach appears as an organizing idea in some textbooks on public policy, such as Ham and Hill's *The Policy Process in the Modern Capitalist State* (1984). They argue that 'the political activities of the state are inextricably bound up with economic developments in society' (1984: 24). Though Ham and Hill reject classic Marxism and question whether each agency of the state automatically represents the interests of the capitalist class, they argue that Marxism offers useful insights for the policy analyst. As with much radical public policy analysis in the 1970s and 1980s, their approach is 'marxiant' rather than an example of the full-blown variety.

There are two main ways to advance the Marxist argument, although the two approaches can be combined. The first stresses the simple power of the capitalist class, particularly the way in which the social and economic division of power in society is reflected by who occupies the elite positions in government, the public sector and quasi-public organizations. The occupants of elite positions are from high social strata and they are closely linked by personal connections to private-sector elites and, in their day-to-day dealings, to the capitalist power structure of the economy. It follows that, as these people occupy powerful positions and largely determine policy, policy reflects capitalist interests. Even though the capitalist class does not directly rule, others rule in its interest by virtue of the many linkages between governing elites and economic leaders. The argument appears in the Marxist accounts of modern politics, such as Miliband's *The State in Capitalist Society* (1969), that describe the connections between elites and the powerful positions they hold in Britain, linking elites in the economy, the civil service, the media, education and the private sector. Domhoff's (1970) account of the elite control of US policy-making deploys a similar argument. The notion resurfaces in empirical examinations of the close networks of public and private elites (Scott and Hughes 1980). Thus instrumental Marxist analysis claims to show the direct and indirect influence of capitalist elites on policy. So, even a measure as apparently radical as the US Social Security Act 1935, which introduced welfare assistance in the USA, was in fact drawn up from the advice of business groups rather than as the result of social-democratic style interest-group lobbying. The argument does not say that marginalized and weaker groups have no influence on policy, but that decision-making as a whole reflects the power of economic interest groups which in turn protects the capitalist system.

The other Marxist approach is the idea that the state produces policy in the interests of capitalism by virtue of its role rather than from the power of the capitalist class and its networks of supporting elites. Politics and the state reproduce capitalism. This approach is often called structural or functionalist Marxism. The capitalist state's function is to protect and reproduce capitalism. Structuralist analysis examines the broader forces that affect the development of the state, particularly as the nature and needs of capitalism change over time. In the early years of capitalism, policies performed the function of social control and set up a broad regulative framework to allow capital accumulation to take place. In mature capitalism, greater state action was necessary to ensure high levels of growth, to foster an educated, well-housed and trained workforce and to accommodate the interests of the working classes who were represented in social-democratic parties. As the chapter shows later, in late mature capitalism the policies and framework in which policy takes place are somewhat different from when Western industrial capitalism was in full swing.

The general idea is that broad changes in the structure of the economy are responsible for shifts in policy and in the framework for exercising power. Public policies in place at any time reflect the role of the state in regulating the economy and in ensuring political and social stability. Policy does not just reflect bargaining between groups (as set out in Chapter 3). Even though rational planning occurs and groups bargain, they do so while reflecting the interests of the wider economic order. Similarly, the behaviour of institutions or the salience of belief systems are epiphenomenal. Policy researchers need just to read off the policies of governments from the economy.

Functionalist Marxist analysis of public policy became popular in the early 1970s. As in conventional policy science, Marxists examine the relationships in a policy sector. In education policy, for example, it is argued that schools, far from rectifying inequality, perpetuate economic divisions in the interests of capitalism as a whole by preparing social strata for their roles in the workforce (Bowles and Gintis 1976). Another example is Piven and Cloward (1979), who argue that US-style welfare policies ensure that the underclasses and the poor are kept from protesting and rioting. They find evidence that welfare policies are often introduced after a period of unrest and/or social dislocation. The difficulty with it, and the debate that followed their work about whether black citizens gained anything out of the urban rioting in US cities in the late 1960s, was not that the US states and federal government increased welfare social spending for the black urban poor after they rioted, as this was found out by empirical research (Button 1978; Fording 1997). The problem is how to interpret these policies. Were the improved and better-funded social policies that resulted from rioting the mark of the ability of a social group to use its power to extract resources from the state, or was it the state acting in its interest to prevent challenges to its power? In some senses both interpretations apply, but in one actors are imprisoned within powerful social forces that automatically disadvantage certain social groups; in the other they respond to the conditions that allow some freedom of choice and a little improvement in their circumstances when the conditions are ripe.

The same problems of interpretation bedevil other Marxist accounts of policy. O'Connor's *The Fiscal Crisis of the State* (1973) and Gough's *The Political Economy of the Welfare State* (1979) offer explanations of the development of policy in capitalist states in the post-war years. O'Connor's classification of state activities into social investment, social consumption and social expenses provides a typology of how the capitalist state serves the interests of the capitalist class in different contexts. Particularly important is the contrast between state expenditure necessary for capital investment and profitability, and that for consumption. While it is interesting to examine the political and economic costs and benefits of different types of expenditure, the problem is that any form of state policy can be considered to benefit the interests of the capitalist class or of capitalism. For example, Marxists consider that the fiscal crisis of the state in the 1970s, characterized by escalating costs of public provision and strenuous attempts to control public expenditure, was precipitated by a crisis of accumulation and state policies that in turn led to a new form of regulation. The explanation relies on the association of the survival of potentially unstable capitalist forms of economic relationships with the parallel development of new policies, with the assumption that the latter perpetuates the former. Association is, however, not explanation.

The criticism that causal mechanisms are not explored in functionalist Marxism can be countered by specifying relationships between the economy and policy-making. Some writers, such as Block (1977) and the neo-pluralist Lindblom (1977), envisage ways in which the capitalist system reproduces itself through the needs of the economy, for example through the state's dependence on economic growth for tax revenues and the importance of the economy for government popularity and hence re-election. Governments also depend on the capital market for government bonds to finance their deficits, and they rely on the power structure in society to implement their policies. Even though policies appear to be radical at their outset, by the time they are implemented policy-makers modify them to reflect the interests of capitalism, and policy initiators refrain from enacting radical policy initiatives in the knowledge that their efforts would be largely futile. States also fear the consequences of private actors making decisions, such as the holders of capital effecting an 'investment strike' if there are measures to regulate markets or to fund costly social policies. More generally, reformist or radical parties in power are prisoners of the market. As they cannot formulate policy independently from the holders of economic power, public policy expresses the interests of the capitalist class. The attempt, however, to spell out the causal relations in the analysis transports the critics right back to the instrumentalist account of public-policy formation. In reality, sophisticated Marxists rely on the access or influence of fractions of capital to show the way in which the capitalist state serves the interests of capitalism. The very problems that modern Marxists wish to escape, the autonomy of the state and the inadequacy of the accounts of a narrow and unified governing elites, return with all their oversimplifications of complex decision-making and governing processes.

While functionalist accounts suggest that the state formulates and implements policy to reflect the interests of capitalism, it is difficult to know whether state policy always benefits the capitalist economy. Thus economic growth need not benefit capitalism if it increases wages and inflation. Policy-makers believe their policies benefit capitalism as a whole, but they may be misguided in the policy tools they deploy. The dependence of government on the capital markets can bias capitalism away from its long-term interests in increased productivity and long-term planning. It is a common argument among Marxists and non-Marxists (e.g. Hutton 1995), that British government policies in the twentieth century have been highly influenced by the City of London to the detriment of the interests of industrial capital. Critics consider that the bias in public policies harms the long-term health of the British economy.

The problem with the socio-economic determinist approach, and of Marxism in particular, is that it does not explain the variation and complexity of public policy. As Barrow comments, 'when structuralists move away from abstract theorising toward institutional and policy analysis, they have found it virtually impossible to make a reasoned case that specific institutions or policies are required by the functional needs of particular capitalist societies' (1993: 71). The dominance of the capitalist class or of the logic of capital does not seem to point to the variety of groups involved with formulating public policy. The monocentric view of the goals of government does not do justice to the multiplicity of social and political objectives expressed in the formulation of public policy. Nor is instrumentalist or functionalist Marxism well placed to account for the differences between policy sectors even when they all involve economic interests. Traditional Marxism does not have much to say about the differences in the content of policies between countries of similar levels of economic development and class mobilization, or between different levels of government, whether local, regional, national or European. The analysis gives little place for accident or an unintended functional role (whereby policy-makers accidentally protect the interests of capitalism) or for error and incorrect policy analysis. Thus, to ensure Marxist accounts capture the kaleidoscopic character of modern policy-making, modern writers modify the classic formulations.

One stream of marxiant writing argues that public policy does not follow just the long-term interests of the capitalist class or the capitalist system. The state is composed of different elements each of which has client groups. Cawson (1982), for example, argues that an important factor in explaining public decision-making is the structure of the state and power relations. In certain policy sectors the state develops close relations with powerful producer interest groups to process key decisions. In economic policy, the state regulates relationships between itself and producer groups in corporatist fashion. Producer groups have a monopoly of access to the policy-making process and in exchange accept the regulation of the state. Other branches of the state, such as local government in the UK, are charged with different responsibilities and incorporate alternative interest and professional groups. Thus, in the bulk of the post-1945 years, the local state represented consumers and professionals, and sought to pursue more redistributive policies than the central state; and this led to conflicts between central and local government. As such, Cawson considers his account to be an escape from the functionalism of earlier Marxist formulations.

The focus on the state produces a more subtle account of public policy than the strictly determinist formulations. Organizational realists focus on the power of state bureaucrats to shape policy design and implementation. The logic of capital accumulation is mediated by the development of institutional structures, and is modified by the motivations and interests of state officials. Writers such as Skocpol examine the role of the state at different times and places in structuring policy. The state may, in periods of crisis and with threats to its survival, act against the interests of the capitalist class. There are historical traditions of the state. Some states, such as Sweden, are strong and resist the interests of the capitalist class by being dominated by socio-democratic parties. Other states, where there is less of a tradition of the autonomy of the state, such as the United States, have a history of public restraint in intervening in social affairs. On the other hand, organizational realists argue that even the United States can develop more interventionist policies owing to the mobilization of political movements and the exigencies of political crises, such as the economic depression of the 1930s, or the conditions affecting a sector like agriculture (Skocpol and Finegold 1982). There is a strong institutionalist emphasis in the work of Skocpol that verges out of Marxism. In particular, her argument that the structure of state institutions, guided by the separation of powers, is important (Amenta and Skocpol 1989) belongs better to the 'new institutionalist' school of writers set out and criticized in Chapter 3.

Marxist theorists reacted to the criticisms of determinism and functionalism by introducing more complexity into their understanding of policy formation and implementation. The policies of a nation-state cannot just be derived from the mode of production. That much is accepted. The solution modern Marxists offer is to accept the relative autonomy of the state and thus of public policy. The state is itself an actor that has clear interests. There are semi-autonomous decision-makers within the state that follow their self-interests that may or may not correspond to the interests of the state as a whole and/or to the capitalist mode of production. There is also the possibility of the conquest of the state by political movements that do not serve the interests of the capitalist class.

The analyses of Block, Cawson, Skocpol and others provide an account of policy that is far more convincing that the 'conspiracy' approach of Marxist instrumentalism or the circularity and over-determinism of functionalist accounts, such as those proffered by O'Connor and Gough. However, as Skocpol's work demonstrates, it is possible that by becoming more realistic the account loses its

Marxist focus and becomes either neo-pluralist or new institutional-ist instead. The Marxist content does not provide a coherent account of how public policy is formed and implemented. Other types of explanations seem to be doing the work. Even if it is accepted that Marxism is a backdrop to the understanding of the way public policy emerges, there remains the problem, common in the approaches discussed so far, that it is not possible from this approach to have a 'meta theory' that tells the analyst when social or political approaches are going to be efficacious or when other influences on policy are salient. As there are many forms of input to the policy process, how can researchers know which one is important?

Functionalist arguments do not seem to explain the radical way in which governments structured policy-making systems in the 1980s, especially in Britain. Margaret Thatcher's administration, elected since 1979 on a gradually intensifying right-wing platform, at first strengthened Marxist analysis. Writers such as Gamble (1988) and S. Hall (1985) identified a peculiarly British solution to the capitalist crisis, what Hall terms 'authoritarian populism'. Authoritarian state structures, such as aggressive policing, extend the capability of the state; populist policies and rhetoric legitimate it. Yet, as the Conservative Party won over the skilled working-class voters, and the political centre and the left slowly accepted the Conservative agenda, so the functionalist account of policy formation looked less and less convincing. It is not possible to label each change away from a left-wing agenda as serving the long-term interests of capitalism. The endless sequences in the causal chain make it improbable, and negate aspects of politics that do not reduce to the interests of market economies. Partly because of these failures, the growing fashion-ability of post-modernism and the return of normative discussions in politics, neo-Marxist approaches have been sidelined. The result is that there are now few purely Marxist accounts of public policy like those of the 1970s, and those that exist have rather different labels.

Regulationist Accounts

Though neo-Marxism's relatively short period of influence on policy studies waned, there have emerged two similar accounts of the salience of the economic relationships on public policy that either are Marxist or draw their central insights from Marxism. The first is the French regulationist school that has as its 'problematic' the role of public authorities in regulating certain 'regimes of accumulation'.

The key writer in this school is Aglietta (1979), with more recent defences by Lipietz (1988; 1992) and, in part, Jessop (1990; 1995). The central insight of the regulationist school is that the structure of the state and the policies it produces reflect and regulate the technological basis to the capitalist economy. The form of technology is part of an overall regime of capital accumulation taking place at points of capitalist development. The regime is the economic, social and political framework that allows capitalism to extract a surplus and to prevent, for a while, capitalism from excessive instability and collapse. The account is not so different to functionalist Marxism as the form of the state and the policies it carries out are unique to a particular stage of capitalism. The difference is that it is technologies of production that structure the regime as much as the intensity of capital accumulation. Thus, in explaining policy change, regulationists draw upon the shift in production techniques and their effect on capital accumulation, the rate of profit, the nature of the state and the regulatory framework of law and policy. In advanced capitalism the spread of mass-production techniques in large factories required a well-developed state bureaucracy to set uniform standards for products and to create the conditions for mass markets. To reap the investment in large factories, there were long production runs based on stable consumer demand. Here again the state was important in ensuring the regulation of the economy. Keynesian economic management techniques of manipulating consumer demand, savings and investment ensure full employment and a stable level of economic growth. The workforce needed to be trained and to have a good standard of health. Hence the large welfare state provided universal education and public health provision. Large factories and organizations mirrored the bureaucratic state, both of which were organized according to rational principles. They had large hierarchies and aimed to produce a uniform product. The result was Fordism.

In the regulationist account, declining rates of profit and the saturation of mass markets precipitated a crisis of accumulation in the late 1960s. A more competitive market drove down rates of profitability. New forms of production were devised based on small production techniques. Enterprises developed specialized or 'niche' products that yield high rates of return. Companies became leaner and more efficient, more flexible and less dependent on long production runs. The ensemble of new practices, restructured organizations and novel technologies is called post-Fordism.

As mass production no longer delivered the profits, so too the regulatory framework lost its legitimacy. The state itself came to reflect the post-Fordist economic structure of the economy, partly through the availability of new technologies, such as information systems, new forms of accounting, and the capacity to contract out, which ensure that the state becomes much like private-sector bodies it regulates. According to this hypothesis, there is also the need to develop a new regulatory framework to assist new forms of capital accumulation and to promote the expansion of the new sectors of the economy. This may involve relaxing planning controls and industrial zoning. As the regulation of product lines becomes less important, it is part of the capitalist logic to deregulate the state's control over the economy, job protection and safety and welfare, and to accommodate the new 'flexible' mode of production. The regulationist account provides an account of the policy initiatives of the 1980s, particularly in the UK with its high level of deindustrialization, but also in other countries as experiments with privatization, contracting-out of public services and the reshaping the bureaucracy spread throughout the developed world, and have been exported to lesser developed countries as well. While the processes are divergent, they produce a new set of policies, revealing a shift to what Jessop (1995) calls the 'Schumpetarian workfare state', where governments design social policy to enhance labour market flexibility rather than follow the social democratic aim of extending citizenship. The use of the word Schumpetarian conveys Schumpeter's (1942) belief that capitalism decays because of social tensions and market failure. The state needs to shore itself up in the face of social breakdown.

Globalization

The second strand of recent Marxist theorizing is about globalization. As with the other modern theories about economic power, the term 'marxiant' is a better account of the way the argument is formulated as it does not depend strictly on Marx's economic analysis, although it borrows some Marxist arguments. Globalization theory seeks to understand the effects of the structure and institutions of contemporary market economies rather than to investigate the economic mode of production. Indeed, the analysis can be regarded as an extension of Lindblom's ideas set out in *Politics and Markets*. What globalization theorists argue is that a series of converging trends since the 1970s transferred economic decision-making away from the arena of the nation-state to that of the world economy (e.g. Picciotto and Radice 1973). First, new technologies in telecommunications and information reduce the space in which economic activity takes place. Second, the deregulation of financial markets means that national control of the terms of trade and movement of money is no longer a realistic course of action. Companies and nations trade on the same terms; capital movements are global and are determined by relative profit levels. Third, the growth of multinational companies has proceeded apace, which means there is less of an association of particular enterprises with the territories of nation-states. As organizations operate on the world scale, they can make decisions, invest and transfer production separately from the wishes of the national governments. Finally, because of the diffusion of information and advances in the scope of telecommunications, the world becomes one culture. The process of homogenization according to Western market values complements the economic pressures reducing the power of nation-states.

The policy implications of the globalization thesis are stark. The autonomy nation-states once had over economic policy diminishes in the face of global processes. Nation-states become like municipal governments competing for capital and adjusting their policies to suit the needs of multinational companies. As with regulation theory, the thesis provides an explanation for policy change since the 1980s. Deregulation, privatization and cutting back welfare derive from globalization. The dilution of the radicalism of social-democratic parties follows too, explaining the centrism and convergence of policies formulated by political parties and executives in many Western countries, whether it is the road to moderation taken by the British Labour Party after their electoral humiliation in 1983, the recovery of the US Democrats at the presidential level or the abrupt U-turn of the French socialists in 1983 after their experiment in nationalization and planning collapsed amid international financial pressures. Here it again was economics determining politics, albeit by a different route from the classic formulations.

The similarity of the position of nation-states to local government suggests a similar type of approach, and much has been written about the relationship between politics and economics at the local level. Peterson (1981) suggests that local authorities follow policies that are in the interests of business because capital is able to migrate away from cities if municipal governments follow welfarist or radical policies against the interests of the private sector. As capital can flee to low-tax and low-service havens, so all municipal governments lower taxes and keep spending low to retain jobs and prosperity in their cities. Differentiation and political choice are not possible when capital is mobile. The process becomes even more accentuated for cities when the globalization of economies is added to the competition. Whereas national governments in European countries used to regulate the decisions of business by directing the location of firms, now the globalized economy means such regulation is no longer efficacious, and ensures that each city in Europe is competing for investment across national boundaries. As a result, the market reigns.

Yet studies of Peterson's idea fail to confirm that local policy-making is constrained by economic conditions. Rather than every city illustrating the logic of pro-growth politics, some are anti-growth (Clark and Goetz 1994). Cities are able to pursue non-growth policies and still develop redistributive policies in a more competitive context (see Clarke and Gaile 1994 for the USA). Similarly, the idea that greater capital flows and a more inter-nationalized economy amount to globalization and spell the end of national autonomy has similarly been challenged on the grounds that the states are still central to world economic and political systems (Hirst and Thompson 1996). Much trade remains within nation-states and occurs between the most powerful ones. It seems that the autonomy and complexity of politics yet again challenges the socio-economic approach to policy formation.

Developmental Accounts

Paralleling the Marxist studies of policy in the 1960s and 1970s were accounts of policy outputs based on the economic modernization perspective. The argument is that as economies become more prosperous so the nature of policy-making changes. For example, there is greater need for public expenditure because of the complexity of markets and a need for more public goods to overcome externalities, such as pollution and damage to health. As economies and societies become more differentiated so there is a need for more regulation; and as economies become more complex, the regulatory framework changes. The relationships between economics and politics is often conceived of as a system with a necessary relationship between the inputs to a political system, the demands and supports, and the outputs (Easton 1965). The argument is similar to the Marxist accounts without the assumption that the capitalist economy is in crisis and needs public policy to prevent its collapse. There is also a parallel between developmental systems accounts and modern Marxist system approaches (Offe 1985). Unlike most Marxist studies, however, the economic approach has been backed up by empirical tests, albeit flawed ones. For example, Dye (1966) finds that measures of economic development, such as urban per capita income, median educational level and industrial employment, remove any apparent relationship between party competition and expenditure levels in US states. The other classic study is by Wilensky (1975), who finds that Gross National Product per capita, the longevity of the social security system and the age structure of the population determines the percentage of Gross Domestic Product devoted to social security in 60 nations. Similarly, Jackman (1975) finds there was no impact of the strength of socialist parties on income inequality in 60 nations. The implication of the relationship is that as countries become more economically developed, so their policies converge, whether it concerns the level of public intervention in the economy or the extent of welfare provision.

Scholars of comparative public policy do not now accept the idea that the level of development largely determines public policy outputs. The 'politics matters' school of research effectively demonstrates that political parties have a major role in shaping policy outputs over and above the influence determined by the level of economic development (Castles 1982). For example, Sweden is developed economically, but its level of social welfare spending in the post-war years was shaped by the long period in office of the Social Democratic Party. At the local level, there is similar research explaining the level of local expenditure and the type of policy outputs. It has been conclusively demonstrated that it is the type of political party in power in a locality that predicts the level of spending as well as other variables (Sharpe and Newton 1984; Boyne 1996). There have been a number of studies disproving the classic studies by Dye and Wilensky, often by comparing a smaller number of more similar countries (see the literature reviews in Castles 1982).

However, rather than showing the primacy of politics over economics, the research shows the complexity of the relationship which varies according to whether it is just developed Western democracies that are being compared or whether less developed countries are included. There are different results according to the policy sector under examination because political and bureaucratic actors have greater autonomy to determine decisions in some areas than in others. The relationship between economics and politics varies over time, as the factors that led to the setting-up of the welfare state (political mobilization) are often different to those that expanded it (economic prosperity). There are highly complex relationships between the different aspects of economic development and the various policy sectors that make the argument about whether politics or economics comes first rather simplistic. In any case the set of choices open to political leaders is limited by the causal relation- ships in a market system and other practical constraints. As Castles puts it, 'while democratic capitalist states may be characterised by a range of different policy outcomes and policy mixes, there are certain structural constraints on the total policy mix' (1982: 17).

As with so many research frameworks, the energy behind the 'politics matters' attack on the socio-economic approach quickly diminished. The finding that the relationship between politics and economics is complex, though largely correct, did not inspire an on- going research programme. The hard edge of quantitative comparative analysis disappears when researchers fear interpreting the results with only eighteen cases (only the developed capitalist economies have good quality data). The result of three decades of research may just be that non-political variables are one among many. There is little consistency about when and where they are important. Even the policy convergence idea has become popular again in policy studies as globalization research frameworks appear in many books and studies. It is often argued that policies are becoming much more similar between nation-states as governing regimes face very similar public problems and have a limited set of policy choices. The insights of the 'politics matters' school need to be reapplied once again as the policy convergence approach contains all the errors of the earlier developmental literature (see Bennett 1991 for a critique).

The 'Funnel of Causality'

In contrast to the sophistication of the 'politics matters' school, some policy analysts deploy a simpler model of how events external to the political system affect public policy, in a way which tries to avoid a narrow determinism of the developmental approach. Hofferbert

(1974) creates a model called the 'funnel of causality'. This is a synthesis of approaches which arise from the assumption that socio-economic structures determine policy outputs and the problems of that premise. Hofferbert argues that political scientists too often deploy a simple input–output model of policy formation which confuses rather than elucidates. Instead, he argues that the inter-action between politics and economics occurs at many different levels because policy responds to several contexts. As such, the account is not much different to Castles' reservation about the assumptions of the developmental perspective. However, Hofferbert argues that, in spite of the complexity, there is a funnel of causality, moving largely from historical–geographical conditions, to socio-economic composition, mass political behaviour, government institutions, to elite behaviour and formal policy conversion, and thence to policy outputs. Hofferbert is interested in explaining the reasons why policies are adopted, such as the expansion of higher education or welfare (the book was written in the early 1970s). The notion is that policy decisions are never made in a vacuum as there is no clean slate from which decision-makers start. The geographical characteristics of an area give a certain backdrop to policy problems, thus a rural location necessarily involves rural public policy; and the socio-economic composition of an area affects decisions, so an above-average number of the elderly requires policies for residential care and support in the community. Similarly, mass political behav-iour, such as a predisposition in the electorate to vote for tax and budget cuts, feeds into political incentives and thus to policy. The conditions 'are a set of circumstances with multiple relevance that the elite can overcome, suppress, or exploit, but not ignore, under normal circumstances' (1974: 253). As such, the explanation is consistent with incremental models of policy-making whereby poli-cies gradually emerge through bargaining and adjustment to decision-makers' environments. The relationship between the vari-ables can vary over time and according to policy sector. As with other approaches to public policy, the analysis draws its insights from Lowi's typology of regulatory, constituency, distributive and redistributive policies (see Chapter 1), and other similar conceptu-alizations.

It would seem that Hofferbert's synthesis admirably fits the main objective of this book, which is to bring together accounts of policy-making. But, unfortunately, the funnel model is really an amalgam of the different perspectives rather than a theory of policy. The model is an unthinking analysis of data with a large number of variables and a set of assumptions rather than a theory about the directions of causation. The conclusion of his book stresses the particularity of the policy-making processes, and the varying factors within each one, without saying why socio-economic conditions are important in one policy sector or at one point in time or in one country and not the others. Hofferbert's revision expands the analytical frame to cope with the empirical finding that politics matters, but the result is that nothing is explained except complexity. The revised developmental approach parallels the Marxist attempts to grapple with the real world.

The Interdependence of Politics and Economics

It is unsurprising that policy analysts start with society and the economy first and then assume the direction of causation is toward the political system. Social science has often assumed that base affects superstructure, whether in the classic sociological tradition or in the Marxist or marxiant accounts. The implausibility of policy simply reflecting the economic and social structures and forces is belied by the complexity of politics and the idea that political actors have autonomy and interests of their own. Modern policy analysts wish to examine the multifarious influences on public policy that include the socio-economic factors but also others that derive from within the political system. However, the problem is that the relationship between the variables is hard to systematize.

It is also natural that writers conceive politics and economics as separate entities. But such a simplification does not do justification to the murkiness and fuzziness of the real world. In reality politics and economics are so intertwined that it is impossible to separate them, partly because of the extensive feedback and interlinking between political and economic decisions. Many of the very objectives of public policy are to shape the economy or society, either as a political objective or to affect political behaviour for party political advantage. In the former case we think of the structure of society as affected by many public decisions. Thus the level of poverty is affected by welfare, but also the level of poverty will affect welfare decisions and the structure of choices faced by decision-makers. In the latter case, governments may target political rewards to certain areas of the country to certain social groups to increase its chances of re-election, such as through discretionary allocation of grants or tax cuts aimed at certain socio-economic classes (Ward and John forthcoming). Models of political–business cycles would also offer complex accounts of policy formation, with politics affecting economics and vice versa. The result is that the logics and demands from socio-economic structures are structured by political choices. It is not possible to separate them. In fact, the way forward for policy studies is to consider all the variables affecting policy decisions in one system with causation flowing both ways. The task of the researcher is to unpack the various impacts and to test hypotheses.

Some Applications

The regulationist approach and UK local government in the 1980s

An example of how the regulationist approach seeks to explain policy change is the reform of local government in the UK. In the 1980s UK central government radically restructured local government with initiatives ranging from requirements to sell public housing; the contracting-out of public services to the private sector; extensive controls over local financial autonomy; restriction of the activities of party politics; the creation of quasi-markets in education; the establishment of new agencies and the taking away of functions altogether in areas like training, higher education, further education and aspects of local economic development (Stoker 1991). One explanation of these rapid policy changes derives from the nature of party politics and party competition. Factors the analyst can point to are the conquest of the Conservative Party by the 'new right'; the resilience, skill and length of tenure in office of a remarkable prime minister, Thatcher; and the electoral misfortunes of the Labour Party during the 1980s. As such, much of the explanation of policy change lies in the approach summarized in Chapter 4. It is the balance of power of interest groups and the role of political parties that is important. Political action through mobilization and strategic manipulation is the essence of politics and can either correspond to ideas about how democratic systems should work or draw attention to defects in the way some groups can easily gain access to the levers of power in a representative democracy.

Some writers remark on the difficulty of seeing the policy initiatives of the Conservative Party as just the long march of the right (Marsh 1995). The Conservatives, when elected in 1979, had a few policy proposals that amounted to a coherent ideological programme. Conservative policies were more a reaction to the policy failures of the previous Labour governments, and consisted of an unconnected list of populist measures, such as the proposal to sell council houses and to control the trades unions. The Conservative approach to government developed as it went along, and policy initiatives were extended when they worked and were reformulated when they did not. Thus the Conservatives' privatization strategy began with the obvious candidates, such as steel, gas and tele-communications, then extended to other more difficult cases, such as coal, railways and water. The formula seemed to work as the privatizations were accepted in the long run. The government gained financially and transferred some troublesome policy prob-lems to the market.

Analogous to its privatization strategy, central government at first very modestly proposed the contracting-out of local authority ser-vices to the private sector and to management buyouts. In the Local Government, Planning and Land Act 1980 it was only direct labour organizations, the in-house departments that were responsible for construction, that had to tender for local government work along-side private contractors. The government gradually extended the policy in subsequent legislation, in particular the Local Government Act 1988, and in 1996 the government required white collar work, such as legal departments and information technology services, to be tendered out as well.

In no sense did the Conservatives plan in 1980 what they did in 1996, yet in an evolutionary way it fell into place, following a logic of events. The argument is that rather than a conscious set of policy choices, the governing party devised policy in response to a favour-able environment generated by previous policy successes. Partly by chance it discovered a policy that worked. Given that politicians are capable of learning and that they wished to capitalize on successful policy initiatives to get re-elected, they extended the strategy so that it eventually became an overriding aspect of government policy. As a learnt system of adopting new policies, by the 1990s, the strategy overextended itself as privatization and contracting-out became more difficult to implement successfully after the easier government activities had been disposed of in the booming stock markets of the 1980s. But, in explaining the progress so far, it can be argued that a favourable socio-economic context drove the reforms and that a non-right-wing government would have introduced some of the same things as the Conservatives. Indeed the election of the Blair government in May 1997 on a platform which did not seek to reverse most of the policies of the Conservative governments, such as privatization, council house sales and delegation of education budgets from local authorities to schools, is an indication that these policies derive from more that just the ideology of the new right. On the other hand, there are several competing explanations for the policies of the Labour government. The difficulty of reversing policies and electoral competition are just two.

The gradualist approach of the Thatcher governments is consistent with a gradual move from a Fordist regulatory order to a post-Fordist one. Stoker (1989) argues that many of the changes affecting local government can be attributed to the move from a Fordist to a post-Fordist governing paradigm, partly because the management of local government is affected by changes in the public sector and because many changes imposed by central government promoted the post-Fordist style organization. Thus, the contracting-out of services to the private sector, the creation of quasi-markets, the availability of decentred cost centres and decentralized offices are part of the move toward the flexible local authority. While these policy initiatives are part of the right-wing agenda, and would seem to limit the autonomy of elected local government, they are also an aspect of the restructuring of the policy-making styles and institutional structures of Western European democracies. Of course, Stoker is no overt Marxist, nor need post-Fordism be necessarily a Marxist account of policy change. When boiled down to its essence it amounts to technological determinism, whatever political struggles and contestations are assumed to constitute the process. From technology flows public policies.

The main weakness of applications of regulation theory is that it has an unconvincing account of the direction of causation and it needs a better account of the transition from economic structures to political ones. This book argues that an evolutionary account can provide the right connection and a convincing story, and one version is set out in Ward's rational choice defence of 'bottom line economism' (1993), which will form a part of the synthesis of approaches in Chapter 8. In essence the idea is that in the economy there are selection mechanisms, particularly through the impact of technologies, and similarly through the evolution of policies there are state strategies that benefit the system as a whole. They succeed largely because they work (Ward 1997). The penultimate chapter of the book covers this argument in more detail.

Tests of the 'policy funnel'

Sabatier uses Hofferbert's model, the 'funnel of causality' (Hofferbert 1974), as one of the drivers for stability and change in his policy advocacy coalition (PAC) framework (Sabatier 1988; Sabatier and Jenkins-Smith 1993). In the 1980s Sabatier developed the idea that coalitions of decision-makers and lobbyists argue for their policy positions. In a policy sector there is likely to be two to four stable PACs, and each one is associated with particular ideas about how to solve public problems (see Chapter 8 for a full account of the framework). These coalitions bestride many levels of government and comprise politicians, bureaucrats, consultants and policy analysts. In essence, the policy-making system is stable as these coalitions exist over many decades. This is because Sabatier assumes that ideas and mutual interests cement policy advocacy coalitions in place for several decades. There are relatively stable parameters to the system that do not change, such as natural resources, the nature of the policy sector/the good that is being supplied, the basic socio-economic values and the constitutional structure though these characters do mediate the changes that do happen. Thus it needs major world shaking changes to unfreeze policy-making systems: 'the core (basic attributes) of a government action program is unlikely to be changed in the absence of significant perturbations external to the subsystem' (1993: 34).

Sabatier uses the Hofferbert model to explain stability and change as the drive to policy advocacy coalitions. He admits the model has its problems. It tends to treat elite behaviour and government institutions as a 'black box' (this is actually an unfair criticism) and the funnel neglects intergovernmental relations. The model also does not deal with 'feedback' and 'loops'; nor does it incorporate the ability of elites to shape public policy. In spite of these problems Sabatier argues that 'the Hofferbert approach constitutes a parsi-monious view of the policy process with clear (if perhaps not always valid) driving forces' (1991: 147–8). The external (system) events are changes in socio-economic conditions, changes in the governing coalition and policy decisions and impacts from other policy sub-systems. The socio-economic conditions may be a major event, such as the oil price shock to the world economy in 1973–4, which fundamentally altered the balance of power in the environmental policy system by increasing the advantages of organizations advo-cating environment-friendly technologies and policy fixes.

Sabatier, Jenkins-Smith and a growing band of researchers have attempted to examine policy change using data (Sabatier and Jenkins-Smith 1993; Jenkins-Smith *et al.* 1991). The key finding that emerges is stability in the coalitions over time. The best example is Jenkins-Smith and St Clair's examination of oil and gas leasing policy between 1969 and 1987 where, coding the beliefs of groups and organizations from their testimonies in congressional hearings, they map the changes in the structure of the coalitions and set out the organizations' relationships to each other. They find that the change in the pattern of the policy advocacy coalitions can only be explained by system shocks as there was a substantial realignment starting in the 1977–8 period which led to a greater polarization of pro- and anti-development coalitions. The shock was the second oil crisis that also shaped the policies of the Carter administration and affected the orientation of the public agencies in the coalitions. As such, the finding produces support for the policy funnel idea, albeit elaborated by the PAC framework.

It is hard to criticize such impressive attempts to map decision-making and how it is shaped over time. The model and method of research offered by Sabatier and his colleagues is an effective way of understanding the relationship between the socio-economic structures and policy change. The defect in the idea is that it does not provide a theory of when the different elements in the model apply. When are ideas more important? To what extent are elites autonomous? What level of socio-economic change leads to policy change or when does change just get simply absorbed by the decision-making system? The problem goes back to the funnel of causality. While it is intuitively plausible that socio-economic changes are funnelled upwards, the model does not indicate when they are transferred, and when they are not. Chapter 8 treats Sabatier's PAC framework in much greater depth.

More 'politics matters' research

Castles and Merrill's (1989) attempt to understand the determinants of public policy is theoretically and empirically well informed. They quantitatively examine the interrelationships between policies and the economy in a small number of economically advanced nations. They analyse a large number of variables, such as national political culture, EEC membership, openness of the economy, age structure, political factors, economic growth, age of programmes,

and happiness. Moving beyond the constraints of the 'politics matters' school, they formulate hypotheses which derive from a range of
theories. They create a 'path' model, where all the theoretically
relevant effects and interactions are measured at once. They make
no assumption that economic variables necessarily influence the
political ones. They argue convincingly that 'that there is no one
"magic key" to unlocking the mysteries of policy causation does not
necessarily mean that a wide range of policy interventions cannot be
located in terms of a general model of the economic, social and
political processes in modern industrial societies' (1989: 177).

They test several hypotheses, and control for the different affects.
They show there is something about English-speaking countries,
such as the UK, New Zealand and Australia, that negatively affects
the economy, which could boil down to the effects of economic
structures and political cultures. Confirming a Eurosceptic position,
they find that the decision to join the EEC inhibits economic growth.
Once countries enter the European Union, their growth rates suffer.
While there are problems with their analysis, in particular the small
number of cases that inhibits generalization, it is a useful way to
integrate the socio-economic approach into the analysis of public
policy. After the slowdown of the 'politics matters' research in the
mid-1980s, there are still some interesting hypotheses to test.

Summing-up

The chapter reviews socio-economic approaches to public policy.
The influential idea is that public policy reflects stability and change
in economic and social relationships. Either consciously or uncon-
sciously, policy-makers' decisions reflect wider forces, either through
the function of governing for the economic and social systems or the
close relationships between elites and the power blocs. There are
several approaches. Highly influential are Marxist accounts. These
range from instrumental to functionalist models that focus on the
role of elites or properties of the economic and political system
respectively. Recently, regulationist and global economy accounts
displace the traditional focus on state policy. Now there is interest in
the role of technology and in the economic effects of international
economic processes, and how these feed into national and local
decision-making. There have been parallel developments in mainstream political science. In the 1960s and 1970s, the level of
socio-economic development was thought to determine public policy

outputs and outcomes. Economic factors have recently re-emerged in discussions of policy convergence across nation-states.

The classic objection to structural accounts of policy change is that they neglect the importance of political autonomy in politics, and they reduce complex policy choices to wide-ranging forces. Structural accounts tend to deploy a circular functional argument whereby political action automatically maintains social and economic systems. Discussions rarely specify the causal mechanisms. As with other accounts of public policy, it seems that the socio-economic approach in public policy claims far too much as an explanation of policy change and variation.

Yet, by the end of 1980s, a more complex picture emerges. Some analysts, such as Sabatier, deploy a policy-funnel model whereby social and economic events can shift policy advocacy coalitions and the stances policy entrepreneurs take. In the 'politics matters' school, researchers such as Castles recognize the complex inter-dependencies between public policy and the wider social and economic world, in particular what counts as a broad set of constraints upon policy choice. While macro socio-economic approaches do not offer an all-encompassing theory of political action, they suggest sets of constraints on action that impact on policy choices depending on the circumstances that decision-makers face.

6

Rational Choice Theory

Introduction

Rational choice theory posits that individual choice is the foundation of political action and inaction. The theory explores how individuals react to and seek to structure the varying constraints on action that occur in political life, whether they are sets of institutions, patterns of group interaction or constellations of socio-economic structures. As well as reacting to structures, rational choice theory examines what individuals do when they are faced with choices made by other political actors, either in the current time-period or at a future date. Rational actor models investigate why people choose to cooperate with others or not, whether they decide to participate in politics or to remain as a spectator. These models can examine the ability of political systems to solve acute public problems like the crisis of the environment. By building up from first principles what individuals are likely to do, the theory addresses some of the central problems in political science and public policy.

While originally the purview of economists, rational choice has gradually taken hold in political science, particularly in North America. As a theory of human behaviour, political scientists now apply its insights to phenomena such as voting turnout, party choice, the strategies of political parties, legislative behaviour and bureaucratic decision-making. Popular because of its parsimony, rational choice focuses on a particular aspect of political behaviour, such as electors voting for a political party in a two-party system or sovereign national governments allocating budgets to local areas, and models how political decision-makers act. Rational choice studies often add to the understanding of the political process because they test hypotheses which may on first sight be counterintuitive, but end up being richer and more consistent accounts of political action than the apparent common sense of much empirical research.

The growth in the popularity of formal models of analysis also reflects the belief that the frameworks which had guided political science up until the 1980s had run much of their course. Institutional, group and socio-economic explanations seemed trapped with an 'infinite regress' of their structures which made them unable to offer coherent accounts of causation.

Moreover, by the end of the 1970s, the social-determinist underpinnings of contemporary social science weakened. The loss of certainty and confidence of traditional forms of explanation allowed researchers to explore new intellectual frames. The socio-political environment of the time no doubt played a role in shifting the course of ideas. As much of contemporary social science, in Europe at least, rested on the belief in socially progressive social intervention and upon the gradual maturing of democratic institutions, once much of that consensus fell away by the end of the 1970s, so the assumptions which underlay the institutional and group approaches attenuated. Researchers were ready for approaches which assumed self-interest and explored the difficulty of achieving cooperation. It seems that the spirit of the age embraced individual choices. While there is no necessary connection between neo-liberal or new-right ideology and rational choice theory, they are both part of a wider shift in ideas.

In contrast to the study of voters, parties and legislatures, rational choice explanations of public policy are rare. The paucity of research is partly a consequence of the nature of the policy process which encompasses so many sets of interconnected decisions occurring in the various parts of the political system. It is difficult to apply rational choice hypotheses which typically model two sets of actors in such inherently messy circumstances. However, while not as common as rational choice analyses of party competition and legislative voting, there are some interesting applications of rational choice to the policy process which show the strength of individual-level analysis and point to a wider application. In spite of the difficulties of operationalization, rational choice modelling can pose the right questions and suggest pertinent hypotheses about the policy process. It is less susceptible to many of the problems of the approaches discussed in earlier chapters, in particular the tendency to redescribe rather than to explain human behaviour. By being sensitive to the diverse circumstances political actors face, rational choice can analyse public policy over time, by sector and in different spatial contexts. However, as the chapter concludes, rational choice theory has some almost insoluble problems of its own.

The Rational Choice Method

Rational choice theory derives its inspiration and method from the discipline of economics. Economists begin their enquiries by constructing models of human behaviour from first principles. More empirically minded economists then try to operationalize the formal models by deriving hypotheses that they test in real-world situations. They refine or reject the models depending whether the tests verify or falsify the hypotheses. From the results of their enquiries, economists elaborate new models that investigators can test afresh.

In contrast to economists, political scientists face two main difficulties when deploying rational choice methods. First, the variables are harder to quantify because political behaviour does not translate so easily into indices like prices and output. Second, the central research questions in political science derive from the nature of the political world. Political scientists are not just interested in allocative efficiency and tendencies toward equilibrium, but in solutions to the difficulties of collective action. They seek to discover mechanisms that can effectively resolve conflicts in interests and ideas. These two problems make rational choice hard to apply, but they suggest challenges for empirical research rather than insurmountable obstacles.

As in economics, political science versions of rational choice deploy some distinct assumptions about human nature. The first is that humans beings have preferences that are, for the purposes of analysis, prior to the social and political world. Individuals are purposive entities rather than just vehicles for wider social and economic forces, and, as such, are capable of choosing their own projects and preferences. Second, rational choice modellers usually assume individuals act in their self-interest rather than for the interests of others, though it is possible to use the same modelling techniques without self-interests in what is called 'altruistic rational choice'. People are instrumental rather than expressive, and they seek to maximize their personal utility rather than to give life to their personal and collective identities. Personal utility is maximized through an optimization process whereby individuals maximize their income or balance out a number of preferences, such as between current and future benefits. Third, people express their preferences as clear goals. Fourth, rational choice theorists often assume individuals have information about the preferences available to them, such as the policy platforms of political parties and the effects of government decisions on the economy. This assumption is not necessary as it is possible to model preferences with less than perfect information, but it makes the initial analysis simpler. Fifth, when individuals examine the information available to them they are able to select the course of action that satisfies their preferences and are able to modify their courses of action when the benefits and costs of choices change. Actors are also consistent in acting on their preferences as their choices are transitive, i.e. if A is preferred to B and B is preferred to C, then A is preferred to C. In short, these assumptions shows that individuals have the capacity to act as rational agents (Ward 1995).

Many rational choice theorists argue that these assumptions do not aim to mirror the world exactly. Instead they offer reasons for action that derive from a simplified model of human behaviour. By examining the relationship between reasons for actions and the structure of human choices, rational choice theorists derive hypotheses that may or may not turn out to be true. Rational choice does not offer an all-encompassing explanation of political behaviour, but examines the implications of an important component of it, and its empirical programme of research aims to see when hypotheses using rational choice apply and when they do not.

Rational choice theory can analyse a wide range of human phenomena. Some of the applications are trivial in the sense that the analysis does not need deductive theory to predict behaviour, but others are non-trivial because the theory generates counterintuitive and unexpected hypotheses. A non-trivial prediction is one that does not assume that preferences unproblematically translate into outcomes but, by using game theory, models how the interaction between choices of decision-makers may or may not produce non-desired results. In many human situations actors increase their level of utility by cooperating with other individuals. There is no problem in exchanging resources or contributing to joint action. All the actors gain in what game theorists call an assurance game. In other circumstances actors choose not to cooperate because they fear what would happen if others decide not to cooperate. This is a verbal description of another game, the prisoner's dilemma, derived from a hypothetical situation where two prisoners are accused of the same crime. They are arrested, put into separate cells and interrogated. The police and criminal prosecution service present the prisoners with the following options: if both stay silent, they each receive a mild punishment; if one confesses and the other does not, the former gets off and the latter receives a severe punishment; and if they both confess they receive a heavy punishment. The game predicts they both confess because they fear that the other one will and they will receive a worse punishment as a result. They are not capable of choosing the outcome that benefits them both because they do not trust each other. The game produces the powerful insight that people do not cooperate to pursue their best interests because they fear others will free-ride on their gullibility.

While the prisoner's dilemma powerfully demonstrates the inter-action of choices, it appears far removed from the practicalities of public policy. The following two hypothetical examples show the power of game theory in the exercise of policy choice. Imagine two countries, A and B, which have a common sea channel between them, and they both face a choice about whether to clear up a pollution leak from an oil tanker. Both countries enjoy benefits if the pollution spill is cleared up; both incur costs if it is not. But they also incur costs by clearing it up, such as the expenditure involved in hiring specialized operatives and equipment. Their levels of expendi-ture are lower if they both share the costs, particularly as there are economies of scale from sharing facilities. It is possible to model this situation as a game whereby each country decides whether to engage in pollution-clearing or not depending on the choice likely to be made by the other country. Figure 6.1 shows the payoffs to each country depending on which of the choices each one makes. As they can both make either of two choices, there are four different types of situation, one where both do not cooperate, another where both cooperate, and two cases where one cooperates and the other does not. The top right and bottom left cells show the relative

		Country B	
		Not clear up	Clear up
Country A	Not clear up	2, 2	4, 1
	Clear up	1, 4	3, 3

Figure 6.1   Prisoner's dilemma game

benefits to each country if one country does not clear up the pollution and the other does. The bottom right cell shows joint action and the top left no action at all. The numbers in each cell represent the benefits minus the costs to A and B respectively for each combination of decisions. The number 1 is the lowest benefit; 4 is the highest.

Even though the benefits of cooperating are greater than not, country A and B choose not to clear up because they fear that the other country will seek to free-ride. The safe strategy is 2, 2 so the channel remains polluted. The choice not to clear up dominates because 2 is preferred to 1 and 4 is preferred over 3. This is because there are no clear advantages from cooperating which outweigh the risk from not, largely because, in this case, there are no economies of scale. However, the prisoner's dilemma is not the only game to be played. Consider Figure 6.2, which shows a very similar set of payoffs.

		Country B	
		Not clear up	Clear up
Country A	Not clear up	2, 2	3, 1
	Clear up	1, 3	4, 4

Figure 6.2   Assurance game

From looking at the payoffs in Figure 6.2, a casual observer might think that each country would still fear being 'taken for a ride' by the other if it decided to clear up because it would bear the whole cost. After all, if one country starts the clearing-up operation it has the benefit of 1 whereas the other country has the benefit of 3. If it did not spend the money on clearing up it remains at benefit level 2. But in this case each country can rely on the other because there are more benefits from cooperating than from not trusting each other. They will always seek to improve their overall level of utility by moving from 3 to 4 because the other country will do the same. This is called an assurance game.

The prisoner's dilemma and assurance games, as examples of the collective action problem, offer powerful insights for social science in

that they question the liberal idea that cooperation naturally follows
from mutual interests. Thus, in the group accounts offered in
Chapter 4, the idea that individuals shape policy on the basis of their
resources and effort does not always follow because members of
interest groups are not able to rely on the collective action of their
members. Such is the central theme of Olson's classic work *The Logic
of Collective Action* (1965). Individuals and groups affected by a
policy problem are not able to agree a solution to it because they fear
other individuals or groups will take advantage of their public
concern. Collective action problems appear in a host of policy
problems, such as the international politics of global warming.
Countries do not act to reduce carbon monoxide emissions that
warm up the planet because they fear other countries will free-ride
on their goodwill. If some countries undertake expenditure to stop
global warming, others can use the situation to improve the competitive advantage of their economies by not taking any measures.
The result is that no country acts because each country fears being
'a sucker'. Though the structure of international institutions can
overcome this problems through rules of unanimous action, it is also
likely that modest solutions to global warming may involve larger
countries shifting costs of compliance onto smaller ones (Ward
1996).

The collective action problem suggests that societies are not able
to solve public problems when they involve common pool resources,
what Hardin (1968) calls 'the tragedy of the commons'. Thus, in the
case of common grazing pastures or fish stocks in the oceans,
economic actors overgraze or overfish the resources because they
fear others will carry on producing if they stop. In policy terms, game
theory suggests that collective action depends on the nature of the
public good. In cases where there are clear benefits in cooperating
and the public interest is served, there is little difficulty designing
new policies and in ensuring compliance. In other examples, there
may be great difficulty in achieving policy change. For example, in
developing a fishing policy it may be hard to ensure the cooperation
of fishing enterprises. In situations where there are clear public
benefits, such as air pollution control, it may be easier to ensure
compliance. In such cases, rational choice theory offers clear explanations why policy-making takes a particular character in a policy
sector.

The institutional structures of most democratic states are designed
to overcome the worst features of the collective action problem

through the executive freedom of governments and bureaucracies to act and through the convention of majority rule. Political leaders act in the general interest and majorities can form to enforce cooperation. On the other hand, no institution in a conventional representative democracy can rule out the collective action problem because there generally needs to be consensus before a policy is decided. There are often cases where a narrow majority forces through a policy but cannot achieve compliance in implementation because there is no will to cooperate. Because of the need for legitimacy there are collective action problems in compliance issues. In addition, governing parties and bureaucracies suffer from internal collective action problems.

The prisoner's dilemma is not just a recipe for inaction or policy disaster. Game theorists argue that collective action problems can be solved, given the right conditions and environments. One solution is through 'supergames' (Taylor 1987), where actors cooperate when they discount benefits over time. Particularly when games repeat (a common feature of policy-making where the same people face each other for long periods), decision-makers learn to weigh up the benefits over time (provided there is no end-point where in the penultimate game it is rational once again to try to take advantage of the other participant). In this way a prisoner's dilemma game turns into an assurance game. Another way to examine cooperation in repeated games is through the analysis of experimentation where actors gradually learn to trust each other by trying different strategies (Axelrod 1984). Thus, in conditions where actions are repeated, there is more likely to be cooperation. Another argument is that decision-makers are more likely to cooperate in small groups where it is easier to enforce norms (Olson 1965). This is because members of the group can easily detect, monitor and punish free-riders.

Another cause for cooperation is in institutional design which can allow for learning and the building of trust (Ostrom 1990). The participation of actors in the design of institutions can assist collective action in the case of common-pool resources, such as fish in the sea. Institutional design may prevent producers from depleting the whole stock of resources because, with the right decision-making opportunities, individual actors, such as boat-owners, agree fishing limits on the basis that they choose the rules by which they can solve problems. There is now a substantial literature analysing the application of common-pool resources to many human problems, such as the maintenance of irrigation systems (Keohane and Ostrom 1995).

Rational choice theorists consider that political culture can help societies adopt solutions to collective action problems. The argument is that long histories of cooperation can create trust in government. If societies solve collective action problems in an early period of their history, they can continue solving them at much later dates. The way trust often continues over time creates a set of attitudes toward government which support public action and create effective policies. In some societies, where there is little 'social capital' (the level of individual investment in cooperation and networks), governments cannot get policies successfully implemented; in others, maybe by historical accident, there are virtuous circles of cooperating behaviour which result in well formulated and implemented public policies (Putnam 1993). Putnam gives the examples of southern and northern Italy, where the north developed a high level of social capital, whereas the south remained trapped in an untrusting political culture. As a result northern regional authorities were able to develop more solutions to collective action problems than their southern neighbours. Recently, the concept of social capital has been applied to solve common-pool resource problems (Ostrom 1994).

It is through examining different solutions to the collective action problem that policy analysts examine change and variation in public policy. The institutional framework and histories of cooperation are important in understanding the way decision-makers solve problems. The nature of the public good is important too. At the heart of public problems are the dilemmas posed by individual choice and strategic interaction, elements of explanation that derive from rational choice theory. Rather than a set of mathematical abstractions that have no application to the real world, modern rational choice theory is sensitive to the importance of cultural and historical contexts. It is the interplay between changing institutions and the choices of actors that provides rational choice with its realism and analytical power.

Rational Choice Theory and the Rational Model of Decision-making

Even though the rational decision-making model emphasizes the criteria for rational action, the level of analysis is organizational or institutional. Rather than model the roles of individuals, the rational decision-making approach aims to explain how a unitary actor, the executive/bureaucracy, makes a public decision, such as reacting to a foreign policy crisis. The assumption is that the political system as a whole, which is made up of bureaucrats and politicians, has objectives, is able to rank them and can select the option that maximizes its interest. As Chapter 2 suggests, most modern public policy research considers the rational model to be an oversimplification of the complexity and limited organizational coherence of decision-making. Even if the political system could adopt a rational decision-making strategy, the costs of reaching the standards required would probably paralyse decision-making processes, frustrate the groups involved in the policy process and limit the opportunities for policy-learning.

Rational choice theory, however, does not predict the same processes and outcomes as the rational model of policy-making. In fact, what policy researchers know about the complexity, messiness and indeterminacy of public policy is exactly what rational choice theory predicts. This is because rational choice theory perceives policy formation and implementation from the perspectives of the individuals making the decisions rather than from those of the organization. Thus what is rational from the point of view of the organization is not necessarily rational from the perspectives of the individuals in it. By focusing on the costs and benefits of cooperating, rational choice theory offers an account of when organizations sometimes achieve ends that are desired by political leaders and when they do not.

Institutional Rational Choice

Chapter 3 criticized the institutional approach to politics because it reduced all political action to institutions. Institutionalism does not seem to offer an explanation of variation between policies, nor does it provide a convincing account of policy change. However, there is a place for the role of institutions within rational choice theory (Dowding and King 1995: Introduction). They are a constraint on the exercise of choice and, as with common-pool resources, they offer a potential solution to the collective action problem. This approach may be termed institutional rational choice.

The use of institutions in rational choice derives from the recognition that the payoffs within games are determined outside the bargaining situation. In the example of the prisoner's dilemma, the punishments to the prisoners are determined by the judicial system not by the prisoners themselves. The reason the actors do not cooperate is because of the costs and benefits of each strategic course of action. If the institutional rules are different, so the game alters. In the policy process, it is possible to examine institutional arrangements, such as voting rules or committee procedures, that affect the choices open to rational choosers. The rules may reflect decisions made by participants in the policy process long ago, and in such a way are 'congealed tastes ... "unstable constants" amenable to scientific investigation' (Riker 1980: 432). By introducing institutions, rational choice analysis becomes more attune to the real world. The advantage over historical institutionalism is that the scope is narrower so there is more of a chance for institutions to explain outcomes through the way structures affect choice. Institutions are less central, but more cogent in their explanatory power.

Institutional rational choice can explain different types of political action, by viewing decision-making on three levels (Kiser and Ostrom 1982). There are some games where actors try to maximize the advantage within the existing set of rules; there is a metagame where they argue about the rules themselves; and there is a meta-metagame where they contest the rules that govern the rules. Kiser and Ostrom argue that actors can choose which game they wish to play, whether just to accept the rule or whether to negotiate to change the rule themselves, and each course of action imposes different costs and is embarked upon for different reasons. Though there is no logical reason to restrict the number of levels in which games are played to three, and a criticism of the framework is that there is a possible infinite regress of levels, in practice it is hard to imagine what kind politics would be talked about in the meta-meta-meta- and meta-meta-meta-metagames.

Though the argument becomes more about values underpinning a political system and less about institutions, interests do not dissolve as the hierarchy is ascended. In terms of bargaining, all that happens is that the rules by which bargaining occurs change rather than political interests. Also the costs of embarking on a bargaining strategy are different at each level. It is easier and less costly to engage in bargaining within the rules of the game than to change those rules, because opposing actors will greatly resist such a change. In addition, actors not affected by the immediate decision can be mobilized by a change in rules of the game as this can affect how they play bargaining games in the future. The argument shows that institutions are not permanent features of the policy environment but arise through choice because different types of games have unique rules. Institutions are lower-level building blocks for analysing public policy. They are important in explaining factors constraining choices, but institutions are created by prior decisions and they can be undone by loss of support or renegotiation. Institutions embody the norms of the political system, but those norms are up for debate.

Some Applications

Macro-economic policy

A simple rational choice explanation of public policy is the management of macro-economic policy in a representative democracy. Governments have a range of choices about how to tax, how to spend and what level of interest rates to set, all of which can affect the level of economic activity in market economies. In liberal democratic theory, economic policy derives from competitive pressures to produce the preferred policy as parties compete on different platforms and voters assess the party best able to manage the economy. Alternatively, an institutional account suggests that economic policy reflects formal structures and standard operating procedures. Countries wish to tax more or less depending on their cultures. Institutional structures bestow on executives different degrees of freedom of manoeuvre. Alternatively, policy could derive from networks of policy-makers, say of influential economists and opinion-leaders or it could be the function of the most powerful economic group or the needs of the capitalist economy.

Another way of explaining the direction of macro-economic policy is to see it as a relationship between party leaders and voters and to assume that voters reward the government that delivers them a stream of economic benefits (Schumpeter 1939; Nordhaus 1975). These benefits may or may not be beneficial to the economy as a whole. In some party systems, such as the UK and the USA, one party and leader may hold office for four or five years and can control the economy by manipulating demand, interest rates and public investment. The idea is that in the period before an election, the party and leader in office stoke up the economy by reducing interest rates and taxes and increasing public expenditure to encourage the voters to reward the government by re-electing it. Because it is likely that a government overheats the economy at the end of the previous election cycle, in the period after an election the government allows the economy to go into a recession. The government re-energizes the economy again when the next election looms. Hence, there is a policy cycle geared to the timing of elections that drives the economy and voting behaviour. As well as being a rational actor-driven model, the political-business cycle also corresponds to popular and media folk wisdoms about how governments run the economy, especially in the UK. For example, it is generally believed that Conservative governments stoked up the economy to win the general elections of 1983, 1987 and 1992, though the strategy did not work in 1997.

The model produces testable hypotheses. There should be associations of the trends in inflation, unemployment and government policy with the political timetable. The surprising finding, however, is that tests do not confirm this simple prediction. There is no evidence that economic cycles correlate with elections, and there is only weak confirmation of the significance of economic policy instruments (see Schultz 1995 for a review). This is a disturbing finding for the model because it only sets out common-sense ideas about how governments and voters behave. If the political-business cycle does not work, then there must be either: (1) a very good explanation for the failure of the model in this case or (2) a better rational actor model to explain what happens or (3) voters and governments are not rationally self-interested in this aspect of political behaviour. It is possible that (1) is the best explanation of why business cycles do not seem to work. Economists using the rational-expectations model of individual behaviour assume that voters are less interested in past benefits, but calculate likely future benefits. The result is that voters do not reward governments for past successes but appraise the likelihood that those successes translate into future streams of benefits. Voters do not reward a government that induces a boom if the fiscal strategy leads to a post-election deflation. Thus governments are highly constrained in the extent they can manipulate macro-economic variables to get re-elected.

Schultz (1995), on the other hand, argues that (2) is the best way forward. He suggests that political-business cycle models do not appreciate the competition governments face. In particular, governments encounter different circumstances at each election because their political needs vary. If governments go into the elections believing that they will be re-elected because they are way ahead in the opinion polls, they do not have an incentive to stoke up their

economies. Governments wish to avoid artificially induced refla-
tionary strategies as these can weaken the voters' perception of
economic policy competence. A poorly run economy affects governments' electability as much as economic downturns. By destabilizing
the economy, governments impair their ability to manipulate it in
time for future polls because the inflation and unemployment consequences of poor macro-economic management take many years to
correct. Long years of high interest rates and taxes may put off voters
in the next poll. Governments weigh up the costs and benefits of
reflating the economy for each election. Schultz tests these results,
finding that the government's lead in the polls predicts the level of
social security transfers over time. He thus confirms a revised, more
subtle model of the interaction between voting behaviour, the
economy and government policy.

Even though rational choice theory does not generate models to
predict behaviour in the first instance, the failure to confirm hypotheses allows theorists to devise more refined models and to test new
hypotheses. The result is a more subtle and complex understanding
of the policy process. Thus the notion of constrained maximization is
a more powerful explanation of the choices politicians face when
dealing with the macro-economy than the simple allocation of a
stream of benefits from politicians to voters. If empirical tests had not
been performed, rejected, and the model revised as a result, then
investigators would not have produced such a rich account of the
policy process.

Bureau-shaping

If rational choice is a distinct theory of public policy, it must offer
explanations that are rivals to the ones that are already on offer. One
of the best candidates for a counterintuitive rational choice account
of policy change is Dunleavy's (1991) bureau-shaping model, which
adapts the more formal work of Bendor and Moe (1985). Dunleavy's
research problem is to explain the fundamental changes in the
structure of the British central state which occurred in the 1980s.
Governments privatized formerly state-run functions and broke up
the hierarchical structure of government departments so that central bureaucrats no longer have clear lines of command to
service-providing organizations. In the place of line-bureaucracies
are agencies of government at one remove from the control of
bureaucrats in central departments. Agencies now administer most

state functions and have their own chief executives. The challenge for research is that political scientists generally assume bureaucrats seek to increase their size of their bureaus rather than to reduce them. Public-choice theory suggests that bureaucrats expand the size of their budgets, mainly because they want to increase their power, patronage, perks of office and financial rewards (Niskanen 1971). In addition, the client groups of a bureaucracy, such as producer interests, press for a rise in the public expenditure of their patron bureau because they receive a stream of benefits from public activities.

It is possible to explain the decrease in the size of the British central state by the power and vision of the reforming Thatcher governments which were able to override the normal bureaucratic resistance to internal reform. But, given what British political scientists know about the power of bureaucrats to determine public policy, especially when it concerns their terms and conditions of employment, it seems likely that senior officials had a role in reconstructing the shape of the state. After all, there has been much written on how bureaucrats subverted the government's attempts to reform the civil service in the early 1970s. When the government tried to implement the mild set of proposals to professionalize and open up the senior appointment in line with the Fulton Committee proposals of 1969, civil servants gradually weakened the proposals (Kellner and Crowther-Hunt 1980). In the context of these conundrums, Dunleavy uses rational choice theory to generate a model that predicts how bureaucrats, under certain conditions, prefer to reduce the size of their bureaus.

Dunleavy argues that bureaucracies face their own collective action problem. Public organizations are not unified, and their members do not necessarily engage in strategies to increase the size of their budgets, particularly as senior bureaucrats tend not to be used to acting collectively. Instead, officials follow strategies based on their individual interests, such as seeking promotion or transferring to other agencies. Dunleavy argues that senior bureaucrats prefer to follow individual strategies because collective ones are harder to organize and they have greater opportunity to alter their conditions of work than lower-level functionaries. Junior officials prefer collective action, such as increasing wages and the size of their bureaus. Senior bureaucrats have less to gain from budgetary expansion because they face higher costs when arguing for more resources than the collectively organized public-sector employees.

To expand their budgets, senior bureaucrats must engage in the public political process, which is something they refrain from doing. Dunleavy argues that senior bureaucrats maximize only certain types of budget, in particular the core budget of their agency, comprising bureaucratic salaries and office expenditure. He argues that:

Rational officials want to work in small, elite and collegial bureaus close to political power centres. They do not want to head up heavily staffed, large budget but routine, conflictual and low-status agencies. (1991: 202)

In contrast to being managers of large organizations, bureaucrats prefer non-pecuniary benefits, such as policy advice and working in small elite units. Dunleavy believes these incentives vary according to the type of bureau as well as with the type of budget and level of the official. Not only does Dunleavy derive a model that predicts that bureaucrats do not necessarily seek to increase the whole budget of their bureaus, he shows how bureaucrats located in different types of agency follow varying strategies. Thus bureaucrats in regulatory agencies have an incentive to maximize their core budgets because they form a very small proportion of the total resources of their bureaus, ensuring the total budget increase as a result of utility-maximizing strategies is very small. Lower-level bureaucrats in these agencies cannot seek large increases in expenditure because these would take up a large part of the public-sector budget. In the UK this generates the prediction that bureaucrats in departments that transfer money to local government or to other agencies do not argue for great increases in the size of budgets. Also, in times when politicians reorganize administrative structures, bureaucrats seek to bureau-shape by redesigning the budget structure in line with their personal utilities. When it is favourable for structural change, bureaucrats offload functions to agencies and to other decentralized bodies so they can increase the proportion of time they spend on core budget activities.

Dunleavy provides some evidence in support of the basic hypotheses of the bureau-shaping model. During the 1980s public expenditure increased, but certain departments – social security, law and order, defence and agriculture – gained more than others. Dunleavy concludes that spending was concentrated in the few remaining large line agencies which have a close relationship to industry so that benefits could be distributed between bureaucrats and interest groups. Other departments do not have these incentives. Dunleavy also reviews the international evidence about the distribution of functions between levels of government and finds that all states tend to shift managerial functions on to other bodies leaving policy work with the key central bureaucrats.

The bureau-shaping model provides an explanation for the way, after the *Next Steps* proposals of 1987, the UK civil service rapidly adopted reforms of the internal structure of the state by transferring a large number of routine government functions to separate agencies but retaining intact the high command of the civil service. Rather than civil servants resisting what might be thought of as a major loss of control of their functions, the evidence suggests they supported and pushed through the changes which reduced their direct involvement in managing large bureaucracies and concentrated their work on shaping policy: 'the hiving off proposals provide senior bureaucrats with a unique opportunity to engage in wholesale reshaping of their bureaus to attain their ideal form of small, elite, staff agencies' (1991: 226).

Dunleavy's analysis meets some of the criteria for a powerful model of public policy-making as it generates testable hypotheses. It is part of rational choice theory because it links individual action to the changing structures that individuals face. Rather than accepting the simple public choice account of an expanding bureaucracy, the bureau-shaping model carefully examines choices from the perspective of the individual bureaucrats who are located in different types of agency and who are at various levels of seniority. From these different situations the bureau-shaping model predicts different outcomes. Rational choice theory proves its worth by, in this case, providing a far more satisfactory account than any other of both change in expenditure and the restructuring of the British civil service since 1987. The model also applies to the privatization strategies of UK governments and to the process of deinstitutionalization, such as the competitive tendering of services in local and central governments. The model nearly explains policy change, something which few accounts of public policy hardly approach. It neatly accounts for contrasts between policy sectors, which vary according to the relative sizes of core and other budgets. The model is able to explain public policy comparatively as countries have different institutional arrangements and thus varying incentives for public officials to engage in bureau-shaping behaviour.

It would be uncharacteristic of this book if it presented a study uncritically. So there are some objections to the bureau-shaping model. The first is a familiar line of criticism in public policy. The model is not really a dynamic account, though it claims to be one. It is possible to say that bureau-shaping is a descriptive device to compare and contrast how different budgets of the bureaus present different incentives to the bureaucrats who have a say in policy. The model on its own does not explain why bureaucrats follow particular strategies at particular points in time. Dunleavy acknowledges that bureau-shaping needs a special set of conditions to take place which are usually external to the costs and benefits of the budget structure. Changes, such as budget growth or administrative reorganizations, introduced by other agents than bureaucrats, explain policy change rather than bureau-shaping behaviour. What bureau-shaping seeks to explain is how bureaucrats exercise choice or assent to reforms when policy changes. This is the familiar problem with the approaches discussed in this book. They often rely on some other factor to explain policy change rather than the approach itself. There is an infinite regress in the reasons for action. The researcher would retort that it is an impossible task to explain all behaviour. An approach that offers a partial explanation in a limited set of circumstances is an advance in social science knowledge. Partial explanation is better than the description that usually passes for theory in public policy.

The second criticism is that there is no mechanism within bureau-shaping theory to explain why bureaucrats engage in bureau-shaping behaviour. Dunleavy relies on the intuitive idea that bureaucrats like policy work but he does not set out under which conditions they choose more policy and less administrative work. As James argues (1995), the model is unspecified (see his approach below). There is a need to separate-out external changes and to model the choices bureaucrats make in response to them.

The third criticism is that Dunleavy does not test the model. Dunleavy presents results which are suggestive but not conclusive as he does not investigate and reject other possible explanations which could account for the behaviour that appears to be explained by bureau-shaping. Dunleavy assumes rather than proves that certain central government departments in the 1980s increased expenditure because of the structure of their budgets. Defence, law and order functions may have increased in size relative to other departments for reasons that have nothing to do with bureau-shaping. Likewise, the finding that the growth of government in the post-war years did not lead to an expansion of direct line agencies is

consistent with many other explanations of the allocation of functions between tiers of government and patterns of decentralization,
such as managerial economies and the political convenience of
offloading functions of government onto other levels of government.
Similarly, the evidence of civil servants supporting reorganization is
secondary and anecdotal. There is no test comparing the support or
opposition of civil servants according to type of agency and proportion of core to other budgets. What is needed is a multivariate model
with all the relevant controls.

The other untested assertion is whether civil servants actually
prefer policy-orientated work, though Dunleavy cites a number of
studies. The bureau-shaping thesis relies on an outmoded distinction
between policy and administration, where the former is about
political choices and the latter concerns just routine administrative
and managerial tasks. But the task of managing a large organization, such as the Benefits Agency, involves a considerable number of
policy decisions that are embedded in administrative and personnel
details, whereas policy advice could mean enslavement to the whims
of the politicians. Thus it is possible to put forward an opposite
hypothesis to that suggested by the bureau-shaping model. It could
be argued that civil servants prefer to work for large-staff bureaucracies because the detail and complexity of the management
function insulates these organizations from political interference. In
contrast, policy-orientated work involves a high level of political
direction and a lack of autonomy. Thus the assumption that bureaucrats prefer policy work needs to be tested. It is likely there are
different sorts of civil servants. Some relish contact with politicians;
others prefer to run a large bureaucracy. Bureaucrats may prefer the
Next Steps-type reforms because they enhance a division of labour.

The final criticism is that bureau-shaping is trivial. Bureau-
shaping does not claim to explain why the state engages in internal
reform or decides to expand the budgets of some agencies and not
others. All that bureau-shaping claims is that once politicians agree
changes in the constraints affecting public bureaucracies, officials,
to the extent they have autonomy to structure their pattern of work,
change their budgets so as to maximize their preference for policy-
orientated work. Even if the finding were true, this claim is hardly
earth-shattering.

Some of the limitations of Dunleavy's formulation are overcome in
James' (1995) reconstruction of the model. He models bureau-
shaping as a process whereby bureaucrats trade-off two types of

utility. These are the level of core budget per bureaucrat and the proportion of a bureaucrat's time spent on policy work. These two types are partly in competition as more of one means less of the other. James presents this situation as a set of trade-offs (indifference curves) where bureaucrats can substitute levels of core budgets for proportions of time spent on policy work so they can maintain the same overall level of utility subject to constraints of the combinations of budget and policy work that are available. If politicians change the constraints, bureaucrats engage in bureau-shaping strategies. For example, if an administrative reorganization alters the amounts of policy work and levels of core budget, bureaucrats alter the combinations of policy work and core budget to maintain their overall level of utility. While politicians change the overall structure, officials bureau-shape by altering the amount of work done by other agencies and the amount of policy work they engage in. There is no collective action problem as they do not need to trust each other to cooperate.

James uses the example of the *Next Steps* reforms in the Department of Social Security to show how the preferences of civil servants shape the organizational structure. James argues that managerial reforms in the 1980s altered the amount of core budget per senior bureaucrat because the government expected civil servants to carry out more managerial work. As a result, the *Next Steps* initiative was a unique opportunity for civil servants to reshape their departments to ensure that they spend more time on policy work.

James' article, while starting off as an attempt to predict bureaucratic behaviour, suffers from some similar defects as the original model. Seeking to separate the activities of civil servants from those of politicians, and to model effectively bureaucratic responses, the account assumes civil servants are like consumers substituting products with the budget constraint as the prices of alternative goods. But the way in which politicians control the civil service does not affect the price of the 'goods' on offer, but shapes the structure of the civil service including the ability of civil servants to reshape their pattern of work. It is highly likely that the choices open to civil servants are affected by these other decisions because bureaucrats interact with politicians in the form of a game. This suggests there needs to be some more complex modelling, such as in principal-agent models. Just like Dunleavy, James presents a case study that relies on intuition rather than evidence. James argues rather than shows that civil servants bureau-shaped in response to the managerialism of the 1980s. It is just as likely that they would have supported the reforms whether managerialism had been introduced or not. James does not show how much discretion civil servants have to alter the time they spend on policy work.

Work welfare programmes

The applications this chapter discusses so far do not use game theory even though the analysis of collective action is the key contribution of rational choice to the study of politics. The two examples above explore the various strategies open to policy-makers without strategic interaction. The bureau-shaping model uses the collective action problem as an adjunct to the main argument to understand how bureaucrats can act without thinking that other officials are going to take advantage of them.

Game theory is hard to apply empirically because it is not easy to measure the payoffs, although it is possible to model them from the rankings of preferences. On the other hand, it is possible to use game theory as a heuristic device to understand policy choices. King and Ward (1992) use game theory to explain the adoption of work-welfare programmes in the UK and the USA. Work-welfare is the requirement that welfare recipients take up employment or participate in a training programme, measures that have been popular with the 'new right' in the USA and UK since the 1980s. Examples include Title II of the Family Support Act 1988 in the USA and, for the UK, the Employment and Social Security Acts of 1988 and the Social Security Act of 1989. These reforms apply a conception of citizenship that is very different from the social-democratic ideal that informed much of post-war policy-making, such as the thinking behind the Great Society social policies introduced in the USA in the 1960s. Whereas social democrats use the concept of entitlement to justify rights and freedoms in social welfare, the new right is more interested in the obligations and duties that justify linking work or training with welfare benefits. In the light of this distinction, the authors use rational choice theory to explain why some countries adopted work-welfare policies and other, social-democratic countries did not.

King and Ward examine three different sorts of programmes: family and community assurance, market provision and state programmes. They use the prisoner's dilemma to understand the choices that individuals face when deciding to help each other or not. In the first case, aid in small communities, mutual reciprocity is founded on the constant iteration of giving. People do not fear others taking advantage of giving because they help each other over time. They give aid freely because everyone recognizes the value of expecting help in the long term. However, as societies became larger, trusting relationships become less easy to sustain. Because of mobility and the weakening of social bonds, free-riders capitalize on these schemes without the obligation to contribute to them when their time comes. Hence, market- or state-led solutions became more feasible.

In market situations individuals purchase insurance from private companies. This is problematic because companies do not know the risks they face so they cannot offer contracts. Individuals seeking to purchase insurance are likely to be those who are job-insecure, yet they are unlikely to disclose their level of job-security. Unlike medical insurance, where there is some semi-objective measure of applicants' health, it is hard for a company to know the likelihood of the claimant losing employment. It also difficult or expensive to detect whether a claimant has access to another job but prefers to claim the benefit. Although there are ways in which the asymmetry of information can be overcome, it is likely that the market will not supply unemployment insurance.

When there is a choice between state benefits and work-welfare, King and Ward argue that, 'depending on the political preferences (new right or social democratic) of the party in office, public policy may be used to generate a partial separating equilibrium in which some claimants identified by the state are discouraged through workfare' (1992: 490). New-right governments do not gain any utility from helping undeserving claimants while social-democratic governments gain some utility, even though both governments want to help deserving claimants more than undeserving ones. King and Ward model this as a principal–agent game between governments and job-seekers, though the mathematics does not alter the essentially intuitive conclusion.

The complex manner in which game theory models policy choices causes problems with the argument. While it is interesting to explore the choices available, it is possible that the mathematics is being applied to a non-problem. New-right governments favour work-welfare schemes because they believe in them. There is enough electoral support for these governments, but the electorate do not want a market-based scheme. Social-democratic governments are going to favour more rights-based schemes because they believe in them too. While there may be some electoral support for work-welfare schemes, if voters elect social-democratic governments, the type of welfare available is unlikely to be a crucial factor affecting a party's strategy. It would only be one item in a large package of policies. It is likely, therefore, that the choice would be based on ideological considerations.

The best aspect of King and Ward's work is the explanation of the failure of community-based schemes in terms of changes in community structure that encourage free-riding. The unavailability of private-sector insurance is interesting too, though the explanation for market failure rests on the economics of insurance rather than game theory (though free-riding questions are important). The most interesting question posed by the research, that the authors do not address, is why work-welfare programmes are introduced at a particular point in time.

Criticisms of Rational Choice Theory

It is impossible to read about rational choice without being aware that it is one of the most criticized methods of social science enquiry. Although this book is sympathetic to rational choice, there are problems with the theory, and empirical applications suffer from operational difficulties. Rational choice is not the knight in shining armour that can save public policy from its problems, as it suffers many of the familiar problems of social science. Applications of rational choice are often more descriptive and heuristic than explanatory, have difficulties in explaining change and are difficult to test conclusively. Hopefully, this chapter shows that rational choice is a superior approach, but policy-oriented research needs to be aware of the limitations of individual-level models. To deal fully with the more pertinent attacks on the theory and method, this section explores the main criticisms.

First, it is often argued that rational choice theory is methodologically individualistic on the grounds that not all behaviour reduces to the preferences of individuals and that rational choice denies the importance of structures. It is true that rational choice places the weight of its explanation upon the individual, but the criticism is misguided because rational actor models seek to explain choice under the constraints of institutions, the logic of group membership, socio-economic structures and the preferences of other individuals (Dowding and Hindmoor 1997). What determines the payoffs to each actor in games, whether they are of the assurance or prisoner variety, are these structural constraints. Rational choice models what actors do under these constraints. Naturally, there is a tendency for individual-level analysis to focus more on the behaviour of each actor in the decision-making process than do other approaches. In the treatment of bureaucratic politics, for example, rational choice theorists examine the preferences and options open to each bureaucrat rather than assume that an entity like a bureaucracy acts in a unitary manner. Such an approach is entirely in keeping with how modern analysts understand the policy process. Whether from the perspective of the policy advocacy coalition framework or the policy network approach, complexity is the current order. In fact, theorists who write about large organizational entities, such as bureaucracies, often make assumptions about the role of individuals in them, but in an implicit and casual manner. Thus, in some formulations, bureaucrats are assumed to be rule-following, as in the Weberian account of bureaucracy; in public choice accounts it is assumed that bureaucrats only wish to expand the budgets of their bureau. In contrast, Dunleavy's model of bureau-shaping sets out bureaucrats' complex motivations in a manner which can be tested.

Second, it is often argued that rational choice is ideological. Critics believe the theory presents a simplified and biased account of politics because of its roots in individualistic and market-based thinking. The criticism is similar to that made against public choice economics. Thus rational choice models are no different from the works of Milton Friedman and, later, the members of the Virginia school, Buchanan and Tullock. However, the strong right-wing prescriptive dimension to public choice contrasts to the analytic claims of rational choice. As the bureau-shaping model shows, rational choice does not necessarily predict an expanding bureaucracy, the overbearing state and the inefficiencies of democracy. Rational choice seeks to provide an analysis of how strategic choices affect action and does not advocate any political arrangement. Thus rational choice has been used to clarify some of the arguments in Marxist analysis (e.g. Elster 1986), such as the account of the structures and choices that could lead to a revolution in capitalist economies. The claims of rational choice Marxism are about as far from the new right as can be imagined.

Third, it is often argued that rational choice does not provide a convincing account of human action. It has no foundation in psychological studies of human behaviour (Kirschner 1996). Psychological tests show that people do not behave as economists assume. They do not choose courses of action that maximize their utility (Quattrone and Tversky 1988). Individuals do not just act in their self-interest, they are capable of altruism and emotional behaviour. They are often not able to select preferences when presented with information about them and frequently do not remember or do not have available information about their preferences. Prospect theory is a better account of individual choice. Choosers frame their choices with respect to the status quo. They are risk-adverse with respect to gains; they are risk-accepting over losses. The evidence suggests that individuals choose strategies that fit their perception of risk rather than maximize utility.

Rational choice theorists retort that their models are not designed to give an exact prediction of all behaviour, but propose hypotheses of behaviour that could apply and hence should be tested (see many of the contributions in Friedman 1996). If it is accepted that rational choice offers a plausible explanation of how actors could behave, then it is a matter for research to find out when they act rationally or not in the manner theorists hypothesize. Rational choice theory offers a research programme to find out the situations where actors act rationally and to ascertain which account of rational action is correct. Human behaviour is complex and multilayered, a context within which actors try to maximize their utility. That people do not arrive at their choices in an exactly rational manner does not mean that their actions are not rational. Individuals often rely on intuition to allow them to choose the best option even though they are not exactly weighing-up costs and benefits. What matters is whether the outcome supports hypotheses derived from rational choice theory rather than whether the process resembles the ideal type.

Fourth, tests of rational choice in political science have often been negative (Lewin 1991). Political actors do not seem to act as rational choice modelling predicts. As shown by some of the applications above, people do not, it seems, vote in a pocket-book manner, they tend to vote for the benefit of the economy as a whole. There is mixed evidence that economic policy follows a political cycle. Bureaucrats do not seem to maximize budgets. But, as the bureau-shaping example shows, the questioning of the initial theory led to a more complex model of bureaucratic behaviour, sophisticated tests and a more parsimonious model. There is a similar development of the model of political-business cycles. It is also not true that tests of rational choice models have only produced negative results. There are both negative and positive results, an outcome which shows an on-going creative research programme rather than an intellectual dead end. Rational choice researchers continuously refine their models and test new hypotheses. There are wide-ranging debates about how to apply rational choice models.

The final criticism is that the applications of rational choice in political science are flawed. Green and Shapiro, in *Pathologies of Rational Choice Theory* (1994), argue that tests of rational choice have not been applied with sufficient rigour. They contend that empirical studies using the rational choice approach have tended to fit their theories to the facts of the case under investigation rather than to develop hypotheses that are either supported or rejected. They argue that rational choice theorists often claim the evidence supports situations, like equilibria, that are not capable of support or falsification. Rational choice theorists do not accept results that challenge rational choice, and they focus on situations where rational actor models work; and when they do not work, they do not believe that the negative findings challenge the theory. In short, Green and Shapiro argue that tests of rational choice theory are shoddy.

The responses to this assault are that tests of rational choice theory are no better or worse than other tests of models in the social science. In all sub-disciplines within political science there is a legitimate debate about which research technique to use and whether supportive or unsupportive evidence confirms or rejects the model being tested. Research in the social sciences is inherently messy and contradictory, and there is a range in the quality of the tests. As political science, and even science itself, cannot live up to the tenets of a superpositivism proposed by Green and Shapiro, it does not make sense to criticize tests of a theory from an artificial benchmark. The adjustment of theory to results is not necessarily a flawed method; on the contrary, it is the basis of scientific investigation provided that each revision is a real test of the hypotheses and researchers create better models. The partial nature of theory is also not a problem as one of the objectives of rational choice is to find out the extent to which generalizations from economic models apply in politics, not to assume that all political behaviour is based on axioms invented by economists.

Summing-up

The exposition and examples in this chapter show that rational choice theory generates powerful models that explain change and variation in public policy. Whether it is seeking to understand what drives macro-economic policy, the way in which bureaucrats respond to the reorganization of the structure of the central state or why certain politicians adopt work-welfare programmes, rational choice does a better job than rival theories. This is because it is rigorous in the way it derives hypotheses from formal modelling which, whether proven or disproven, tell analysts what kind of relationships to expect between various possible factors explaining human action. Because the theory is based on human choices, rational choice offers cogent reasons for action. There is no difficulty of trying to build a micro-level foundation to the operation of collectivities, the main problem of most approaches in the social sciences. Because rational choice theory models individual choices within the context of institutions, groups and macro socio-economic constraints, the theory provides a dynamic link between the micro and the macro levels. This causal link is often missing in other approaches.

In spite of its advantages, rational choice theory cannot offer a complete explanation of human behaviour. This is because it generally explains action by assuming a set of preferences; and rational choice has great difficulty showing where preferences come from, though this is not impossible. Thus, in terms of public policy, rational choice is good at explaining what actors do once the objectives of a policy are set, but is often silent on why decision-makers select a particular course of action. Thus, in the bureau-shaping example, rational choice theory examines the responses of bureaucrats to an exogenously determined change, such as the government's decision to introduce the *Next Steps* agencies, but says little about why British governments introduced such agencies at a particular point in time. Thus there is a tendency in rational choice to expend a large amount of effort in explaining decisions that are less important than the initial policy choices.

Rational choice can examine the reasons for major policy initiatives. For example, the chapter briefly covers the way Ostrom and her associates investigate the way in which rational actors choose which type of institutional mechanism is appropriate to solve common-pool resource problems (Ostrom 1990; Keohane and

Ostrom 1995). The other approach is to examine the evolution of preferences over time and how they may be shaped by bargaining, mutual learning and trust. There is much to commend these approaches, but it still leaves out why a policy should be desirable or not over and above the interests of the actors involved. On the other hand, it could be the case that the content of policy, and the ideas which it represents, are embedded in the choices and preferences of the actors in it. Thus it is possible to have rational choice accounts of the type of governing regime in place in a nation-state, such as whether a polity is socio-democratic or market-based (Milner 1994), and that these fundamental social values determine policy choices. But it is a plausible line of argument to claim that political agents make choices because of the validity of the ideas just as much as that the structure of bargaining influences political values. The next chapter explores the idealist claim.

7

Ideas

Not ideas, but material and ideal interests, directly govern men's conduct. Yet very frequently the 'world images' that have been created by 'ideas' have, like switchmen, determined the tracks along which action has been pushed by the dynamic of interest. (Weber 1948: 280)

Introduction

It is impossible to imagine politics without ideas. Ideas constitute the world to the extent that all human agents, and thus decision-makers, have to use concepts and images if they are to act. The problem is not that ideas are not important, but that such a large number of cognitive processes are classified under the term. Ideas can be statements of value or worth; they can specify causal relationships; they can be solutions to public problems; they can be symbols and images which express private and public identities; and ideas can be world systems and ideologies. Commentators not only differ in the extent to which they think ideas influence or constitute actions, they refer to different things when they talk about ideas. Writers can refer to one or any combination of these definitions when they write about ideas. These differences, and the swift transfer between one meaning and another, make the debate complex and often confusing.

What is interesting for the theorist of public policy is not that ideas exist, but whether they have an independent role in the policy process. Do the conceptions, form of knowledge, beliefs and norms of human actors explain what happens in addition to the role of political institutions, groups, individuals and wider social and economic structures? Ideas are important in public decision-making because, while participants in the policy process agree about many ideas, more usually they dispute which one is best and they contest which explanation best fits the facts of the case at hand. Ideologies and world systems are typically in conflict. In addition, there are disagreements based on competing moral outlooks or ideologies, such as between social democrats, who believe in the primacy of equality, and market liberals, who do not believe in state inter-ference with the individual's freedom to acquire property. More fundamentally, there are disagreements about the causal relation-ships that people use to explain the empirical world, such as how economic aggregates relate to each other. Thus a monetarist believes that the only way to control inflation is to reduce the size of the money supply; a traditional Keynesian believes that it is possible for the state to manipulate the level of consumer demand and government expenditure to achieve the same effect. These disagree-ments can be based either on the imperfection of human knowledge in the social sciences or on wider differences about how human agents know the empirical world or about how differing values and beliefs affect the selection of knowledge.

The policy process is permeated by ideas about what is the best course of action, and by beliefs about how to achieve goals. Because politics is defined by disputes about how to follow the good life and the means to get there, participants in the policy process advocate contrary ideas and engage with others to try and win their case. In health policy, for example, there are many lobbyists for policy change, some arguing for radical positions, such as alternative medicine and community treatments, while others put forward conservative preferences, such as arguing for the primacy of tech-nology and hospital medicine. These advocates may be agency bureaucrats, experts, legislators and politicians as well as members of interest groups. Ideas-based approaches in public policy contend that it is the ideas these actors bring to the public sphere that are the reasons for policy change and stability. The reason why there are particular policies is because people believe and try to influence decision-makers on the basis that there is a right course of action. Advocacy is a causal factor over and above the effects on policy of political institutions and interests. Majone, in his book *Evidence, Argument and Persuasion in the Policy Process*, argues that 'We miss a great deal if we try to understand policy-making solely in terms of power, influence, and bargaining, to the exclusion of debate and argument' (1989: 2). An example he cites is the issue of poverty in the USA, which was a minor issue in public consciousness in the 1950s, but by the 1960s had become central to the political agenda and influenced the policies followed by the decision-makers, such as the war on poverty led by President Johnson. During the 1960s there was no evidence that the material conditions of the poor had altered, thus alerting public and elite opinion. What had changed were elite and mass attitudes toward poverty, which had been influenced by social-scientific research and popular debates about the structural causes of deprivation.

Some writers go further. They argue that political action is constituted by ideas. Public policy can only be understood as discourse which includes the functioning of institutions and groups and how the actors in these collectivities conceive of themselves as agents. Though the claim about the importance of ideas is consistent with interest-based or institutional explanations in public policy, in its most radical incarnation, ideas are an alternative way to understand political action. This difference of view about causation reflects one of the classic debates in social science and philosophy. Is it interests or ideas that is the fount of human agency?

Agendas and Public Policy

Even though the discussion of ideas in public policy is novel, the notion that politics and administration is about argument and discourse is old. For example, Vickers, in his classic book *The Art of Judgment* (1965), argues that policy-making is an appreciative system where decision-makers continually make judgements and learn as they negotiate the policy-making process. The process of judging is as much about ethical and moral issues, and about seeking meaning, as a response to changing conditions. Vickers' work belongs to a pre-behavioural generation of public administration researchers who considered political behaviour, institutional arrangements and moral issues to be part of the same subject of inquiry. Scholars in the 1990s are reforging the links between moral argument, institutions and political behaviour, if in a different manner.

As well as being part of the traditional study of public administration, the other approaches in this book give some play to the importance of ideas in the policy process, though often in a manner which makes ideas consistent with the approach. Institutional analysis, for example, stresses the importance of ideas. While traditional institutionalism implies that ideas are unimportant, the new version argues that they constitute institutions. Thus, when comparing the way in which Western countries respond to economic crises, P. Hall (1993) points to the different ideas embedded within political institutions as the key factor explaining policy change. In fact, the complaint against new institutionalism is not that it pays insufficient attention to the ideas of political life, but that it broadens out the concept of an institution so much as to make the account ideas-based rather than institutional (see Chapter 3).

Ideas also play a role in group and network accounts of public policy. Pluralists argue that there is a political marketplace in ideas which reflects the balance of group power in society. Each group has a fair chance of influencing the public agenda by advancing its case and mobilizing its ideational and cognitive resources. Of course, most political analysts, including the pluralists, do not assume the political agenda automatically reflects an equal balance of power between the groups in the policy process. In fact, research on agenda-setting suggests that the type of the situation, such as the proximity of the event to the audience, influences whether an idea gets on the political agenda or not (Cobb and Elder 1972). Alternatively, ideas have a natural life-cycle from initial public interest to eventual saturation, which then leads to their fall from fashion, what Downs (1972) calls the issue-attention cycle. Even though the agenda is not just shaped by group power, but by outside events or by luck, agenda-setting models do not say that ideas have an independent existence, merely that a variety of factors conjoin in numerous and diverse ways to shape the political agenda.

Elitists argue that, through group resources and institutional power, some groups shape the agenda and ensure decision-makers discuss a limited set of ideas. As with the pluralists, the distribution of power is the underlying factor, but it is more normal in radical accounts to stress the salience of ideas and political language which marginalizes certain interests and ideas. Power is expressed through the hegemony of certain ideas. Created by the middle or upper classes and by economic interests, ruling ideologies ensure that certain issues are off the agenda and others are on it. An example of an elite theorist who focuses thoughtfully on the importance of language in public policy is Edelman (1964). Edelman argues that, rather than there being a transmission of public demands into public policies, elites respond to public concerns by symbolic political actions which are designed to reassure but not to deal substantively with policy problems. Through political language political leaders often create public expectations which they can 'fulfil' by symbolic political actions which again leave aside the real problems. Edelman

(1977) focuses on the role of language as a way in which reality is structured so as to marginalize the interests of excluded groups, such as poor people. Edelman argues that words such as 'welfare' create images in the mind of the public which cause them to reject the claims of the groups which need assistance and help. Even though Edelman believes that ideas operate in the interests of the elites, his analysis veers off from straightforward elitism, with almost no reference to the power of decision-makers. He almost becomes an interpretivist, seeing ideas and language as an independent factor in political life.

Policy network theory, to a greater or lesser degree, assumes that ideas as well as interests bind together the groups and individuals in a policy sector. It assumes that what keeps a network functioning are common ideas about solutions to public problems. Networks would not function unless there was some agreement about what the main policy problems are and how to solve them. If there are major conflicts within networks, informal bargaining and transmission of ideas within them do not occur as there would be an inside group which holds on to power and weaker members would be excluded. Modern network theorists have gone even further and argue that some relationships over policy are primarily about sharing values.

The international relations theorist Haas (1992) identifies communities of experts in international relations as 'epistemic' in that they transmit and maintain beliefs about the verity and applicability of particular forms of knowledge. Ideas are important because 'the diffusion of new ideas and information can lead to new patterns of behaviour and prove to be an important determinant of international policy coordination' (1992: 3). An example is the community of experts who identify problems and propose solutions to the international problems of the environment, such as the depletion of the ozone layer or the number of whales in the oceans. Haas identifies the profusion of government agencies, policy analysts and experts that have emerged since the mid-twentieth century as one of the driving forces behind these communities. The increasing complexity of public issues and a more unpredictable policy-making environment than hitherto lead decision-makers to participate more in epistemic communities to resolve policy dilemmas. As a result these bearers of ideas can limit the policy choices being made at other tiers of governance, such as at the level of the nation-state. As with the new institutionalists and agenda-setting writers, the analysis becomes not an example of the network approach, but one in which ideas take the central place in structuring policy, though Haas distinguishes his approach from interpretivism.

Macro socio-economic theorists also give some play to the role of ideas, but often as an expression of power relationships in the society at large. Unlike the pluralists, and more like the elitists, Marxists and others believe that systems of ideas – ideologies – explain the way in which economic and political power-holders maintain their power and reproduce the social-economic system. Hence, the ideologies characteristic of capitalism derive from the private ownership of the means of production. More profoundly, ideologies derive from the form of knowledge capitalism creates. Market societies emphasize the centrality of the individual in political and social life. The importance of liberal ideas in turn legitimizes the system of economic production. The link between science and capitalism ensures that methods of enquiry, such as the means–end instrumental rationality, dominate, that policy options are limited to measurable outcomes and that the system of public regulation controls rather than liberates human beings. As with new institutionalism, modern Marxist accounts allow a wider role for ideas than more traditional writers. Gramsci (or rather the way followers of Gramsci have interpreted him) argues that civil society legitimates social and economic arrangements, but also contains ideas which can challenge the dominant order. The objection to these accounts is that if ideology or discourse is not really an expression of the economic system, any form of recognizable Marxism recedes.

It seems that analysts, in their attempt to explain the world in terms of their approaches, either assume that ideas follow from whatever structure they think is important in political action, or give such a weight to ideas that the observer is left wondering why the original approach is so important. Rather than institutions, groups, networks and socio-economic structures, there are ideas which seem to govern how those aspects of political life operate. Conceptions about participation and public actions exist independently of interests; policy ideas and solutions to policy problems cement networks together; instead of socio-economic structures, there are ideologies which govern how power is exercised. Thus the argument becomes less about how to incorporate ideas into an existing model of change, than about understanding how they act as an independent factor.

Ideas-based Empiricism

Researchers in comparative politics and public policy have long been worried that the existing tools of enquiry are not sufficient to explain the variety and complexity of modern political systems. King's reflective essay on why different governments pursue different policies is an example of the way in which barefoot empiricists have stumbled on the importance of ideas (1973; 1974). He explores why governments in different countries follow the policies they do. He notes that there is a wide divergence in the type of activities regulated by the state in developed Western countries, with the exception of the United States, which regulates much less than European countries. This is a restatement of the old problem of explaining US exceptionalism, which stretches back to Louis Hartz and beyond to de Tocqueville. King approaches the variation in public policies in a novel fashion, seeking to explain the relative impact of elites, demands, interest groups, institutions and ideas in comparative public policy. In identifying five factors, the approach is rather like this book, though with some differences which reflect the period when he wrote the article.

King rules out the difference of elites as they are essentially the same between Western countries, and similarly he regards mass publics in developed countries as similar in their outlooks and in the demands they place on political systems. While interest groups seem to be different between the USA and European countries, King argues that North American ones are not as distinct as the conventional wisdom suggests, even though they are more vocal and public than their European counterparts. Significantly for ideas-based analysis, King argues that US groups articulate more abstract public ideas than in other countries. With regard to the fourth factor, institutions, naturally King is aware of the different framework in the USA, as its divided government and federal constitution appears to influence the pattern of policy-making. But King downplays this factor because he believes institutions are not an insuperable obstacle to introducing new policies. Instead, he argues that policies differ between the USA and elsewhere because Americans want them to be different. US citizens believe in the limited state, except in the case of public education because it promotes their belief in equality of opportunity. King's argument about institutions and political cultures is not particularly convincing because there are important differences in institutions which seem to explain much about public-policy-making, whether it is the influence of the courts or the importance of the separation of powers. But King is right to believe there is a gap in standard interest-based accounts of policy change and variation.

Policy Transfers, Learning and Design

The notion that ideas are important has influenced important sub-literatures in the policy sciences. The first is the investigation of the transfer of policy from one country to another or from one period to another (Rose 1993). Policy-makers examine the negative and positive experiences of others, and seek to apply the policy to their own contexts. Though there are conditions by which policies can be transferred, and some countries and groups may be better searchers than others, what is being transferred is ideas.

For example, British urban policy since the 1970s is littered with direct copies of US programmes from Community Development, to the Urban Programme and the Urban Development Corporations. These policies have had equivocal effects, partly because they were originally developed in different economic and political contexts. It is difficult to specify the reason why US urban policy has been so frequently adopted in the UK. Perhaps much has to do with the importance of urban policy in the US states because of the entrepreneurial role of governors and mayors in developing new policy initiatives and the investment in urban policy research in the USA. UK politicians picked up on these ideas because of visits to the USA, and there has been extensive contact between US and UK urban researchers. Even though the transmission of policies is contingent, it is still the ideas themselves which are important.

A second sub-literature which emphasizes the importance of conscious choice in public policy is the policy learning literature. Pioneered by Heclo (1974), the idea is that policy-makers are not automatons driven by electorates or institutional routines but respond to the changing contexts of policy. They are capable of learning from the implementation of policy, and policy changes as a result. This insight has produced a now large literature which has investigated policy adaption and learning (e.g. Hall, P. 1993; John 1994). In turn the expansion of research has provoked the charge that researchers are collapsing a wide range of activities into the elastic concept of learning (Bennett and Howlett 1992). The critic could heighten the scepticism as there are few situations where decision-makers do not seek to learn and adapt. The term 'learning' is insufficient to specify when policy-makers are able to learn or learn correctly. Nor does the theory say what they are learning. Is it new techniques, new explanations of how the world works, values or norms of behaviour?

A third sub-literature is about policy design. Though not always geared to understanding policy change and variation, changes to the design of a policy can affect outputs and outcomes. The insight draws on the literature on policy tools or instruments (e.g. Hood 1986), and seeks to understand how intentions behind a policy affect policy change (Goggin and Orth 1997). There is a variety of instruments available. Examples include subsidies, taxation, symbolic instruments, capacity-building instruments or learning instruments, though to an extent these categories merge or cross over depending on the classification scheme. Policy-makers select instruments according to their theories of how the world works. 'Policy design, like any kind of design, involves the pursuit of valued outcomes through activities sensitive to the context of time and place' (Bobrow and Dryzek 1987: 19). Lower-level policy-makers affect policy design by reacting to events and creating a policy redesign in the form of a loop. By linking together theory and values, the reactions of policy-makers and audiences to the changing battery of policy instruments, the policy-design literature aims to be an intentions- and ideas-based account of policy change. The causal factor is the process of selecting a particular battery of instruments rather the notion that the choice is predetermined by social structures or ideologies.

Reconciling Ideas and Interests

The most sophisticated exposition of ideas-based empiricism is by foreign-policy scholars in the USA. Though the discussion is about international relations issues, the debates are readily applicable to national and sub-national contexts. Particularly illuminating is a collection of essays edited by Goldstein and Keohane (1993), written largely within the realist rational choice framework of analysis which assumes that international relations are composed of states following their interests. The starting-point for these writers is that ideas can account for policy changes which interests do not seem to explain. The mere fact of human self-interest does not explain changes in world-views, such as the growth of individualism, the prevalence of principled beliefs, the opposition to slavery and the spread of democratic freedoms.

Ideas-based empiricists do not seek to replace interests by ideas, but they aim to generate a theory of public policy which encompasses both. They seek to explain human action in a way which makes sense of the quotation from Weber at the head of this chapter. They outline three 'pathways' which are causal mechanisms to explain the influence of ideas on action. First, ideas can act as 'road maps' which help agents determine their own preferences in a complex world. Ideas can guide behaviour under conditions of uncertainty, such as limited information and when the choices open to actors do not yield a clear course of action which is beneficial to them. Second, Goldstein and Keohane deploy the folk theorem, which is an idea in rational choice theory to describe the lack of a unique equilibrium in repeated games. The theorem suggests that outcomes are indeterminate in many situations. Rather than offering a course of action to maximize the utility of the participants, ideas alleviate coordination problems by providing a solution. In short, when rational choice fails as an explanation, ideas have their place. Third, ideas become embedded in institutions and practices and may shut off courses of action through habits of action and political routines.

Thus 'ideas influence policy when the principled or causal beliefs they embody provide road maps that increase actors' clarity about goals or ends–means relationships in which there is no equilibrium, and when they become embedded in political institutions' (1993: 3). Though Goldstein and Keohane are generous in assessing the influence of ideas, there is no doubt that they consider interests are primary, with ideas filling any gaps which interest-based explanations happen not to fill. In this way, the realist underpinnings of much of the analysis of foreign policy are not disturbed. Ideas show their mettle because they add to rather than challenge rational actor models.

The advantage of Goldstein and Keohane's framework and the well crafted examples in the edited volume is that they try to specify causal relationships. However, as Philpott (1996) comments, the notion of ideas is rather eclectic, meaning different sorts of things in different cases. Ideas do not amount to a theory like rational choice. Ideas-based accounts do not produce hypotheses and predictions as they are more like partial 'explanatory gadgets'. The road map idea is also problematic, because it is not always appropriate to think of ideas as responses to uncertainty, particularly when beliefs are highly principled. The other problem is that ideas-based accounts often rely on association rather than causation because they assume elite ideas cause a policy (Yee 1996). Studies never prove there is a transmission of these ideas into action. This is, however, not so much a problem with the Goldstein and Keohane collection, partly because the authors of the case studies carefully consider the range of other possible explanations of the phenomena under study.

The main problem with the approach is the automatic assumption that ideas are only important when interests fail. This premise seems to rule out studying cases where ideas might influence policy and forces ideas to be an adjunct of rational choice theory. While it is plausible to argue that political actors generally look after their interests when they conflict with ideas (except in extreme cases such as religious fundamentalism), Goldstein and Keohane misapply Weber's switchman metaphor. Weber argues that the ideas may shape interests, not that they are additional. The switchman shifts the course of action. Similarly, the way in which actors conceive of their interests is affected by ideas. Further, if ideas shape the empirical world in some way, the actors' actual interests are shaped by what is created. There is an everlasting interplay between ideas and interests. Neither necessarily dominates.

The Rediscovery of Policy Analysis

Contemporary writers often argue that ideas count on their own. They do not just emerge when interests are indeterminate. The relegation of the role of interests in politics reflects the rediscovery of ideas, language and discourse in parts of social science, particularly since the early 1980s. There has been a rejection of the claims of rational or public choice that politics boils down to the interplay of interests, and a similar retreat from economistic Marxism. Public ideas, such as concern for the poor and belief in international justice, count (Reich 1988).

In the policy sciences, the growing interest in discourse has led to a rebirth of the study of policy analysis, albeit in a different form than before. Whereas policy analysis was about how to apply rational techniques, such as cost–benefit analysis, to solve policy problems (see Chapter 2), the new policy analysis investigates the power of language, persuasion and argument which often masquerades as rational policy analysis. Researchers reject the rational model as it is unable to solve basic public problems, such as effective budgeting or environmental degradation. The rational model is based on a false conception of human behaviour, and there is very little empirical evidence to show that the experiments using the technique ever worked.

Yet policy-orientated research found plenty of evidence that expert knowledge is an important part of the policy process. Particularly in the USA, policy analysis became an essential part of the decision-making process and it is used by any public organization seeking to bring about policy change. Rather than a crude interplay of interests, new policy analysts argue that public decision-making forums, such as congressional hearings, are about the weighing-up of different forms of evidence and attempts to find solutions to policy problems. The reasons for policy change are not about the relative power of interests, each with resources and strategies which would be able to influence outcomes in the policy process, but about the quality of the arguments which the lobbyists and government agencies present to other public decision-makers, to the media and to other experts. The ability of participants to argue, to use rhetoric and to marshal evidence is crucial. Even if these activities are not scientific and hide real interests, the conditions of public discourse demand objective and research-based argument. Advocacy, however, elaborates and stylizes such arguments while not challenging their rationality.

The work of Sabatier and his associates shows the importance modern policy researchers place on the role of analysis and ideas in the policy process (Sabatier and Jenkins-Smith 1993). The members of each policy advocacy coalition (PAC) in a policy sector share values and forms of knowledge which distinguish the alliances from others. The PAC framework, following a Lakatos model of knowledge, distinguishes between a deep core of fundamental normative axioms, a policy core of fundamental policy positions and a multitude of instrumental decisions necessary to implement the policy core. Thus a policy position is based on claims about knowledge and causation. Sabatier argues that the fundamental core of axioms and policy positions resists change over time. Core positions lead to stable coalitions unless blown off course by a large event. Hence PAC analysts recommend that researchers examine the impact of coalitions on policy for a decade or more. Different policy advocacy coalitions advance their ideas from within these knowledge citadels. The focus on policy stability in the absence of exogenous change suggests that ideas play a static role in the model which make the PAC approach apparently unable to explain policy change, a charge Sabatier and Jenkins-Smith (1996) are very sensitive to. The PAC approach does give knowledge an independent role, partly from the operation of 'policy-orientated learning' which mainly affects the secondary aspects of belief systems, but they still hold that core beliefs only change as a result of an external shock to the policy system (see the discussions in Chapters 5 and 8).

A radical perspective on policy analysis is offered by Majone (1989). He argues that policy analysis primarily has an argumentative function. This is because it is impossible to separate values from rational analysis. Thus people who argue for policy change need to engage in moral as well as scientific argument. He argues that 'policy analysts and researchers are often deeply involved in the process of norm setting' (1989: 25), so that knowledge and values advance together and influence policy outcomes such as in the example of the war on poverty cited above. Once a decision has been taken, arguments and justification, often provided by policy analysts, are needed to legitimate a policy and to ensure effective compliance by other actors. Majone slightly undermines his account by arguing that policy analysis often justifies a course of action once it has been decided. Thus, in the USA in the 1930s, Franklin Roosevelt did not need Keynesian ideas to think of the New Deal. He had this plan anyway, and Keynesian ideas were helpful in giving it intellectual substance and legitimating it. Yet, in the long term, Keynesian ideas ensured that the fiscal stimulation of the economy became a paradigm for government intervention rather than a short-term response to a crisis. In summary, Majone's argument is that 'objective analysis, unassisted by advocacy and persuasion, is seldom sufficient to achieve major policy innovations' (1989: 36).

With Sabatier, Majone and other 'new' policy analysts, the purview of the study of policy expands. Policy analysis and the use of evidence brings in new actors into the political process, a much larger range of participants than in traditional institutional, group or network accounts. Experts, analysts, technicians, journalists, television programmers, researchers and academics all have a role. The policy process is characterized by arguments about norms and evidence which, in the end, structure policy outcomes.

Post-positivist Public Policy

It is clear where the argument now leads. Moving from the modest claims of ideas-based empiricism, the new policy analysis makes claims about the primacy of ideas and the indeterminacy of knowledge. Rather than rational actors following their interests, it is the interplay of values and norms and different forms of knowledge which characterize the policy process. It is only a small step from the argument that language is central in policy-making to the claim that ideas are only real because they give meaning to those who use them. Policy is a contest between forms of discourse which are based on the quest for power and the search for meaning. Systems of ideas construct decision-makers' interests. Political action is about language which is a system of signification through which people construct the world (Hajer 1993). By being the way in which people frame questions, give meaning to the world and propose solutions, ideas have a life of their own. They are independent in the sense that discourse has its own rules which structure how the public and policy-makers perceive policy issues, such as the idea that a public problem takes the form of story, with a beginning, middle and an end with the end being successful government intervention (Kaplan 1993).

Even when the policy theorist drinks the heady brew of discourse, there are moderate or radical ways to approach the role of language in the policy process. A mild form is the social constructivism used by Deborah Stone to say that 'our understanding of real situations is always mediated by ideas; those ideas in turn are created, changed and fought over in politics' (1989: 283). Political actors articulate narratives, images and symbols. Participants in politics contest these ideas and seek to define the boundaries and classify the concepts. These complex disputes are embedded in different 'scientific' causal stories, but in fact they advance political values. The identification of a cause is vital in the policy process because it can become the way in which policy-makers identify a policy problem. The side that wins the scientific and expert argument has its policy preferences satisfied in the form of policy programmes. Ideas, in effect, create the policy. Stone limits the autonomy of ideas as she argues that the outcome of arguments about responsibility and blame are policy decisions that reflect power relationships in society.

More radically, writers such as Fischer and Forester (1993) have developed a post-positivist analysis of public policy whereby rationality, instrumentality, interests and causation are elements of the various discourses at play. Policy-makers deal in images, symbols and narratives through which they seek meaning. Coalitions of actors try to use a certain form of knowledge to dominate decision-making. History shows the continual interplay between different types of discourse, though with a tendency for certain forms of language to become dominant. In particular, the production of knowledge in modern capitalist societies reflects the development of a rationalistic, technocratic society based on market principles and scientific methods. Dominant interests have a monopoly on the production of knowledge. In this way, the use of policy analysis is not an 'objective' aid to the political process but is ideological.

On the other hand, some post-positivists believe the discourses which create and legitimate public policy can liberate as well as oppress. Given an institutional site which permits discussion and communication, interests may discuss an issue in a way arguments which advance human freedom and emancipation can win. Discourse coalitions, the participants in the political process sharing the same frames of reference, argue about the norms, values and causal relationships in policy choices. The process of argumentation can embody more humane and participatory ideas if actors are brought into the political process and if the democratic values implicit in many modern institutions are to be rediscovered.

In its most radical formulation, post-positivism regards the whole notion of policy as part of the discourse (Yanow 1996). Yanow's version includes not only the discourse about policy as part of systems of meaning and language, but the whole policy process: 'policies and political actions are not either symbolic or substantive. They can be both at once . . . even purely instrumental intentions are communicated and apperceived through symbolic means' (1996: 12). The creation and implementation of a policy is about the manufacture of symbols, with programme names, rituals and organizations, and even the decor in buildings being part of the language. In this formulation, notions of cause and effect disappear, there is no task of 'explaining public policy' as it is not possible to separate any concrete action which could be explained. Everything is interpretation.

So far the chapter has summarized the different aspects of the 'ideas' approach to understanding public policy. In fact, the divergence between the authors that fall into the category of ideas-based means that the terms 'approaches' best covers the literature. It may be the case the interpretivism of Yanow has nothing in common with the extension to rational choice of Goldstein and Keohane, except the rejection of a narrow conception of interests. Authors use the blanket term 'ideas' to cover a range of ideational processes from knowledge, beliefs, norms and causal stories to world systems and ideologies. Because of these differences, the following discussion of applications of ideas in public policy is designed to capture the different claims being made.

Some Applications

The Canadian forestry sector and policy-learning

Canadian forestry strikes the casual observer as a sector where technological and expert considerations dominate the regulation of the industry. But a recent piece of research is a neat example of the ideas in public policy approach, particularly in the way it claims to apply the policy advocacy coalition framework, and how the research prompted a counterattack that questions the validity of the policy-learning approach. The research of Lertzman, Raynor and Wilson (1996) seeks to explain the rapid change in the sector beginning in the mid-1970s. The story is of attempts by policy-makers to diversify land use, and of the resistance of economic interests to the proposed change. Public-sector decision-makers wanted to enlarge the area under long-term tenure and, in the 1990s, to respond to environmental concerns. In contrast, land-owners and forestry enterprises wanted to continue to maximize profits. The researchers argue there are coalitions of actors in the policy sector aligned to these value positions. In the period of change, there was a realignment of the coalition associated with continual learning and adaption. Officials and other members of the network of actors implemented the policies, and they refined and adapted the available policy instruments. The official belief system based on maintaining a sustained yield of wood dominated the governing network until the late 1960s. Then an environmental coalition began to form which engaged in policy-learning, and became stronger in the context of general world-wide arguments in favour of biodiversity. The economic coalition responded, but not enough to counter the more environmental direction of policy. Observing these changes, they argue that 'interest based explanations really do need to be supplemented or even supplanted by

knowledge-based accounts of policy change' (1996: 125). The core
ideas informing policy shifted from economic justification to environmental awareness. They argue that Sabatier may be wrong in
assuming that the basic forms of knowledge in a sector can only
change as the result of an external shock. There was a gradual
evolution of change through learning and adaptation, although the
authors believe they do not have enough evidence to say there was
a 'paradigm shift'.

Presented as a gradual evolution of learning and coalition-
building based around different ideas about what policies should be
followed, the forestry sector appears to be a neat example of the role
of ideas in public policy. However, it is not clear that the researchers
have shown the primacy of ideas in the formulation of public policy.
As the first paragraph in this chapter indicates, ideas are always
present in any public decision. In this case the disputes in the forestry
sector were consistent with a group or network account of public
policy-making, with new interests coming to the fore in the period of
policy change. In the criticism of Hoberg (1996), the authors
assume that if one set of actors wins the argument, that must show
the salience of ideas. New voters, an incoming government and
structural changes in the forestry industry and international action
all stimulated policy change and need not be regarded as ideas. This
is not to argue that cognitions are not important, but they are one
cause among others. A better conception of policy-making in forestry is to consider the importance of the embedded communities
that shape decisions against a background of new ideas and debates
which gradually shift the power bases of the actors involved (Howlett and Rayner 1996).

The single European market

In 1986 the European Union embarked on a fundamental change in
the way it makes policy. It moved from being an international body
with limited powers in certain policy sectors to one with a full
capability to act. The policy change was the move to the single
market captured in the Single European Act which liberalized economic transactions in Europe but at the same time introduced new
regulations in areas such as procurement, occupational health and
working conditions. Rather than examining change within the
confines of the nation-state, understandings of European Union
public policy need to incorporate relationships between nation-

states, to understand how national preferences interact with the decision-making framework of the final European decision-making body, the Council of Ministers, and also to comprehend the role of other European institutions, such as the European Commission, European Parliament and European Court of Justice. It is for the ambitious task of explaining rapid policy change that Garrett and Weingast (1993) use an ideas-based approach, though one linked to rational choice, and part of the scheme elaborated by Goldstein and Keohane.

Garrett and Weingast begin from the difficulties of rational choice theory in explaining cooperation, in particular the stringent conditions whereby the repeated prisoner's dilemma game can satisfy all participants. There are multiple paths toward cooperation and no prior way of knowing how the actors converge on one solution. In addition, the information requirements for successful repeated prisoner's dilemma games are unlikely to exist in the real world. Garrett and Weingast accept the argument that an element is missing from purely interest-based accounts. The gap suggests the importance of ideas. At the same time, they are critical of the notion that ideas matter on their own. Explanations resting on the salience of ideas need to explain why one idea is successful while other ideas fall by the wayside. The solution they offer is that ideas help players cooperate: 'ideas are important because they play a role in coordinating the expectations that are necessary to sustain cooperation among a set of players with divergent preferences' (1993: 205). Although social cooperation is a function of the gains to be expected, it also derives from what actually expresses the cooperation, which is the idea, and the way the idea is translated into a shared belief system which is a set of institutions. Thus Garrett and Weingast seek to map out the relationships between benefits, ideas and institutions as an integrated explanation of policy change. Ideas are not salient without a means whereby they are translated into practices and vice versa. Institutions mediate between ideas and interests by providing a focal point for decision-making, by freezing the past and setting out solutions for the future. For institutional regulation to work, the formal rules and organizational behaviour need to embody and maintain a normative system.

In the context of the move to the single market, Garrett and Weingast show that it is not possible to explain radical change in EU policy from the short-run self-interests of member states. While there were strong economic reasons for wanting to push ahead, such as strengthening the European economy against international competition and taking advantage of the gains from trade, there was no one path toward trade liberalization and, without some sort of institutionalization of practices, nor was there any method of preventing defections. On the other hand, though many writers on the development of the EU emphasize the importance of ideas, such as of greater European unity or federalism, the institutions in Europe which promote these ideas, such as the European Commission and the European Parliament, have been weak political actors. Garrett and Weingast argue that what explains the single market is the operation of a normative system that helps the players cooperate. This normative system is articulated through a developing legal framework regulated by the European Court of Justice, particularly through the rule of mutual recognition of national practices laid down in the *Cassis de Dijon* court case of 1979. At first sight the presence of the court and its developing jurisprudence, which has encroached onto the sovereignty of nation-states, is puzzling. As in the famous case in 1991, about British fishing rights, whereby a British court protected the common fisheries policy, a decision later upheld by the European Court of Justice (*Commission* v. *United Kingdom*), it would seem bizarre that nation-states would allow themselves to be regulated in this manner. Yet member states willingly accepted the Single European Act. The authors argue that the legal principles are an efficient form of decentralized regulation of the market system. The normative principles assist cooperation and prevent free-riding. In the large and complex European societies and economies it is not possible for actors to know what the others are doing, hence they rely on the efficiency of legal regulation. They argue that rapid policy change is inconceivable without this underlying set of normative principles.

The difficulty of the account is whether it shows the importance of ideas. As the authors admit, there were reasons why the main countries cooperated. The UK wished to deregulate because of the ideological stance of the Thatcher government. The strong German economy expected to gain from a single market and the French government rejected Keynesian economic management policies after the failure of the early 1980s socialist experiment. Were the countries embracing an idea? In a tautological sense they were, as without ideas there are no policies. But this is different to saying the idea was driving the policy or shaping the interests, as it could just as easily be interests which drive the policy which create the ideas.

The second possible problem is the opposite to the first. It is possible to construct a model to show that ideas were important in a way which did not foster the self-interests of the participants. The classic case was the UK. The government led by Thatcher believed in the single market so much that it signed away veto powers as part of the deal. Yet in a few years the same government was unable to stop EU legislation it did not want or think was in its country's interest. Was the move irrational or ideas-based? It is possible to argue that the British stand on the SEA was a suspension of self-interest or a misperception of self-interest on the part of the government. It was this short-run blindness to the consequences of its decisions which allowed countries in whose interests it was to gain from integration. Thus countries like Germany and France followed integration to benefit their economies and either hoodwinked or bought off the rest to follow the single market policy.

Thirdly, Garrett and Weingast's account of the policy development smacks of functionalism, whereby the actions of decision-makers are explained by the logic of the economic and political system and are supported by a guiding normative framework. But the reality of European integration is rather messier both in intention and, as the authors admit, in implementation. Intentions did not lead to predicted outcomes. It is possible to model the interests of some of the actors, but not all of them. Nor is it possible to comprehend an underlying functional logic. To better defend themselves, the authors could have presented some more evidence about the decision-making process. Nonetheless, their model is an impressive account which mixes interests, institutions and ideas and comes close to articulating a theory of public policy.

Public inquiries and child abuse

At the polar opposite to the study of the single European market, both in subject matter and in approach, are studies of policy-making carried out by official bodies charged with inquiring into crises of public policy. The focus is back to the national or even the local level, though it need not be. The approach which has commonly been used is to see inquiries as ways in which challenges to the existing established pattern of interests are managed and processed. There are variants of this approach, often using Edelman's symbolic politics framework, showing how commissions of inquiry can defuse challenges to the status quo by buying time and offering concessions which governments mildly implement. The classic study of this process is Lipsky and Olson's *Commission Politics* (1977), which shows how the US federal government used commissions to defuse the crisis which followed the 1960s urban riots in the USA. As such, these studies are examples of elitist approaches which acknowledge the importance of language through the way in which meanings and understandings filter demands on the policy process and affect how policy-makers perceive problems. However, because of the importance of argument and evidence in the resolutions of political conflict, some writers use inquiries as a particular exploration of the way in which discourses of power are embedded in institutional and political practices. Public policy embodies theories of knowledge about how society works which have their origins in scientific epistemology. Feminism and other discourses can challenge this hegemony, especially when there is a crisis which exposes the contradictions within the dominant order. The argument is that public inquiries and commissions restore policy continuity. Governments adopt modest reforms and changes which reflect and uphold the intellectual order.

Ashenden (1996) uses the work of Foucault to understand the way in which policy-making on the family is governed. She starts with the existing consensus which stresses the need both to protect children and to uphold personal privacy. The existing regulatory framework sets up a public/private distinction which is institutionalized by professional practices about whether to intervene or not. These policies express what Foucault calls the governmentalization of the state, a process based on new forms of knowledge and state rule that emerged at the end of the eighteenth century. This form of knowledge sees the family as the object of scientific and expert intervention guided by the state, particularly concerning the management of populations.

Professionalization establishes the boundaries of social and political intervention and thereby is the framework which guides public policy. The ambiguity and artificiality of the public/private distinction is a fundamental contradiction, yet it is protected by power of rationality embodied in law and in political institutions. At times of crisis, new forms of knowledge and practice can challenge the legitimacy of the existing framework. Public inquiries are a means to resolve such problems because they are 'objective' ways of producing 'facts' which they can then 'judge', a process which normalizes knowledge: 'the Inquiry operates as a means for the repositioning of knowledges and practices which maintain the relationship between public and private spheres' (Ashenden 1996: 73).

Ashenden analyses the limited policy recommendations of the Cleveland inquiry of 1987 which followed a public crisis about the decisions of health professionals and social workers in child abuse cases. The charge is that the professionals were over-zealous in the use of their powers to protect children from sexual abuse; in particular it was argued that the diagnostic technique was incorrect. Ashenden argues that the inquiry was a way to restore normality through a reasoned account of the issues and events. This is a radically different approach to understanding the emergence of public policy from an interest-based account. Policy is not the result of the interaction of individual or group interests, nor does it reflect some social and economic base or institutional determinism. It is knowledge itself which is driving the policy arguments, and in the end the policy outcomes. Policy cannot be seen as the expression of a neutral rationality, but it is the expression of knowledge as power. Thus the recommendations of the inquiry were designed to uphold the legitimacy of scientific and medical objectivity rather than to engage with the underpinnings of the discourses. Since the inquiry used this framework, so the solution to the policy problem requires the reapplication of technical expertise.

The research examines the text of the inquiry and the evidence submitted to it, rather than the wider context. So it is hard to conclude whether the methods of the approach sustain the importance of discourse in the policy process as a whole. It is difficult to know if there is a normalization of policy caused by the inquiry. Policy stability could also be explained by the power and interests of the professionals and politicians and not depend on the discourses at work. While the analysis of argument, text and evidence shows the extent to which discourse is important in understanding how public institutions react to crisis, it is hard to know if an approach which relies on analysing discourse can find out the effect of ideas.

Summing-up

The three examples of ideas-based policy change or stability are very different. Their contrasting starting-points, methods and conclusions illustrate both the advantage and the problem with the ideas approach. The diversity of situations and methods seems suited to the complex world of policy. The problem is that once interest-based claims are relaxed, there is a broad spectrum of frameworks ranging from the Foucauldian to the modification of rational choice theory. Which ideas-based approach assists the quest to explain public policy?

As with the other approaches in this book there is a tendency for one element in the explanation to dominate. As a result it is impossible to know whether what is being claimed is correct or not. In post-positivist and/or interpretivist public policy everything is transformed into discourse. If the empirical world is to be investigated, it cannot be seen as a seamless connection of ideas. The policy analyst needs to cling on to the claim that ideas affect the empirical world rather than that the empirical world is constituted by them. Although in a tautological sense the latter statement is true, the political process sorts ideas so that some are influential and others fall out of favour. It is the process by which ideas become important in structuring outcomes that interests scholars of public policy. Thus the ideas of Goldstein and Keohane, Haas and Sabatier are useful, whereas the interpretivism of Yannow and Stone and the post-positivism of Fischer and Forester are circular and cannot explain.

Yet, much as the rational choice ideas of Goldstein and Keohane are interesting, they limit the applicability of ideas to when interest-based models fail. It is counterintuitive to argue that powerful ideas like the 1960s US war on poverty and 1980s neo-liberal proposals succeed when game-theoretic models yield indeterminate outcomes. Naturally, political decision-makers, as much as they are able to know what course of action benefits them, do not follow ideas which are against their self-interest. But to realize their self-interest they need ideas to give meaning in politics and help shape their identity in the political world. It seems that at the same time that ideas constitute interests, interests gave reality to ideas. Though there are politicians and bureaucrats who simply aim to maximize personal wealth, fame or the size of their bureaus, most political actors are attached to political ideas which help their careers and launch them into the political world. In the soup of ideas there are always political agents which will attach (and detach) themselves to some of them. It is this symbiosis between ideas and interests which is at the heart of change and stability in public policy. This form of explanation is dynamic and protean, and captures the complex and multilayered nature of the political world. Approaches which link ideas and interests in public policy are the theme of the next chapter.

8

A Synthesis through Evolution

We need a name for the new replicator, a noun which conveys the idea of a unit of cultural transmission, or a unit of imitation. 'Mimeme' comes from a suitable Greek root, but I want a monosyllable that sounds a bit like 'gene'. I hope my classicist friends will forgive me if I abbreviate mimeme to *meme*. (Dawkins 1976: 206)

The Need for a Synthesis

The main theme of previous chapters is that the single approach fails to explain policy change and variation. Even though the five approaches are often complex and multidimensional, they usually offer partial accounts of political action. They concentrate on examples best placed to illustrate their perspectives. As a result they often leave out much of the practice of decision-making. Sometimes a theory is good at explaining stability, such as policy network theory, yet is unable to explain change. Alternatively, researchers, aware that their method covers only a range of examples, seek to expand the number of phenomena an account explains. Yet, by introducing different forms of explanation, the framework either becomes too general and *ad hoc* or collapses into other forms of explanation. An example is the new institutionalism which transforms conventional accounts of institutions into norms and values, such as Hall's explanation of economic policy change. The result of the 'concept expansion' is that the approach loses its original parsimony and becomes a set of labels which is descriptive rather than explanatory.

This chapter throws off the constraints of one perspective. The underlying theme of this book is that policy change and variation emerges from the interaction of processes. For example, individual choice interacts with institutions; and ideas become important when they interplay with individual interests. This book, however, does not welcome an unreflective amalgam of different approaches. If the theorist is not careful, approaches can be fashioned to fit any possible policy context. The result is an 'over-determined' set of explanations. The critic can never disprove the way an approach is applied because it is so flexible. Moreover, such a medley of accounts does not do justice to the different assumptions upon which they are based, such as about human nature and the effect of structures.

The argument of this book is that the approaches can be linked together if the analyst distinguishes between constraints on action and causes of action. Thus institutions, patterns of interest-group and networked relationships and socio-economic structures are limits to human action though sometimes they change autonomously. Individual actors are the drivers for change and the foundations for human action. Ideas, on the other hand, give human agents purpose and are the way they express their interests. The secret is to uncover the way each of these processes interacts with the others over time and in different places.

Previous chapters discuss a few theorists who seek to integrate levels of explanation. One example is Garrett and Weingast (1993), who combine ideas, interests and institutions in their account of the emergence of the Single European Market. Another is multilevel rational choice institutionalism (see Chapter 6) that explores how individuals choose rules depending on whether they are operational, collective or constitutional choices (Kiser and Ostrom 1982). This is a neat way to integrate the rational choice and institutional/ constitutional perspectives, and to categorize the choices of actors as they seek to influence the future. It is also an interesting way in which rational choice can incorporate constitutional and normative approaches to policy-making. Through self-interest actors choose an institutional framework that is unlikely to disadvantage them at some future date. The analytical distinction can be the driver for political action as it allows actors to solve collective action problems by seeking agreement of rules of decision. However, as Sabatier (1991) comments, the approach is rather partial as it neglects the role of information and does not deal with the complexity of the policy process. While it makes some progress in integrating a new institutionalist and an institutional rational choice approach, it is not a theory of public policy.

There are other writers who integrate approaches. This chapter reviews three of them. They represent the 'state of the art' in 1990s US policy studies, and have many common features. They have long complex titles! They seek to encompass the complexity and changeability of the US policy process. They reflect a concern in contemporary policy studies to be 'multitheoretic' as they have, in part, emerged in reaction against the domination of the single approaches covered in Chapters 3 to 7. While there are problems with each framework, they come close to being theories of policy change and variation. In the way they all partly fail, they suggest new avenues for research and theory. In particular, they need to push their insights further, and this is where evolutionary theories find their potential.

Sabatier's Policy Advocacy Coalition Framework

A powerful candidate for the integrative approach is Sabatier's policy advocacy coalition (PAC) framework. It already appears at various junctures in the book either as a socio-economic or as an ideas-based approach. Indeed, Sabatier regards the model as integrative, and he synthesizes many insights from accounts of public policy, such as institutional rational choice, the socio-economic determinants of public policy and the new policy analysis.

Sabatier (1991) and Sabatier and Jenkins-Smith (1993) begin from the importance of policy subsystems in policy formulation and implementation. Like many US and European policy scholars, they stress the importance of relationships within policy sectors as the key to understanding how decision-making works. As such, the PAC framework has much in common with the policy network school. Like many network accounts, the PAC framework regards policy-making as a continual process with no strict beginning and end. The coalition, however, is a broader set of processes than that evoked by the network metaphor. In the PAC framework a coalition is an alliance of bodies holding the same ideas and interests for the purpose of arguing against other coalitions within the same policy sector. Coalitions include more participants than the traditional 'whirlpool' or 'triangle' of decision-makers. There are journalists, policy analysts and researchers as well as the more familiar bureaucrats, politicians and interest-group representatives. They all play a role in the dissemination of ideas. Unlike the policy-network account, participants bargain and form alliances within networks. The PAC framework does not assume policy-making systems are consensual or are dominated by stable crosscutting elites.

Sabatier and his associates use their framework to explain change.

The idea is that normally two to four competing policy advocacy coalitions, each with its own ideas about policy content, compete for dominance in a subsystem. Knowledge plays a crucial role because the coalition is a reflection of the ideas and interests about a set of policy issues. The analysis, while seeming to be about relationships, is about values and conceptions, a subject tackled in Chapter 7. The argument of this book is that the articulation of ideas is consistent with the individual and group interests if the analyst properly specifies the relationship between the two. Sabatier himself is rather coy on this point, arguing that it is better for actors to indicate their opinions to researchers than for researchers to investigate why they hold those opinions (Sabatier 1988: 142). In fact, it is possible that short-term interests lead to some strange ideological bedfellows (Hann 1995) as, for example, groups such as feminists and conservatives can ally on their opposition to pornography. It is true, however, that coalition partners will usually be of the same political hue rather than being selected just to win, as is shown by the extensive research of how coalitions form and which partners ally (Laver and Schofield 1990). A key dimension to the framework is that the participants learn over time. Sabatier and his colleagues argue that policy change needs to be observed over a decade or more to find out how policy analysis shapes the agenda and learning takes place. However, as Chapter 7 discusses, the PAC framework assumes ideas are stable unless they are disrupted by a major crisis. Core beliefs do not change because decision-makers can interpret events in the world in a fashion which does not challenge the axioms of knowledge. In a crisis, it is possible that a set of beliefs is no longer sustainable because there are events which are hard to explain.

The framework is not just a synthesis of networks and ideas. It involves other aspects of the political system. Institutions play a role through the salience of levels of government and the interaction of government agencies and committees. Constitutional rules are 'relatively stable parameters' within which policy change takes place. Overall, however, the PAC framework does not emphasize institutional constraints. PACs are more about ideas and networks than structures. Nor does the approach say much about human choices. Sabatier and his associates believe that ideas and interests socialize individuals into patterns of behaviour. Strategic choice and interaction do not play much of a role.

Much more important is the role of the economy and social change. Sabatier and his colleagues argue that policy-making depends on change and stability in the wider political system, in society and in the economy. They utilize Hofferbert's 'funnel' model of policy innovation, whereby changes in the economy or society feed into public opinion which in turn affects the policy positions of political parties and interest groups, and thence the ideas and preferences of policy-makers (see Chapter 5). While Sabatier and his co-researchers are careful to reject a deterministic model of policy change, they argue that rapid change in the external world gives 'shocks' to the policy-makers by disrupting stable patterns of interests and exchanges. Though economic and social conditions act as 'stable external parameters' for long periods of time, crises can change the salience and meaning of ideas. Sabatier gives the examples of the 1973 oil crisis and the election of president Ronald Reagan in 1980 which fostered rapid policy changes. The advocacy of new solutions to policy problems can disrupt the pattern of interests that cement a policy advocacy coalition together and can create new relationships between actors. The result is policy change, such as the energy-saving measures of the 1970s or the market-based policies of the 1980s. The long-term outcome is a new, stable set of coalitions and hence a particular approach to solving policy problems.

Sabatier and Jenkins-Smith have pioneered research methods to map the structure of coalitions over time. For example, Sabatier and Brasher (1993) code the policy actors in land use and water quality at Lake Tahoe Basin. Looking at a wider range of groups than Jenkins-Smith and St Clair, they uncover the emergence of an environmental coalition and the development of a pro-growth/ business one. The advantage of these quantitative studies is that they map change over time and set out the exact structure of the coalitions. The criticism, as so often with quantitative studies, is that the intensive research effort often only proves the most straightforward and common sense of hypotheses. By including several more traditional case study approaches in *Policy Change and Learning*, the authors accept that qualitative as well as quantitative methods can investigate policy advocacy coalitions.

By examining the interaction between external changes and ideas the approach is an effective account of public policy-making which is almost capable of meeting the tough criteria of explaining policy change. If Sabatier and associates stress the constraints of institutions and include a model of human action, the PAC framework could be a full explanation of policy change and stability. Indeed,

Sabatier indicates that he draws on and mirrors some of the ideas of
institutional rational choice. However, there are a number of defects
in the account.

First, the PAC framework may not explain policy change. At its
heart is the assumption that some relationships in the policy-making
process are stable. This is the idea that policy-making systems divide
into two or more long-term ideas-based coalitions. Although Sabatier argues that these coalitions learn, he stresses they follow
strategies within a context of stable core values and beliefs. Like the
policy network approach, the PAC framework on its own only
explains stability, even if the coalitions are active and in conflict with
each other. Sabatier needs factors external to the model to understand when change arises. What happens is that an event, such as
an economic crisis, redistributes the resources within the coalition to
ensure change. It is much rarer for cognitive change to affect the
policy-making system. In spite of the complexity in the way Sabatier
and his allies explain the PAC framework, it boils down to a simple
formulation. Policy-making is stable until a large socio-economic
event changes the coalitional pattern. If this understanding of PACs
is accepted, then the model becomes rather too similar to policy-
network theory. It thus suffers some of the similar defects. In spite of
the attempt to build a causal theory the PAC framework ends up as
descriptive.

Second, the PAC approach, while a great advance on previous
theorizing, is not as integrative as it claims and does not incorporate
all the aspects of policy change and variation. While ideas, socio-
economic conditions and networks are at the centre of the model, it
neglects institutions and individual choices. The only institutional
factors that Sabatier stresses are intergovernmental relations. Sabatier tends to regard individuals as features of policy subsystems and
their attendant ideas, rather than as shaping their own destinies.
Sabatier criticizes rational actor models, except those deployed by
Ostrom and her colleagues.

Third, the PAC framework tends to overemphasize external factors through its use of the time-series method. External shocks are
easy to measure in time-series analysis, so it is possible Sabatier and
associates neglect the role of interests and strategies of coalition-
formation. In fact, the results of this kind of research are not entirely
supportive of an external shock model, as they acknowledge. Several
of the external events fail to have the desired effect on coalition-
formation, suggesting other important explanations.

↳ Fourth, the style of group interaction, with a large number of actors, particularly new ones, such as policy analysts and journalists, is not so applicable outside the USA. Western European countries have more closed policy communities. However, European policy communities are starting to fragment as the number of actors in the decision-making process increases and there is a greater complexity of policy. Particularly at the European level, the fluidity of networks and the importance of new ideas in shaping policy mean that the policy advocacy coalition framework is a useful way of analysing policy. *OBS*

Kingdon's Policy Streams Approach

Kingdon's book, *Agendas, Alternatives and Public Policies* (1984), is one of the few treatments of public policy that examines the political system as a whole, and embraces the relative importance of individual agents, ideas, institutions and external processes. Rather than beginning with stability, Kingdon's policy streams approach assumes continual policy change. All the elements to the policy-making process shift and change, and policy outcomes arise from the continual interplay. Kingdon's policy streams is as close to an adequate theory of public policy as has so far been surveyed in this book, so it is worth setting it out in detail.

Kingdon's problem is the folk wisdom that people in the policy process do not know where policy ideas come from. Attempts to trace an idea back in history usually end up in an infinite regress of causes. There is often no starting-point. Policy solutions seem to come from 'anywhere'; they emerge because the time for an idea has come and they often disappear as rapidly. Ideas are not uniquely associated with one person or organization, but they arise from the sharing of agendas between decision-makers. Kingdon takes the very messiness of the policy process, with its complexity and apparent unpredictability, as the baseline. Unlike many policy analysts, he does not impose a rigid conceptual scheme.

Kingdon regards policy-formation as the result of a flow of three sets of processes or streams: problems, policies and politics. Problems are public matters requiring attention, such as fiscal crises or environmental degradation, that may or may not get defined as important or not. Policies are proposals for change based on the accumulation of knowledge and development of interest among the specialists in a policy sector. Certain highly motivated people, the policy entrepreneurs, propose solutions to policy problems. Policy entrepreneurs mobilize opinion and institutions, and they try to ensure the idea does not fall off the agenda. They can be politicians, bureaucrats, analysts, consultants, journalists and academics. Third, political processes, such as election results and swings in the popular mood, influence how the media and other opinion-formers define public problems and evaluate the potential solutions.

Kingdon argues that each of these processes acts as an impetus or a constraint on public policy by putting a proposal on or off the agenda. It is the circumstances under which these three streams combine to make a policy happen that is Kingdon's research task. He argues that agendas are not an automatic reflection of the power of the participants in the policy process. Policy formation is based as much on luck and chance as on intention. While incrementalism summarizes some aspects of the process, the contingency of the interactions between the streams can cause discontinuity or sudden agenda change. An idea often 'catches on' and moves rapidly onto the political agenda, especially when there is what Kingdon calls a 'policy window', which is an opportunity, such as a new policy-problem or a new administration in power, for policy advocates to press home their ideas. As Kingdon writes, 'windows are either opened by the appearance of compelling problems or by happenings in the political stream' (21). These windows may not be open for long, so participants in the policy process must act swiftly before the opportunity passes by. Because of boredom, symbolic political actions and the natural course of the issue attention cycle, the windows often close as rapidly as they open. Kingdon gives the example of the adoption of Medicare, a healthcare policy for the elderly in the USA, which the federal government introduced in 1965–66. There was an opportunity because the Republicans were discredited after the Goldwater candidacy for the presidency and there was a large Democrat majority in Congress. If the policy advocates had waited, they would not have had such a chance while President Johnson became embedded in the Vietnam War and Republicans regained popularity.

Kingdon deploys a version of Cohen, March and Olsen's (1972) 'garbage can' model of organizational choice to understand the way the streams join together. The model examines how decision-makers 'dump' problems in an organization. What happens is that problems emerge to engage some of the people who take decisions. In the next sequence these decision-makers move on to try to solve other problems. But, in the meantime, the decision creates new problems which involves another set of actors who make more decisions that affect a further group of decision-maker actors and so on. The result is a chaotic style of policy-making as decision-makers deal with a changing array of problems and solutions. They then leave the problems behind for others to pick up. While the garbage can is capable of explaining organizational choice, Kingdon applies the idea to the wider political process that has the characteristic of 'organized anarchy'. The process of continual change and the intermittent involvement of all kinds of decision-makers, whether politicians, bureaucrats or others, is the base point for a policy system that is as far away from the sequential model of policy-making as can be imagined.

The policy streams approach celebrates the importance of ideas in public policy, but also seeks to explain how ideas emerge by their adoption and rejection by the many decision-makers involved. Kingdon also investigates many of the other processes discussed in this book, but he approaches them in the dynamic framework. Thus institutions are important in shaping change and the evolution of policies and policy problems, particularly when they are highly fragmented and allow for the flow of ideas. Rather than ideas in public policy just reflecting power relationships, they originate from a number of contingent and often contradictory selection process. At the same time as the policies and problems are symbiotically floating in their 'policy primeval soup', so the political stream exercises a powerful influence on agendas. These political factors include electoral trends, partisan interests and pressure-group dynamics. Changing agendas affect policy selection via ripples of influence through policy systems. There are 'spillovers' from one policy sector to another. New principles set precedents, successes breed successes and policy-makers learn from each other.

The policy streams approach is a major step forward in understanding policy formation. The book is a convincing explanation of why policy changes, though it has less to say about why policy varies. One criticism of the book is that it is, like the PAC framework, based on the US policy process, though it applies increasingly to the more open and fluid national policy-making systems, and can easily be transferred to the unpredictable EU policy arena (Richardson 1996). The ethnocentric charge, so common to US-dominated political science, is less applicable nowadays. The policy streams approach needs only a partial correction to be applicable to the unitary Western European states and their more integrated policy-making systems.

The main difficulty of the book for the policy researcher is that it concentrates too much on agendas and not enough on how ideas feed into the implementation process and back again. This criticism is perhaps unfair as the book is largely about agendas, but, as Chapter 2 argues, it is rarely appropriate to separate out the factors that affect policy formulation from those that influence policy implementation, as the two processes are almost fused. It is the interaction between different types of actors over both policy definition and implementation that is the correct way to conceptualize policy. Rather than thinking the model only applies to agenda-setting, it explains the role of all the actors in the policy process partly because each of them creates issues and agendas of their own. Even lower-level bureaucrats, who mainly have an implementation role in public policy, can, through the discretion they exercise and the interaction they have with people who have more of a policy-formulation role, propose policy solutions and respond to policy problems in much the same way as the media and legislative committees. Kingdon needs to extend the evolutionary method to deconstruct all the key features of the political system, such as the implementation process. Thus the executive is just a disaggregated set of decision-makers, and public opinion is evolving in time. The fluid policy communities of specialists and policy analysts evolve in a wider interactive context. The streams of policies, problems and politics are ubiquitous.

The Punctuated Equilibrium Model

Similar, in some respects, to the policy streams approach is Baumgartner and Jones' punctuated equilibrium model of policy change set out in their book *Agendas and Instability in American Politics* (1993). Their starting-point is the presence of both change and stability in policy-making in the USA. Whereas, on the one hand, traditional accounts of policy-making emphasize the stability of policy-making in elite policy communities, on the other, writers like Kingdon stress continual change and adaptation. Instead, Baumgartner and Jones are interested in the presence of both characteristics in policy formation over time. In a policy sector there are long periods of stability followed by periods of public interest, media scrutiny and public action.

Baumgartner and Jones are particularly interested in the rapidity of the change between periods of partial equilibrium and of issue-expansion, hence the idea that stable periods of policy-making are 'punctuated' by policy activism. It is the explanation of the shift in the rates of change in policy-making subsystems that is the essence of how policies change and vary: 'The forces that create stability during some periods are the same that combine during critical periods to force dramatic and long-lasting changes during other periods' (1993: 237). Their research task relates to the central objective of this book: to explain policy change, stability and varia-tion. The authors seek to explain how decision-making is about the interaction of institutions, interests, socio-economic factors, individ-ual actors and ideas, so the punctuated model comes close to an ideal way of analysing public policy.

Public-policy writers have often observed that decision-making takes various forms and need not be continuous. Such is the claim of Braybrooke and Lindblom (1963) in their account of disjointed incrementalism. While it is the norm that policy-makers compare current policy choices with those that went before, this can involve high or low understanding, and incremental or large change. How-ever, rather than being a refinement of incrementalism, the punctuated equilibrium model is about the shifts in the rate of policy change and why they occur at particular points in time. Baumgart-ner and Jones deploy the finding from social choice theory that equilibria are rare in politics. Disequilibrium and change are more likely to be normal features of political systems. In public policy, interest groups and bureaus can institutionalize themselves to create stable policy monopolies in relatively secure subsystems. As Chapter 4 discusses, policy communities of actors in policy subsystems pursue limited policy objectives for extended periods. However, by focusing on agendas, Baumgartner and Jones explore how ideas become prominent and institutionalized in a policy system. Institu-tions do not just exist in a vacuum without a grounding in ideas about policy. Likewise, institutions and the influence of power elites ensure that a particular policy can remain in place, supported by the beliefs of other elites in the political system, favourable reports in the media and a supportive public opinion. In this case, policy changes only incrementally. Yet, given favourable conditions, agendas can shift very rapidly, upsetting the consensus of established ideas. New agendas feed into policy outputs, and these sets of ideas can intro-duce new decision-makers and groups into the political system. In

time these actors shift the rules about decision-making that institutionalize them into the policy process. Thus changing agendas in the
political system create new monopolies which other agendas and
groups challenge at a later date.

Baumgartner and Jones are particularly interested in the rapid
fashion in which instability replaces stability. What generates the
shift is the process of positive feedback. When an agenda begins to
expand, the process of change accelerates through the adoption of
the issue by new decision-makers, organizations and, in time, the
public. Because of the serial processing capacity of organizations,
they can only concentrate on one thing at a time. So there is a
tendency for all the decision-makers in a political system to focus on
one issue to the exclusion of others. Thus there is a virtuous circle of
interaction between policy entrepreneurs who stand to gain from a
change in policy, the media who discuss an issue and public opinion
that can fuel change. Each process feeds on the other. There is a
bandwagon effect as a new idea takes hold. Ideas and policies diffuse
across sub-national political systems. Once the issue expansion is
unstoppable, the monopoly is challenged and the partial equilibrium
is punctuated. The media is particularly important because of the
way in which journalists and editors respond to each other. Also, a
policy issue, like the effect of pesticides, may be confined to specialist
sections, such as science pages. But when it becomes a public issue
the topic transfers to the central sections and to the front page.

The authors explore the expansion and stability of agendas in
environmental, agricultural and urban policy in the USA over
several decades. They plot the attention newspapers give to a topic,
whether the coverage is negative or positive; they map public
opinion; they examine the extent to which congressional committees examine the issue, and they investigate whether there is an
effect on policy outputs, such as public expenditure. They find a
relationship between these sets of processes. In particular, there is a
tendency for an issue to shift dramatically from low positive coverage to high amounts of negative coverage in the media. There is
also a relationship between public opinion, media coverage, political
interest and policy outputs, suggesting the diffusion and expansion
of issues. These two findings confirm the model of punctuated
equilibrium.

They examine several examples, such as cities as a national policy
issue. Cities have social and economic problems which can be met by

positive governmental action, such as measures to counter unemployment, to alleviate urban deprivation, to quell urban unrest and
to limit racial discrimination. In the 1960s US cities emerged onto
the public agenda in a sudden jump associated with a high level of
media attention. There followed a period of intense political interest
that resulted in rapid increases in national public expenditure for
cities. There was a clear transmission of an agenda from a public
crisis from the media to the political process and thence to policy
outputs. There later followed a backlash. Public support for urban
initiatives declined and the media reported the issue less frequently.
Congressional attention waned and policy outputs diminished.

In sub-sectors in urban policy and other sectors, like nuclear
power, Baumgartner and Jones discover different relationships suggesting, as in the tradition of studying public policy, that policy areas
differ and no pattern exactly replicates itself. Sometimes public
opinion, political interests and outputs are closely related; at other
times they are not. In some sectors, like food control, the punctuat-
ing of the equilibrium allows for the institutionalization of new
groups and alternative ways of defining public problems; in other
sectors, like urban policy, the fall in public interest and political
backlash deinstitutionalized the interest-group coalition and per-
mitted the contraction of national urban policies.

The punctuated equilibrium model connects together in a
dynamic framework the various elements of the decision-making
process covered in earlier chapters. Institutions are important
because they freeze a set of political participants into the policy
process and exclude others. Institutions help ensure that problems
are defined in a particular manner and not in another. They set the
agenda. On the other hand, institutions are not omnipotent. They
are often shaped by the effects of a shift in the agenda. While
Congress appears to have rigid jurisdictional boundaries which
ensures issues are processed in a manner supportive to particular
coalitions of groups, when issues change, the jurisdictional boundaries alter rapidly to reflect the changed balance of power.
Institutions can create partial equilibria, but only for short periods of
time.

Interests and networks are important in the model because, along
with the institutional framework, there are patterns of association
which help cement agendas and determine the definition of problems. In addition, changes in agendas are often associated with new
interest groups and coalitions which may become important in

setting the agenda. Changes in the interest-group system are important in shifting the policy-making style and the way in which
agendas emerge. Thus, the changes in the behaviour of interest
groups which occurred at the end of the 1960s, in particular the
explosion in the number of interest groups and the weakening of the
hegemony of producer interests, creates a more fluid policy-making
environment. With a larger number of groups of differing ideological
orientations, it becomes more and more difficult for policy-making
monopolies to insulate themselves from agenda change.

Social and economic factors are important but not central to the
punctuated equilibrium model. Problems, like urban unrest, can
communicate messages to the policy-makers that may result in
symbolic political action, but more often they can help focus attention on an issue and shift a policy problem up the agenda. Long-term
changes can affect policies across the entire political spectrum as
there is a feedback between and across the policy sectors.

Individual actors, and their interests, are crucial. The shift in
agendas is driven by the way in which the policy system rewards
some and excludes others. Thus certain actors strive to maintain
the partial equilibrium because they benefit from the policy monopoly. Other policy entrepreneurs seek to overturn policy monopolies
because they get a benefit if the political system adopts their policy
solution. Policy entrepreneurs can take advantage of 'slack resources' in the form of people who are outside the policy-making system
and who would prefer a different policy but who only mobilize if the
entrepreneur makes the first move. Entrepreneurs seek to place
items on the agenda and to seize opportunities when they arise.
Political leaders also seek to guide agendas.

Ideas are also vital. They are the building-blocks of agendas.
Baumgartner and Jones argue that policy-makers and the institutional framework shape the way policy problems are defined. They
adopt insights from the work of Stone (1988) on the way problems
are defined. Policy-makers interpret a problem in the context of an
agenda. Thus the same event can be given a different slant or
meaning depending on the person perceiving it. External events, like
urban protest, can be interpreted as a signal for more generous
federal social policies if there is a liberal consensus. Alternatively,
these actions may precipitate law and order measures if the dominant agenda is conservative.

As with other approaches, there are some limitations to the
punctuated equilibrium model. First, as the authors admit, the

account is mainly descriptive. The quantitative analysis suggests associations but not necessarily causal relationships between agendas of public opinion, the media, political forums and policy outputs. Baumgartner and Jones could be measuring identities rather than relationships. If there is causation, it could be in either direction or in both ways.

Second, there is an assumption that the debates in the media and/ or public opinion influence politicians and thereby policy outputs. Although Baumgartner and Jones suggest that the construction and maintenance of policy agendas gives full rein to the potential for bias in public policy-making, their model is essentially 'bottom-up'. The assumption is that people outside the policy process, if there are favourable conditions, can challenge the prevailing pattern of decision-making. And although there may be a tendency for agendas to fall back or for the challengers to the systems to become the new elites as a sort of elite circulation, the order is always capable of reform from below. But the model neglects the way in which political decision-makers can shape preferences from above. Dunleavy (1991) argues that UK Conservative governments in the 1980s shaped preferences by selling off public housing and privatizing state industries that may have had a long-term impact on the opinions of voters and interest groups. Political leaders influenced the framework within which individual citizens exercised their choices.

Third, when seeking to explain policy change, as with so many public policy approaches, the authors have to reach outside their model. Thus, it is not the expansion and change in agendas in urban policy, and their subsequent contraction, that explains policy change, but the window of opportunity provided by the Johnson presidency's reform programme, and America's post-war prosperity encouraged politicians and publics to think in terms of resolving social problems. The expansion of the agenda is a result of changes occurring elsewhere and due to the importance of political events. This problem is not fatal, as it is the conjunction of interests and expanding agendas that is the motor behind policy change. It is a fortuitous set of factors that allow the partial equilibria to punctuate. It is this combination between the various elements in policy formation, and how they combine differently, that is the beauty of the approach.

The fourth criticism may be unfair. It is that, like Kingdon, Baumgartner and Jones do not pay enough attention to policy-implementation decisions. Because implementation decisions are so closely bound up with policy choices, and usually are policy choices, they have much the same characteristics of agenda stability and instability. Though Baumgartner and Jones discuss policy outputs, they do not take into account the complex implementation process, and the feedbacks and interconnection between the processes. However, as with Kingdon's account, the punctuated model is not undermined by considering these issues. In fact, such a perspective could complement and rebalance the tendency to deal too much with the media and public opinion as the drivers for change.

Many of these criticisms just carp at what is an excellent and theoretically well informed model. The model starts from the complexity of decision-making, both its changeability and stability, explores a model of issue expansion and contraction and provides some powerful tests of hypotheses derived from the model. The model is not just a device for understanding agendas, but is part of a wider analysis of the multidimensional nature of choice, the way in which individuals have limited capacity to make decisions and the manner in which political systems tend to fix attention to a small range of solutions to public problems. The limits to human and institutional capacity mean that, once a new issue comes out into the open, for a while the energy and logic of the system is directed upon it (Jones 1994). In other words, the punctuated equilibrium model derives from a theory of public decision-making.

Evolutionary Theory

Rather than explaining public policy from stable patterns of association and the institutionalization of interests, the policy streams approach and the punctuated equilibrium model explain how the various participants in policy-making systems interact with and respond to each other to produce forms of political action and inaction. They each claim to be an integrated account of policy-making and implementation because they synthesize the various elements that cause policy change. Single-level approaches focus on one key principle as the foundation for the political system, and they often assume that political systems are stable as a result. What may be called evolutionary theory regards all these elements as continually interacting with each other over time. The institutions are sets of constraints upon actors that can sometimes be reshaped if actors so choose. Interests are important because they structure the sets of choices for other actors. Economic power structures similarly offer alternative choices. Individual self-interest drives the machine and interacts with the constraints. Ideas provide solutions and meanings for policy-makers. But what drives policy is the continual interaction between these features. And evolution is the direction in which integrative accounts of public policy are heading. Thus Kingdon regards his approach as evolutionary. Similarly, Baumgartner and Jones hint at an evolutionary model that guides the periods of equilibrium and disequilibrium in policy formation: 'an evolutionary model is more relevant to politics than is the regularity implied by a theory of cycles' (1993: 245–6).

It is important to be careful in using the process of evolution in discussions about public policy, as the term draws its original meaning from the Darwinian idea of a competitive struggle for the fittest and from the Victorian notion of progress. A modern account of evolution, both in science and, more controversially, for societies and political systems, does not assume there is a competitive struggle between organisms or social and political actors. The various elements interact and modify their behaviour either by competing or by cooperating to achieve the survival of their gene or idea (Dawkins 1976). They compete or cooperate in various contexts that may be very different, but what makes the process evolutionary is the process of selection at work whereby some genes or mimemes fail and others succeed. There is no assumption that the process is teleological because evolution can lead to progress or not depending on what drives the selection process. Evolutionary theory generates a causal explanation rather than just a description of change. Thus, if we examine the unit of analysis, the policies, which are ideas concretized by political action (i.e. interests), it is possible to explain the success of a policy in evolutionary terms. As against another possible policy, it succeeds because there is a coalition behind it and that solves the public problem behind it (at least in the way in which the public problem is defined at that point in time). There is a chance conjunction of events that make it successful. It is an idea that works.

Chapter 6 presents a rational choice version of cooperation, the iterated prisoner's dilemma game whereby actors who fear that other actors will take advantage of them come to cooperate through repeatedly interacting with each other (Axelrod 1984). Even though the Axelrod game is limited to individual actors interacting with set preferences and a simple set of constraints, it is fairly easy to extend the idea. Institutions, groups, economies and ideas evolve together through the changing preferences of individuals that shape and are shaped by their external environment. Indeed, Kingdon footnotes Axelrod and Dawkins when he compares the process of generating alternatives and proposals in a community with natural selection (1984: 122–3). Ideas in the policy system resemble molecules that float in the 'policy primeval soup' before coming into being. He regards this process as evolutionary: 'while many ideas float around in this policy primeval soup, the ones that last, as in a natural selection system, meet some criteria. Some ideas survive and prosper; some proposals are taken more seriously than others' (1984: 123). This is similar to Riker's argument in *Liberalism Against Populism* (1982). Riker argues that disequilibrium is a constant in politics: 'the world of political issues can thus be better compared to the world of organic nature than to markets ... the rise and fall of issues is a process of natural selection, in which politicians, like genes, seek to survive and flourish' (1982: 210). As Riker suggests, interests and ideas combine so both survive. Thus the most propitious idea fuses with its proximate interest to have the best chance of survival.

The attraction of evolutionary theory is that chance plays an important role in the policy process. The other advantage, as Kingdon points out, is that the analyst does not need to import the rational model to explain the adoption of a policy idea: 'the policy primeval soup does not closely resemble a rational decision-making system with a few well defined alternatives among which decision makers choose. Instead ... a very large number of propositions are considered somewhere along the line' (1984: 130). Evolutionary theory neatly deals with some of the main defects in rational choice theory in that it can provide an account of how preferences are shaped over time. The notion that preferences change does not undermine the conception of the rational choosing individual, but seeks to place rational choices within a dynamic perspective, and to explain how ideas attach themselves to individuals. Because of the stress on adaption of policy-makers' strategies, the evolutionary model depends on actors learning over time as they adjust their strategies to new situations. Although the diversity of policy solutions depends on the existence of people who are prepared to stick to an unpopular idea in the hope that other policy-makers adopt it at a future date, for the political system to adopt the idea other policy-makers need to be able to shift their strategies. Thus in one time-period an outlandish idea appears to lack sense, but through the failure of previous policies and changes in media and public opinion, in a subsequent period policy-makers shift their preferences to the newly accepted policy choice. The evolutionary process is different to the classic Darwinian selection mechanism in that human actors are capable of consciously adapting to their environment. The process is Lamarckian rather than Darwinian because the organisms are partly succeeding through their own efforts (Koestler 1971), though chance and competition are no less important. Ironically, modern evolutionary theory now incorporates the idea that some organisms have adaptive capacity and learn strategies to evolve (Hodgson 1993).

The evolutionary model of public policy is an extension of the ideas of Kingdon, Baumgartner and Jones because the process explains the adoption of proposals to deal with public problems. The symbiosis of problems and policies defines the nature of agenda-setting. However, as well as agendas and policy-formation, policy outputs and policy outcomes are part of the same process. Just as policy proposals are part of the soup, so too are implementation strategies. Policy-makers cannot control the implementation of their policies because personnel down the line are autonomous. Bureaucrats and their allies seek to implement various implementation strategies that are in themselves policy choices. Because making policy is a continuous activity that precedes and lasts long after a much-trumpeted policy initiative, lower-level bureaucrats, agencies, local authorities and quasi-public and private organizations are all involved in a continuous process of policy-formation and implementation that involves conflict over objectives and the constant circulation of problems and policies. In fact the practice of policy-implementation mirrors that of agenda-setting. The activities are completely intertwined. The only difference is that some actors are exclusive to agenda-setting (the media, some politicians) and others are just policy implementors (some bureaucrats and some politicians). Thus the evolution of agendas characterizes the whole of public policy-making.

The evolutionary mechanism explains the interaction of the many ideas–interests which compete within the institutional, cultural, group-based and socio-economic environments. The constraining factors have less evolutionary potential. Institutions tend to be stable over time, especially over the life of a policy or during a period of policy change. Group patterns of politics and networks may be similarly constrained as these have often emerged in stable patterns of interest and institutional relationships. Economies change slowly, and, for the most part, social relationships are embedded. Thus it is better to see the emergence of policy as an evolution of ideas and interests within generally preset institutions, patterns of group politics and socio-economic constraints. Indeed, if we are looking at the contrast between policy sectors or between countries, it is the different forms of evolution in contrasting institutional and socio-economic frameworks that explains the variation of policies across space and time rather than just the evolutionary process itself. Thus it is better to speak of structured evolution.

On the other hand, it is important not to discount the evolution of institutions, group patterns and socio-economic structures. Institutions gradually change because of reform, system-change and the way groups and individuals make use of formal structures. Well designed constitutions are flexible enough to respond to change. However, though it might be relevant to compare the evolution of institutions across many nations, generally there is only one set of institutions which is responding to change, so there is not enough competition and cooperation to generate an evolutionary model. The exception is at the sub-national or state level, where ideas about constitutional change may float and be adopted by a range of different organizations, such as local authorities. Once there is a success, the idea catches on.

To a certain extent the structure of group politics or networks is not particularly evolutionary unless the sub-national level is considered. In terms of nations it could be argued, like constitutions, policies which emerge from a certain group structure are more successful than others, thus a certain type of arrangement is likely to become dominant. But it is likely that this sort of process is slow and does not affect the selection and adoption of policies.

In contrast, the wider society and economy evolve in a similar way to ideas and interests. There are a large number of actors and ideas about how to organize economic and social life. It is highly likely that political actors pick up on these ideas and seek to design policies based on them. Thus the adoption of new working practices based on flexible technologies may have its expression in advocates seeking to introduce new policies to encourage these practices. Policy advocates point to the success of the idea in society at large as a reason for adopting it. In fact, the economic, social and political forces are an overlapping set of evolutionary subsystems. Thus evolutionary models can overcome some of the basic problems of economic determinism (Ward 1997).

As the book offers some reservations to every theory or approach, the author's preferred one should be no exception. Critics are likely to argue, with some irony no doubt, that evolutionary theory has all the same faults as other approaches in public policy. Just as other chapters have taken issue with the causal claims of research frameworks, it is possible to argue that, rather than being a theory of human action, evolutionary theory is at best a metaphor or a heuristic device which can illuminate the policy process but not explain it. In particular, there does not appear to be a clear causal mechanism in the theory. What is exactly doing the work? Is it popular opinion, group alliances or expert judgements? It could be said that evolutionary theory disguises these more familiar mechanisms. Moreover, it can be argued that evolutionary theory is overdetermined in the sense that it predicts all human phenomena at the same time. It is not a parsimonious theory, for every policy automatically is produced by the evolutionary mechanism. As a result researchers cannot test hypotheses because the theory does not produce any.

Political scientists are often suspicious of theories which do not seem to have a theory of power at their centre, and evolutionary theory may be a disguised functionalism which assumes that the policy-making process is a self-regulating mechanism. Evolutionary theory may not take into account the importance of human agency and argument on the one hand, or manipulation and exclusion on the other. Social scientists have attacked theorists who uncritically imported ideas from the natural sciences because the human world is completely different.

Policy evolutionists would resist such charges. The attraction of evolutionary theory is that it does map out causal mechanisms. There is no automatic process whereby some ideas and interests are favoured, and others are not. It depends on continual interaction and the changing nature of the policy environment. Evolutionary theory is not functionalist because it does not assume that policy-making and implementation are good for the political system as a whole. Evolution does not create stability, for example, but can cause disequilibrium as easily, and evolutionary pressures can just as easily lead to policy disasters as successes. What does the causal work in evolutionary theory is the selection mechanism. Policies are caused by a continual sorting of successes and failures of policy ideas. But as well as policies which benefit society as a whole, environments may create policies which are successful for some groups and not others, and in some extreme circumstances create policies which worsen the condition of society, though these may not last very long if there is an effective democracy. Even where there are improvements to welfare from the selection process, it is possible that the success of a policy may respond to just local and particular conditions and in reaction to each other rather than being any systematic response to overall conditions (Elster 1989: 72–3). This is because the environment is dynamic and the selection process is non-linear (Jones, B. 1994: 206). Thus evolutionary processes create all the conflict, inequality and incoherence of Western democracies rather than progress and order.

The criticism that evolutionary theory is over-determined is also not correct. It is possible to test whether evolutionary processes occur at all by examining the way in which policy ideas succeed and fail. Then it is possible to investigate how strong are these processes. A more advanced research programme would be able to find out under what conditions certain types of evolutionary process appear, such as when policy evolution benefits society and when it does not. The potential ramifications of the research programme are vast. Nevertheless, evolutionary theory needs further refinement. In particular, the nature of the selection process should be further investigated. What is the role of powerful elites in selecting policies? What is the function of groups and public opinion? What opportunities are there for policy entrepreneurs to buck probability, and create the circumstances for their ideas to succeed? There are many possible types of evolutionary process, so social science research needs to investigate if one is dominant or whether the types of selection also evolve too. These many questions suggest a vital and productive research programme ahead.

An Application: the Poll Tax in the UK

The process of evolution as a selection mechanism for ideas and interests can explain policy failures in the same manner as policy successes. Thus a policy might survive and beat its competitors but damage the body politic given a particular set of circumstances. An interesting example was in 1986 when the UK Conservative government proposed a single-person local tax, the 'poll tax', to replace the property-based system, the rates. The rates system had been an unpopular local tax for the Conservatives because it appeared to penalize its supporters who owned large properties. Also because of the rebate system, the rates burden fell even more on those with higher incomes, and on single people particularly. Because the system was based on rental values, there were further distortions. The government delayed revaluing properties, so much of the information used to calculate the rates was out of date, adding to the injustice. However, though the Conservatives proposed abolishing the rates in 1974 and partly in 1979, they could never find a practical alternative. An example of policy stasis was in 1981 when the government published a green paper reviewing the options. It proposed the retention of the rating system as the only sensible course of action.

The interesting set of events to explain is the government's adoption four years later of the poll tax. The idea had become 'successful' in that the government believed the practical difficulties of collecting a person tax from a continually adjusting register of people could be overcome. The regressiveness of the tax would make it more a charge for services, rather than the more conventional idea that local taxes partly redistribute resources between rich and poor. As such, the tax proposal fitted in with the objectives of the Conservative Party at that time. Party leaders and ideologues aimed to cut back the welfare state and create a more market-led society and economy. Moreover, the tax had some newly discovered benefits. As it applied to all adults and at a uniform level, reformers believed citizens would easily understand it, hold to account the expenditure decisions of their local authorities and compare taxes and services with those provided elsewhere. With these arguments and convictions, the government abolished the rates and introduced the community charge or poll tax in Scotland in 1989 and in England and Wales in 1990.

In the opinion of all commentators, the policy was an abject failure. It had to be repealed and replaced by another local property tax, the council tax, coming into effect in 1993. The poll tax was based on a flawed conception of accountability, as tax levels did not reflect spending decisions but the vagaries of the central-government grant system. It was impossible to administer since it proved to be highly unpopular. Public opinion and political protest killed the tax. Given that the policy was such a failure, and that every academic commentary and even the previous government green paper had rejected the options as unworkable, why did the government introduce it? How do the approaches in public policy help in accounting for this radical policy change? Why did supposedly rational actors who sought to maximize their utility propose such a measure?

The five approaches go some way in offering an explanation. First, institutionalists argue that the structure and norms of the British political system allowed an inappropriate policy proposal to be introduced. Butler, Adonis and Travers' detailed study of the poll tax, *Failure in British Government* (1994), concludes that the lack of accountability of the British parliamentary system of government prevented critical scrutiny of the proposal. The unlimited power of the governing party to control the parliamentary timetable meant that it was able to propose and push through the measure and cast aside any opposition and professional objections to it. This reflects a long criticism of British parliamentary democracy as an 'elective dictatorship'. Once a party is elected and gains a majority in Parliament, it can do what it pleases for four to five years. Butler, Adonis and Travers note the lack of consultation and parliamentary scrutiny of the proposal and the lack of effectiveness of constitutional conventions, such as of the role of elected local government. Certainly, such a proposal would be unlikely to emerge in political systems where local power is entrenched nationally (France) or where there are checks and balances on the exercise of power (the USA).

While the institutional reasons contributed to the emergence of the tax, they do not explain it. After all, Britain has had the same institutional structure for much of the twentieth century, which has produced stable, consensual even unimaginative policies, many of which benefited locally elected institutions. While the charge is that there were rapid unstabilizing policy changes induced by changes of government in the years from 1945 (Finer 1975), policy was stable for much of the post-war period (Rose 1980). The idea that Parliament is not capable of scrutiny has been challenged by many British parliamentary scholars either of backbench rebellions (Norton 1975; 1980), or of select committees (Drewry 1989) and by Adonis (1993) himself. The potential weakness of the executive was shown demonstrably in 1990 by the fall from leadership of Thatcher herself, partly owing to the poll tax. The same system that had created the poll tax also replaced it with a more acceptable local tax. The question to ask is not why the political institutions functioned so badly but why they functioned poorly at a particular time.

It is hard to apply group and network accounts to the poll tax episode, mainly because this approach better explains policy stability than change. The only attempt to explain local finance from this perspective is R. Rhodes' (1992) essay. He argues that the perpetual reform of local government finance and its failure was a misguided attempt by the central state to break away from government by policy communities. The government tried a top-down model that failed. The Conservatives paid a price for their ambition. As a piece of policy analysis which evaluates the failure of the reform, there is no doubt that the exclusion of experts contributed to the failure of the poll tax. The more interesting question, however, is why did the government ignore the policy communities if they were so powerful in first place?

It is very hard to find a coherent socio-economic account of the emergence of the poll tax. The only contributory factor is the fiscal crisis of modern states which grew after the world economic disruptions of the 1970s. Given the importance of central governments in funding local services, fiscal austerity precipitated financial cutbacks and a greater reliance on the local tax-base. The other macro-social factor is the effect of the crisis of the 1970s on the politics of the 1980s. The crisis fractured the welfare state consensus and helped the rise to prominence to the left and right in the main political parities. Radical new-right policies at the central level and new-left policies at the local level were the result. The poll tax could be seen as an expression of this conflict introduced by the centre to control the local level. However, the socio-economic account offers more a set of background conditions than an explanation. The only other way to approach the reform is to take a Marxist functionalist perspective and to see the poll tax as part of the state regulation of the capitalist system. The tax's manifest failure, however, rules out a functionalist view.

As with the other approaches, it appears hard to apply rational choice analysis to the reform. It was an incompetent vote-maximizing attempt by party leaders. It may have been the case that the Conservative political leadership believed the poll tax would have been popular policy and that, like the privatizations, its initial popularity would turn into long-term success. It is possible to suggest that the reform was an attempt to shape the vote by changing the structure within which local electors exercised their choices, an attempt that did not have enough time to succeed. Had the tax been introduced with more central government funding, and thus lower tax levels, it may have had a chance to bed down and in the long run help electors strictly judge the financial decisions of their local authorities. However, this argument sets up an untestable series of propositions.

More supportive of the rational actor account is the role of ministers and bureaucrats in the episode. Junior ministers, such as William Waldegrave, led the reform. It is possible that ministers used the proposal to advance their careers. In British government, one way to achieve promotion is to be associated with a successful new initiative rather than just to manage a departmental brief. The enthusiasm with which the ministers adopted the policy change reflected a calculated risk. The potential prize was high office. The same analysis can be applied to the civil servants who sat on the study team that drew up the proposal. They were relatively junior, and stood to advance their careers by taking the risk. Another person who was involved with the proposal was Sir Christopher Foster, an economist and partner of Coopers Lybrand. In Kingdon's formulation these people can be regarded as policy entrepreneurs who seek advantage from the replacement of an existing policy with a new one. The existence of people who stand to gain can explain why the proposal gained momentum and energy as there were people willing to argue for a controversial policy. But the explanation is not sufficient because there needs to be a link between the actors arguing for a policy and the condition of the political system which must accept it. Entrepreneurs need backers.

Many commentators believe that the poll tax emerged because of the influence of new ideas. The proposal was one in a long line of new-right or public choice measures adopted by the Conservative governments since 1979. From council house sales, privatization, parental choice in education and quasi-markets in healthcare, the tax was one point in the long march of right-wing ideas in British politics. This account can be backed up by acknowledging the importance of the think-tanks in government policy. For example, the Adam Smith Institute supported the reform.

While ideas are important in that the poll tax was an invention of public choice economists, the tax was not a stage in a sequence of reforms. Firstly, the Conservative government often stumbled half-accidentally on many of the policies it introduced in the 1980s, such as contracting-out and the privatizations (Marsh 1995). The government tended to follow policies that seemed to work rather than to act from a preset ideological strategy. The same could be said of the poll tax. Rather than following an ideological blueprint, the policy arrived almost from nowhere. The study by Butler *et al.* shows that the think-tanks did not have a direct impact on the reform. The idea lurked in the background, and was mentioned in a little-known pamphlet published in 1980 and in an academic study of local government finance published in the same year (Foster *et al.* 1980).

But even during the fiscal crisis of the early 1980s, the government rejected the option. What happened was that, by the mid-1980s, a long period of crisis in local government finance pushed the government to consider more radical options. In the mid-1980s there had grown up a culture of policy experimentation that relied on rejecting conventional wisdom and reaping the possible rewards of risk. Politically, by the mid-1980s, the strong leadership of Margaret Thatcher gained ascendancy; this threw off the constraints of more conventional political colleagues and encouraged more radical initiatives.

John Kingdon's policy streams approach seems to capture the way the government adopted the policy. The proposals for local tax can be regarded as policy solutions existing in their policy primeval soup. Professionals and many academics believed the rating system to be the most practicable solution; other academics, local authorities and Liberal Democrats proposed a local income tax; some Conservatives favoured complete centralization of the local tax system; and a few academics advocated a local sales tax. The poll tax was the least important idea floating in the policy primeval soup. Only a few economists mentioned it. But, in the mid-1980s, a 'window' opened that allowed the policy entrepreneurs, particularly Sir Christopher Foster, to propose the reform. Other entrepreneurs, the politicians and the bureaucrats, seized on the idea to fill the policy vacuum caused by the failures of the reforms of local government finance. Once the entrepreneurs had identified with the policy solution, the proposal gathered momentum. The consensus that the old system was the only feasible option broke down, and the issue expanded in the Conservative Party so that it became unstoppable. It gained its own logic and energy.

The agenda model works well when identifying the conditions where policy change can come about. Under certain conditions policy advocates can argue their case more effectively and punctuate the existing agenda. As the chapter argues, to understand the change more fully, evolutionary models fill the implementation gap.

Interests and ideas evolve over time. In this case the poll tax has the status of a 'mutant' that survived and flourished because policy-makers had 'learnt' from previous policies that apparently unworkable measures can succeed and that there was no other feasible option.

Whereas agenda-setting theory examines the adoption of the proposal, the tools of evolutionary analysis can follow through the policy. Thus, in the policy-implementation stage the idea was still evolving but this time out of existence. As the policy rapidly started to fail there was no alliance of interests to keep it in place. In the end the only reason for keeping it in existence was the identification of the measure with the prime minister. The unworkability and unpopularity of the measure contributed to the resignation of Mrs Thatcher as party leader in 1990. The policy died and a new tax evolved because policy-makers had learnt from the policy error and sought the most workable solution. By regarding the formation of policy as a dynamic process involving the interaction of ideas and interests in a socio-economic and institutional context, the analyst can construct a convincing account of policy change.

Summing-up

A synthetic approach is the only coherent way to explain policy change and variation. Approaches relying on one process to explain why decision-making takes a particular course are too narrow and relegate other factors to aspects of some dominant principle. The common view of contemporary social sciences is that there is no one general principle governing social and political life. Instead, social scientists need to make sense of the complexity, variation and changeability of the empirical world which is constituted by conflicting ideas. As such, theories of policy variation and change must incorporate and account for continuous change and adaption. It is not possible to say that only institutions count or that social and political phenomena reduce to economic processes. Reality is a messy confluence of the five processes the book outlines in Chapters 3 to 7.

There are three authors who try to synthesize these processes. They are Sabatier (policy advocacy coalition theory), Kingdon (the policy streams approach) and Baumgartner and Jones (the punctuated equilibrium model). The first seeks to combine ideas and networks in public policy, where policy subsystems are driven and sometimes fractured by large socio-economic or external events. second is based on the continual interplay of problems, solutions and politics in the garbage-can model of policy choice. The third is a model of agenda-setting, seeking to describe how agendas and policies move from periods of being highly stable to times of rapid change and fluidity. All three models are contemporary because they place ideas at the centre of their analysis. The time when writers believed that only interests drive public policy is now over. Conceptions, discourse, beliefs and norms define the process of policy-making. Yet, unlike some of the ideational theories described in Chapter 7, Sabatier, Kingdon, and Baumgartner and Jones seek to place ideas with the complex interplay of individual choice, networks, institutions and socio-economic changes. Thus each framework has all these elements.

In keeping with the critical approach of this book, none of these authors quite succeeds in creating a theory of public policy. For all the role of knowledge and advocacy in Sabatier's approach, the PAC framework is too static, as it is driven by outside events. Kingdon's approach is highly attractive, but it relies too much on change and fluidity. Baumgartner and Jones neatly contrast stability and instability in the account of policy-making over time, but in the end it is not entirely clear that they explain the transition between stability and change and back again.

To remedy some of the defects of the policy streams and punctuated equilibrium models, the book proposes an evolutionary theory of policy change and variation that encompasses all the activity associated with public decision-making. The evolutionary approach understands that the elements to policy systems continually interact over time. Combinations of ideas and interests constantly seek to dominate decision-making and to interact with institutions, patterns of interest groups and socio-economic processes which are also slowly changing and evolving over time. The notion is that some ideas are successful in this context, but that change defines the nature of modern public policy. Investigators need to appraise this context and find out exactly how all the elements fit together.

9

Conclusion

This book explores the difficulty of explaining policy change and variation. The chapters are a continual quest for better accounts of decision-making in policy sectors, such as education, the environment or economic policy-making, and an exploration of why decision-making varies between sectors and from place to place, such as between the USA, France and the UK. The task is difficult because of the nature of policy itself. Unlike other subjects in political science, the study of policy focuses on the whole political system and its external environment. Whereas studies of legislatures, parties, bureaucracies and local governments focus on decision-making in one political institution or compare how the institution works in different countries, the study of public policy follows a 'slice' of political action in a particular sector of activity. The numbers of decisions, from agenda-setting to policy implementation, are large. The relationships across the many organizations involved are highly complex. The task of explaining the process whereby political systems create concrete action (i.e. policy) can easily defeat the political scientist. Rather than explaining, many writers prefer to use labels to describe and simplify what happens. Even when theorists offer explanations, in fact they often turn out to be elaborate policy stories.

To make sense of the complexity, traditional approaches to public policy identify separate characteristics of the decision-making process. The most influential is the stages heuristic approach, the idea that policy moves from agenda-setting, policy formulation, rule-setting to policy outputs and policy outcomes. Although the idea remains an attractive simplification device, the policy process rarely divides up into neat stages. Reality is messy. Policy ideas can come from anywhere. The notion that policy-making can be summarized by a distinction between rational and incremental models is another over-simplification. While decision-making and implementation sometimes resemble the classic accounts, more often policy-making shifts rapidly between radical action and periods of incremental change. What is needed is a theory of public policy that can explain why policy changes from one decision-making style to another.

Policy researchers and policy-orientated political scientists have applied broader frameworks to try to explain the policy process. Usually, they take a single approach to reduce the phenomenon under question to an underlying principle. The book identifies five sets of approaches or theories that researchers often use: the institutional; the group and network; the macro socio-economic; the rational choice; and the ideational. Institutional approaches assume that formal structures and their norms process decisions. Group and network approaches assume the pattern of political association explains policy stability and variation. Macro socio-economic approaches try to explain political processes as reflections of changes in society and in the economy. Rational choice theory explains policy from the strategic choices open to individual actors. Ideas-based approaches explore the salience of argumentation, discourse and advocacy in the policy process. Each approach or theory does not always say that all politics is the expression of the dynamics of their principle, but they do try to fit behaviour into the overall scheme. Thus the institutional approach does not say that institutions are the sole basis to policy-making, but that institutions are more important than strategic choices or policy networks. Rational choice theory does not neglect the importance of institutions. On the contrary, individuals select choices on the basis of institutional and other constraints. But rational choice theory focuses on the strategic choices of individuals as the driver behind behaviour, rather than values, norms or cultures.

The book argues that each approach has advantages and disadvantages. The main advantage is that political action results from a clear underlying principle. The policy-making system lights up as a result of the clarity of focus provided by one single account of causation. When the policy world is composed mainly of networks and groups, researchers can map and understand them. When policy-making is the result of strategic choices, research projects can hypothesize whether, for example, officials bureau-shape or not. The key disadvantage is that the single account oversimplifies the complexity of the policy-making process in its attempt to impose a conceptual scheme. While it is important in the social sciences to simplify the world in order to explain it, the problem with public policy is that analysts need to take as the baseline the changeable and multilevel nature of the research subject. In the attempt to impose its conceptual scheme, the single approach tends to describe policy rather than to explain why it changes and varies across sectors and spaces. Also there is a tendency to neglect the importance of interaction in public policy. Public-policy writers tend to believe policy-making systems are static, governed either by institutions or networks which process policy. In fact, public policy changes rapidly. There is a continual interaction of processes which form policies which then in turn affect other policies. In the world of multiple influences, it is not clear why one set of processes, such as institutions, should be primary. Policy research needs to take change as the baseline and to investigate why the different elements to decision-making interact in the way they do.

While the approaches have some similar defects, they vary to the extent they explain public policy, and the type of public-policy problem they consider. Institutional approaches are better at explaining policy stability than change through the way in which the 'rules of the game' or the 'standard operating procedures' constrain choices. If there is not enough push for change, institutions can keep a political system stable by, for example, limiting the impact of new interest groups and ideas. Institutional approaches are not particularly good at explaining the differences in policy-making across sectors as most political systems have similar frameworks for making policy in each area of activity, though there are some differences such as the level of government charged with responsibility for providing services. More importantly, institutional approaches are essential in explaining the difference between countries as national legal systems, constitutions and bureaucracies differ and impact on how decision-makers make and implement public policy. On their own, institutional approaches do not indicate how important are formal processes as opposed to cross-national and sectoral factors.

Interest-group and network approaches are similar to institutionalism in that they generally explain policy stability better than policy change. Patterns of interest-group interaction explain how issues are processed by political systems, particularly the way in which they mediate the operation of formal institutional structures. But it is not clear from the way in which networks operate how change comes about. In contrast to institutions, group and network approaches are effective in drawing attention to the differences in policy-making across sectors. Some sectors are dominated by producer groups, while others are more open and crosscutting. On the other hand, network approaches have little to say about how policy varies across countries except that there are different styles of interest-group activity.

Macro socio-economic approaches are good at explaining both change and stability, at least in broad-brush terms. Slow adjustments of social relations and habits underpin policy-making systems. Stable economic growth can create incremental and accommodatory social and economic policies. On the other hand, rapid socio-economic change can disrupt these stable policy-making systems and create new interests, incentives and values. Such changes may have their origin in the instability of market economies or can originate from other political systems. Macro socio-economic approaches have something to say about differences in policy-making between sectors, partly because society and the economy intersect in different ways with the various fields of public activity. Thus, in a private-sector-dominated economy, policy-making in sectors which affect the productivity of private enterprises is different from decision-making for activities which are not so connected. However, given the way in which analysis of the political system rests on one principle, macro analysis is likely to regard variations within the state as apparent rather than real. Macro-social analysis tends to have limited things to say about why policy-making is different across nations except that it reflects differences in the operation of societies and economies.

Rational choice theory effectively explains both policy stability and change through the choices available to the participants, though it tends to be better at explaining shifts in decision-making within a set of constraints and preferences than changes in the goals and objectives of policy. It has a good account of why policy differs across sectors through the varying incentives and possibilities for collective action. Rational choice tends not to explain why policies vary cross-nationally, though it can explain such phenomena. The overall limitation is that rational choice tends to take preferences as given and models political choices given those preferences. It pays less attention to how preferences come about.

Ideational approaches are good at explaining policy change through the process of advocacy and persuasion, though the approaches do not explore the change in the rate at which policies change. Ideas-based approaches do not deal so much with the variation across sectors and nations. The difficulty is that the notion of ideas can appear loose and formless as it can refer to almost any mental activity or thought-process. Often ideas-based approaches do not specify the relationship between ideas and interests.

The differences between the approaches are illustrated by Table 9.1. The five approaches run along the top of the table; the four types of explanation are on the spine. Each cell of the table evaluates the contribution of an approach to one of the four types of explanation. There is a three-point scale of poor, fair and good.

Table 9.1 The explanatory power of approaches to public policy

	Institutional	Group & network	Macro socio-economic	Rational choice	Ideas-based
Stability	good	good	fair	good	poor
Change	poor	poor	fair	fair	good
Sector	poor	good	poor	good	poor
Country	good	poor	poor	poor	poor

The table is general and does not do justice to the subtleties of the approaches. The levels of performance are broad as well. Nor does the scheme deal with the conflicts between the approaches. Nevertheless, the variation between them is interesting, and if researchers in public policy wish to focus on a particular problem in explaining public policy, they can select one approach. The first three approaches are good at explaining policy stability, but are poor at explaining change. The last two approaches account more for policy change, particularly the ideas-based approach. In certain problems, one approach seems to stand out. In explaining the variation according to country, the institutional approach is best placed to deal with the differences. With regard to policy sectors, the group and network approaches stand out. In policy change ideational accounts are salient. Overall, while not comprehensive, rational choice theory performs better than the others.

It might be thought that policy researchers should choose an approach to deal with the explanatory problem at hand. For example, researchers interested in policy stability can choose group and network approaches; comparativists can choose an institutional account; and those interested in policy change can choose an ideas-based account. But such an eclectic strategy would be misplaced, partly because of the defects of the approaches, and also because the research problems are all aspects of the same quest for explanation in politics. Thus it is not possible to separate out the problems of policy stability and change, as both are mirror-images of each other. The reason why policy changes often lies in the preceding period of stability. Stable power-structures are sometimes inefficient and sow seeds of discontent. Likewise, periods of change come to an end, and stability returns once more. While most studies of policy examine just one or two sectors in one country, it is also important to set national policy-making processes within the context of other experiences. To neglect the particularity of a nation-state's traditions, practices and cultures would lead to a meagre understanding of decision-making. To reach the potential of research, even single case studies must be comparative. Thus all good research, to an extent, combines the four types of explanation, even though it may emphasize one of them. To concentrate on one level of explanation neglects the complexity of the interaction between the sets of processes. And because no one approach can explain the four problems of change and stability, and of variation according to sector and country, the book proposes a framework which synthesizes the five approaches.

Several public-policy scholars propose frameworks to cope with the multilevel nature of policy change and variation. There are three which excel. Sabatier's policy advocacy coalition framework offers a connection between ideas and coalition formation in policy systems. The PAC framework seeks to map changes in the coalitions that are often driven by external changes. The second is Kingdon's policy streams approach, where the three streams of policy problems, policy solutions and politics interact to produce policy change. The third is Baumgartner and Jones' punctuated equilibrium model of agenda stability and change, exploring agenda expansion and the potential for disequilibrium in policy-making systems. Finally, drawing from these synthetic models, but also seeking to overcome their limitations, the book outlines an evolutionary theory of policy change and variation. Evolutionary theory suggests that ideas join with interests to try to succeed in a potentially fluid environment, and it explains why policy is stable for long periods of time. Certain interests–ideas become institutionalized in interest group and institutional frameworks. The approach can also explain why policy suddenly changes as a new set of ideas emerge.

Table 9.2 places the four synthetic approaches into the same grid as Table 9.1. As with the unitary approaches, there is some variation in performance. As shown by its similarity to policy network theories, the PAC model is good at explaining stability and at accounting for the differences between sectors. It says less about policy change, and nothing about country variation. The streams approach, as expected from a dynamic model, is good at explaining change, but is less effective in explaining stability and sectoral differences and, similar to other US-based frameworks, makes no contribution to understanding cross-national differences. The punctuated equilibrium model is good at explaining both change and stability, and accounts for sectoral differences, though again has nothing to say about cross-national differences. Evolutionary theory draws the best from these synthetic theories and seeks to incorporate the dynamic interplay between factors for change and adaption (ideas and some interests) and constraints on that action.

Table 9.2   The explanatory power of synthetic theories of public policy

	PAC	Policy streams	Punctuated equilibrium	Evolutionary
Stability	good	poor	good	good
Change	fair	good	good	good
Sector	fair	fair	fair	good
Country	poor	poor	poor	fair

The progression of the book shows that good explanations of public policy can incorporate the contrasts between policy change and stability, and understand the differences between policy sectors and countries. Rather than impose a tight conceptual scheme on one part of the policy process, a comprehensive approach has some advantages. It takes the complexity, fluidity and changeability of the modern policy process as its baseline. It seeks to understand the relative importance of different processes in policy-making systems. It offers a convincing account of causation. The cost is some loss of simplicity. Given that the policy process is complex by definition, the quest to explain both change and stability in its cross-sectoral and cross-national context is a difficult task. But if the endless cycles of labels and approaches is to turn into more than elaborate redescription of policy events and styles, a more analytical approach is needed. In the works of Sabatier, Jenkins-Smith, Kingdon, Jones and Baumgartner, policy studies is starting to meet the challenge.

Glossary

agenda   a set of issues which, at a particular moment in time, the public, the media and the politician actors believe needs government intervention. See *issue–attention cycle*.

behaviouralism   the school of political study, prominent in the United States in the 1950s and 1960s, that believed that politics could be studied by only observing behaviour.

bottom-up model   an approach to the study of *implementation* that stresses the involvement of lower-level bureaucrats and others who carry out public decisions. The ideas and influence of these actors feed back to the peak decision-makers to influence policy choices.

bounded rationality   the notion that decision-making is constrained by habit, the costs of collecting information and the limits to knowledge.

collective action problem   the difficulty most societies face in providing *public goods*.

disjointed incrementalism   a refinement of the concept of *incrementalism* which stresses the unplanned nature of decision-making and the varieties of decisions that occur.

epistemic community   a description of the communities of actors who share common values or solutions to policy problems. It is similar to *policy advocacy coalition* and *policy community*.

feedback   the effect of policies on the decision-making process.

front-end policy-making   a style of policy-making aiming to prevent and anticipate decisions rather than to react to them.

garbage-can model   a model developed by Cohen, March and Olsen (1972) to explain the chaotic and unplanned manner in which organizations process decisions. See also *policy primeval soup*.

gatekeeping   the practice where decision-makers, particularly bureaucrats, seek to regulate and limit the extent to which people and organizations participate in the policy process.

mechanism an institutional practice which helps system function by storing collective intelligence. It promotes *policy-learning*.

implementation the stage in the policy process concerned with turning policy intentions into action.

incrementalism a model of decision-making based on the idea that policy-makers, operating in a group context, usually make gradual changes from the existing state of affairs.

inputs the factors outside the political system that affect public decision-making, such as voting, public opinion and interest-group pressure.

issue–attention cycle an idea developed by Downs (1972) to describe the tendency for *agendas* to wax and wane.

issue network a loose collection of actors and organizations which influence decision-making in a *policy sector*.

negotiated order a set of values and assumptions about the practice of governing which stresses consensus and compromise.

new institutionalism a school of thought, developed in the 1980s, which reasserts the importance of institutions in political life. Institutions comprise values and norms as well as procedures.

policy a process of public decision-making leading to (or appearing to lead to) actions outside the political system.

policy action framework a term which describes the inter-action between decision-making and the effects of those decisions, particularly as they unfold in the implementation process.

policy advocacy coalition a coalition of actors within a policy sector who share and advocate common ideas about how to solve public problems.

policy analysis policy-orientated research which aims to improve public decision-making.

policy community a restricted set of actors and organizations which influence decision-making in a policy sector.

policy cycle the idea that policy proceeds in distinct stages from *policy formulation* to *implementation*.

policy entrepreneur a political actor who gains benefit from providing a potential or an actual *public good*. They are important because they can help solve the *collective action problem*. They often exist in a *policy primeval soup*.

policy formulation the setting of objectives and the means to achieve them.

policy instrument a tool governments use to implement public decisions.

policy-learning the process whereby decision-makers revise their current policy choices in the light of past mistakes or successes.

policy mess a failure of policy intentions caused by such factors as contradictory policies, *feedback* and the power of *policy communities*.

policy network the collection of actors and organizations which influences decision-making in a policy sector. Types of policy network are *policy community* and *issue network*.

policy-orientated approach a term advocated by Lasswell to describe a way of looking at politics from the viewpoint of the actions public decision-makers produce. It combines different methods and approaches. It can have an explanatory or a normative emphasis or both.

policy outcome action or non-action, occurring outside the political system, intentionally or unintentionally produced by public decision-making.

policy output a discrete decision or set of decisions that produces or aims to produce a *policy outcome*.

policy primeval soup a term developed by Kingdon (1984) to describe the existence of a large number of competing ideas about how to solve policy problems. These ideas are usually advocated by *policy entrepreneurs*. The existence of *policy windows* allows certain solutions to rise out of the soup to become adopted policies.

policy sector a field of decision-making concerned with a certain type of public problem, such as agriculture, energy or the environment. It is almost identical to *policy subsystem*.

policy streams a term coined by Kingdon (1984) to describe the continuous interplay of problems, policies and politics.

policy style a pattern or habit of decision-making that is shaped by a country's political traditions.

policy subsystem a field of decision-making concerned with a certain type of public problem, such as agriculture, energy or the environment. It is almost identical to the term *policy sector*.

policy transfer the conscious adoption of policies developed in another geographical location. It is linked to *policy learning*.

policy window an term developed by Kingdon to describe the combination of events which, sometimes only momentarily, can lead political systems to adopt a solution to a policy problem. Policy windows are useful opportunities for *policy entrepreneurs*.

public goods   a stream of benefits which are not divisible and thus cannot be provided by the market.

punctuated equilibrium   the idea that *agendas* and public policy-making proceed though periods of stability interrupted by rapid change.

rational decision-making   the method of choosing policies which maximize the utility of the decision-maker.

stages heuristic   the assumption that policy proceeds in discrete sequences. It is heuristic because the assumption simplifies in order to explain policy-making clearly.

supergame   an iterated rational choice game. The behaviour of the participants usually changes over time because they calculate the stream of benefits accruing to them from the game as a whole.

top-down model   an approach to the study of implementation that stresses the perspective of higher-level bureaucrats and executive decision-making. Policy is decided by the centre. Then lower-level organizations carry it out or not as the case may be.

Bibliography

Adonis, A. (1993) *Parliament Today*. Manchester: Manchester University Press.

Aglietta, M. (1979) *A Theory of Capitalist Regulation*. London: New Left Books.

Allison, G. (1971) *The Essence of Decision: Explaining the Cuban Missile Crisis*. Boston: Little Brown.

Ambler, J. (1987) Constraints on policy innovation in education. *Comparative Politics*, **19**: 85–105.

Amenta, E. and Skocpol, T. (1989) Taking exception: explaining the distinctiveness of American public policies in the last century. In F. G. Castles (ed.) *The Comparative History of Public Policy*. Cambridge: Polity.

Ashenden, S. (1996) Reflexive governance and child sexual abuse: liberal welfare rationality and the Cleveland Inquiry. *Economy and Society*, **25**: 64–88.

Atkinson, R. and Moon, G. (1994) *Urban Policy in Britain*. Basingstoke: Macmillan.

Axelrod, R. (1984) *The Evolution of Cooperation*. New York: Basic Books.

Barrett, S. and Fudge, C. (eds) (1981) *Policy and Action*. London: Methuen.

Barrow, C. W. (1993) *Critical Theories of the State*. Madison, Wis.: University of Wisconsin Press.

Baumgartner, F. and Jones, B. (1993) *Agendas and Instability in American Politics*. Chicago: University of Chicago Press.

Beer, S. (1965) *Modern British Politics*. London: Faber.

Bendor, J. and Hammond, T. (1992) Rethinking Allison's models. *American Political Science Review*, **86**: 301–22.

Bendor, J. and Moe, T. (1985) An adaptive model of bureaucratic politics. *American Political Science Review*, **79**: 755–74.

Bennett, C. (1991) Review article: what is policy convergence and what causes it? *British Journal of Political Science*, **21**: 215–33.

Bennett, C. and Howlett, M. (1992) The lessons of learning: reconciling theories of policy learning and policy change. *Policy Sciences*, **25**: 275–94.

Benson, J. K. (1982) A framework for policy analysis. In D. Rogers, D.

Whitten and Associates, *Interorganisational Coordination*. Ames, Iowa: Iowa State Press.

Bentley, A. (1908) *The Process of Government*. Chicago: University of Chicago Press.

Birch, A. H. (1964) *Representative and Responsible Government*. London: Allen and Unwin.

Block, F. (1977) The ruling class does not rule: notes on the marxist theory of the state. *Socialist Revolution*, **7**: 6–28.

Bobrow, D. and Drysek, J. (1987) *Policy Analysis by Design*. Pittsburgh: University of Pittsburgh Press.

Bowen, E. R. (1982) The Pressman–Wildavsky paradox: four addenda on why models based on probability theory can predict implementation success and suggest useful tactical advice for implementors. *Journal of Public Policy*, **2**: 1– 22.

Bowles, S. and Gintis, H. (1976) *Schooling in Capitalist America*. New York: Basic Books.

Boyne, G. (1996) Assessing party effects on local policies: a quarter century of progress or eternal recurrence? *Political Studies*, **44**: 232–52.

Braybrooke, D. and Lindblom, C. (1963) *A Strategy of Decision*. New York: Free Press.

Browne, W. P. (1995) *Cultivating Congress*. Lawrence, Kan.: University Press of Kansas.

Butler, D., Adonis, A. and Travers, T. (1994) *Failure in British Government*. Oxford: Oxford University Press.

Button, J. (1978) *Black Violence*. Princeton, N.J.: Princeton University Press.

Castles, F. (ed.) (1982) *The Impact of Parties*. Beverley Hills: Sage.

Castles, F. and Merrill, V. (1989) Towards a general model of public policy outcomes. *Journal of Theoretical Politics*, **1**: 177–212.

Cawson, A. (1982) *Corporatism and Welfare: State Intervention and Social Policy*. London: Heinemann.

Chester, D. N. and Bowring, N. (1962) *Questions in the House*. Oxford: Oxford University Press.

Christiansen, L. and Dowding, K. (1994) Pluralism or state autonomy? The case of Amnesty International (British section): the insider/outsider group. *Political Studies*, **42**: 15–24.

Clark, T. and Goetz, E. (1994) The anti-growth machine: can city governments control, limit or manage growth? In T. Clark (ed.) *Urban Innovation: Creative Strategies for Turbulent Times*. London: Sage.

Clarke, S. and Gaile, G. (1994) Globalism and the new work of cities. Paper presented to the conference, *Shaping the Urban Future*, School for Advanced Urban Studies, University of Bristol, July.

Cobb, R. and Elder, C. (1972) *Participation in American Politics*. Boston: Allyn and Bacon.

Cohen, M., March, J. and Olsen, J. (1972) A garbage can model of organisational choice. *Administrative Science Quarterly*, **17**: 1–25.

Dahl, R. (1961) *Who Governs?* New Haven: Yale University Press.

Dahl, R. (1991) *Modern Political Analysis*. New Jersey: Prentice Hall, 5th edn.

Dawkins, R. (1976) *The Selfish Gene*. New York: Oxford University Press.

Domhoff, W. (1970) *The Higher Circles*. New York: Random House.

Dowding, K. (1995) Model or metaphor? A critical review of the policy network approach. *Political Studies*, **43**: 136–58.

Dowding, K. and Hindmoor, A. (1997) The usual suspects: rational choice, socialism and political theory. *New Political Economy*, **2**: 451–63.

Dowding, K. and King, D. (eds) (1995) *Preferences, Institutions and Rational Choice*. Oxford: Oxford University Press.

Downs, A. (1957) *An Economic Theory of Democracy*. New York: Harper Collins.

Downs, A. (1972) Up and down with ecology: the issue attention cycle. *Public Interest*, **28**: 38–50.

Drewry, G. (1989) *The New Select Committees*. Oxford: Clarendon.

Dunleavy, P. (1990) Reinterpreting the Westland affair: theories of the state and core executive decision-making. *Public Administration*, **68**: 29–60.

Dunleavy, P. (1991) *Democracy, Bureaucracy and Public Choice*. Brighton: Harvester Wheatsheaf.

Dunleavy, P. and Rhodes, R. (1990) Core executive studies in Britain. *Public Administration*, **68**: 3–28.

Dye, T. (1966) *Politics, Economics and Public Policy: Policy Outcomes in the American States*. Chicago: Rand McNally.

Dyson, K. (1980) *The State Tradition in Western Europe*. Oxford: Robertson.

Easton, D. (1965) *A Systems Analysis of Political Life*. New York: John Wiley.

Eckstein, H. (1960) *Pressure Group Politics: The Case of the British Medical Association*. London: Allen and Unwin.

Edelman, M. (1964) *The Symbolic Uses of Politics*. Urbana, Ill.: Illinois University Press.

Edelman, M. (1977) *Political Language Words that Succeed and Policies That Fail*. New York: Academic.

Edwards, G., Barrett, A. and Peake, J. (1997) The legislative impact of divided government. *American Journal of Political Science*, **41**: 545–63.

Elster, J. (1986) *An Introduction to Karl Marx*. Cambridge: Cambridge University Press.

Elster, J. (1989) *Nuts and Bolts for the Social Sciences*. Cambridge: Cambridge University Press.

Feigenbaum, H., Samuels, R. and Weaver, R. (1993) Innovation, coordination and implementation in energy policy. In R. K. Weaver and B. A. Rockman *Do Institutions Matter?* Washington, D.C.: Brookings.

Fenno, R. (1959) *The President's Cabinet: Analysis in the Period from Wilson to Eisenhower*. Cambridge: Harvard University Press.

Fenno, R. (1973) *Congressmen in Committees*. Boston: Little, Brown.

Finer, S. (1966) *Anonymous Empire*. London: Pall Mall.

Finer, S. (1975) *Adversary Politics and Electoral Reform*. London: Anthony Wigram.

Fischer, F. and Forester, J. (eds) (1993) *The Argumentative Turn in Policy Analysis*. London: UCL Press.

Fording, R. (1997) The conditional effect of violence as a political tactic: mass insurgency, welfare generosity, and electoral context in the American states. *American Journal of Political Science*, **41**: 1–29.

Foster, C., Jackman, R. and Perlman, M. (1980) *Local Government Finance in a Unitary State*. London: Allen and Unwin.

Freeman, G. (1979) *Immigrant Labour and Racial Conflict in Industrial Societies: The French and British Experience 1945–1975*. Princeton: Princeton University Press.

Freeman, G. (1985) National styles and policy variation: explaining structured variation. *Journal of Public Policy*, **5**: 467–96.

Friedman, J. (ed.) (1996) *The Rational Choice Controversy*. New Haven: Yale University Press.

Gais, T., Peterson, M. and Walker, J. (1984) Interest groups, iron triangles and representative institutions in American national government. *British Journal of Political Science*, **14**: 161–85.

Gamble, A. (1988) *The Free Economy and the Strong State: The Politics of Thatcherism*. London: Macmillan.

Garrett, G. and Weingast, B. (1993) Ideas, interests and institutions: constructing the European Union's internal market. In J. Goldstein and R. Keohane (eds) *Ideas and Foreign Policy: Beliefs, Institutions and Political Change*. Ithaca: Cornell University Press.

Glennerster, H. (1995) *British Social Policy Since 1945*. Oxford: Basil Blackwell.

Goggin, M. and Orth D. (1997) Using the design framework to understand policy change. Paper to ECPR Joint Sessions, February 27–March 5, Bern.

Goldstein, J. and Keohane, R. (eds) (1993) *Ideas and Foreign Policy: Beliefs, Institutions and Political Change*. Ithaca: Cornell University Press.

Gough, I. (1979) *The Political Economy of the Welfare State*. London: Macmillan.

Green, D. and Shapiro I. (1994) *Pathologies of Rational Choice Theory*. New Haven: Yale University Press.

Haas, P. (1992) Epistemic communities and international policy coordination. *International Organisation*, **46**: 1–35.

Hajer, M. (1993) Discourse coalitions and the institutionalisation of practice: the case of acid rain in Britain. In F. Fischer and J. Forester (eds) *The Argumentative Turn in Policy Analysis*. London: UCL Press.

Hall, P. (1986) *Governing the Economy: The Politics of State Intervention in Britain and France*. New York: Oxford University Press.

Hall, P. (1992) The movement from Keynesianism to monetarism: institutional analysis and British economic policy in the 1970s. In S. Steinmo, S. K. Thelen and F. Longstreth (eds) *Structuring Politics*. Cambridge: Cambridge University Press.

Hall, P. (1993) Policy paradigms, social learning and the state. *Comparative Politics*, **25**: 275–96.

Hall, S. (1985) Authoritarian populism: a reply. *New Left Review*, **115**: 115–24.

Halpern, D., Wood, S., White, S. and Cameron, G. (1996) *Options for Britain*. Aldershot: Dartmouth.

Ham, C. (1992) *Health Policy in Britain: The Politics and Organisation of the National Health Service*. Basingstoke: Macmillan, 3rd edn.

Ham, C. and Hill, M. (1984) *The Policy Process in the Modern Capitalist State*. Brighton: Harvester Wheatsheaf.

Hann, A. (1995) Sharpening up Sabatier. *Politics*, **15**: 19–26.

Hardin, G. (1968) The tragedy of the commons. *Science*, **162**: 1243–8.

Hayward, J. (1974) National aptitudes for planning in Britain, France and Italy. *Government and Opposition*, **9**.

Hawthorn, G. (1991) *Plausible Worlds*. Cambridge: Cambridge University Press.

Heath, A., Jowell, R. and Curtice, J. (1985) *How Britain Votes*. Oxford: Pergamon.

Heclo, H. (1974) *Modern Social Policies in Britain and Sweden*. New Haven: Yale University Press.

Heclo, H. (1977) *A Government of Strangers: Executive Politics in Washington*. Washington, D.C.: Brookings Institution.

Heclo, H. (1978) Issue networks and the executive establishment. In A. King (ed.) *The New American Political System*. Washington: AEI.

Heclo, H. and Wildavsky, A. (1974) *The Private Government of Public Money*. London: Macmillan.

Heidenheimer, A. (1985) Comparative public policy at the crossroads. *Journal of Public Policy*, **5**: 441–65.

Heinz, J., Laumann, E., Salisbury, R. and Nelson, R. (1990) Elite networks in national policy subsystems. *Journal of Politics*, **52**: 356–90.

Hill, K. Q. (1997) In search of public policy theory. *Policy Currents*, **7**: 1–9.

Hirst, P. and Thompson G. (1996) *Globalisation in Question*. Cambridge: Polity.

Hoberg, G. (1996) Putting ideas in their place: a response to learning and change in the British Columbia forest policy sector. *Canadian Journal of Political Science*, **29**: 135–44.

Hodgson, G. (1993) *Economics and Evolution*. Cambridge: Polity.

Hofferbert, R. (1974) *The Study of Public Policy*. Indianapolis: Bobbs-Merrill.

Hogwood, B. and Gunn, L. (1984) *Policy Analysis for the Real World*. Oxford: Oxford University Press.

Hogwood, B. and Peters, B. (1985) *The Pathology of Public Policy*. Oxford: Clarendon.

Hood, C. (1976) *The Limits to Administration*. London: Wiley.

Hood, C. (1986) *The Tools of Government*. Chatham, N.J.: Chatham House.

Hood, C. (1994) *Explaining Economic Policy Reversals*. Buckingham: Open University Press.

Howlett, M. and Raynor, J. (1996) Do ideas matter? Policy network configurations and the resistance to policy change in the Canadian forest sector. *Canadian Public Administration*, **38**: 382–410.

Hutton, W. (1995) *The State We're In*. London: Jonathan Cape.

Immergut, E. (1992) The rules of the game: the logic of health policy-making in France, Switzerland and Sweden. In S. Steinmo, S. K. Thelen and F. Longstreth (eds) *Structuring Politics*, Cambridge: Cambridge University Press.

Jackman, R. (1975) *Politics and Social Inequality: A Comparative Analysis*. New York: Wiley.

James, O. (1995) Explaining the Next Steps in the Department of Social Security: the bureau-shaping model of central state reorganisation. *Political Studies*, **43**: 614–29.

Jenkins-Smith, H. (1990) *Democratic Politics and Policy Analysis*. Pacific Grove, Cal.: Brooks/Cole Publishing Company.

Jenkins-Smith, H., St Clair, G. and Woods, B. (1991) Explaining change in policy sub-systems: analysis of coalition stability and defection over time. *American Journal of Political Science*, **35**: 851–80.

Jessop, B. (1990) *State Theory*. Cambridge: Polity.

Jessop, B. (1995) Towards a Schumpetarian workfare regime in Britain: reflections in regulation, governance and welfare state. *Environment and Planning A*, **10**: 1613–26.

John, P. (1994) Central–local relations in the 1980s and 1990s: towards a policy learning approach. *Local Government Studies*, **20**: 412–36.

Johnson, N. (1975) The place of institutions in the study of politics. *Political Studies*, **23**: 271–83.

Jones, B. (1994) *Reconceiving Decision-Making in Democratic Politics*. Chicago: University of Chicago Press.

Jones, C. O. (1979) American politics and the organisations of energy decision-making. *Annual Review of Energy*, **4**: 99–121.

Jones, C. O. (1994) *The Presidency in a Separated System*. Washington, D.C.: Brookings Institution.

Jordan, G. (1990) Sub governments, policy communities and networks. *Journal of Theoretical Politics*, **2**: 319–38.

Jordan, G., Maloney, W. and McLaughlin, A. (1994) Characterising agricultural policy-making. *Public Administration*, **72**: 505–26.

Judge, D. (1990) *Parliament and Industry*. Aldershot: Dartmouth.

Judge, D. (1993) *The Parliamentary State*. London: Sage.

Kaplan, T. (1993) Reading policy narratives: beginnings, middles and ends. In F. Fischer and J. Forester (eds) (1993) *The Argumentative Turn in Policy Analysis*. London: UCL Press.

Kassim, H. (1994) Policy networks, networks and European Union policy-making: a sceptical view. *Western European Politics*, **17**: 15–27.

Kato, J. (1996) Review article: institutions and rationality in politics: three varieties of neo-institutionalists. *British Journal of Political Science*, **26**: 553–82.

Kellner, P. and Crowther-Hunt, Lord (1980) *The Civil Servants: An Inquiry into Britain's Ruling Class*. London: MacDonald.

Keohane, R. and Ostrom, E. (1995) *Local Commons and Global Independence*. London: Sage.

King, A. (1973; 1974) Ideas, institutions and the policies of governments: a comparative analysis, I and II. *British Journal of Political Science*, **3**: 291–313; 409–23.

King, D. and Ward, H. (1992) Working for benefits: rational choice and the rise of work-welfare programmes. *Political Studies*, **40**: 479–95. Reprinted in K. Dowding and D. King (eds) (1995) *Preferences, Institutions and Rational Choice*. Oxford: Oxford University Press.

Kingdon, J. (1984) *Agendas, Alternatives and Public Policies*. Boston: Little Brown.

Kirschner, K. (1996) Irrational game theory: using psychological perspectives in an interactive environment. Paper for the American Political Science Association annual meeting, San Francisco.

Kiser, L. and Ostrom, E. (1982) Three worlds of action: a metatheoretical synthesis of institutional approaches. In E. Ostrom (ed.) *Strategies of Political Inquiry*. Beverley Hills: Sage.

Knoke, D., Pappi, F., Broadbent, J. and Tsujinaka, Y. (1996) *Comparing Policy Networks*. Cambridge: Cambridge University Press.

Koestler, A. (1971) *The Case of the Midwife Toad*. London: Hutchinson, reprinted by Picador.

Lasswell, H. (1951) The policy orientation. In D. Lerner and H. D. Lasswell, *The Policy Sciences*. Stanford: Stanford University Press.

Latham, E. (1953) *The Group Basis of Politics*. Ithaca: Cornell University Press.

Laumann, E. and Knoke, D. (1987) *The Organisational State*. Madison: University of Wisconsin Press.

Laumann, E., Knoke, D. and Yong-Hak, K. (1985) An organisational approach to state policy formation: a comparative study of energy and health domains. *American Sociological Review*, **50**: 1–19.

Laver, M. and Schofield, N. (1990) *Multiparty Government*. Oxford: Oxford University Press.

Lembruch, G. and Schmitter, P. (1982) *Patterns of Corporatist Policy-Making*. London: Sage.

Lertzman, K., Raynor J. and Wilson, J. (1996) Learning and change in the British Columbia forest policy sector. *Canadian Journal of Political Science*, **29**: 111– 33.

Lewin, L. (1991) *Self-Interest and Public Interest in Western Politics*. Oxford: Oxford University Press.

Lindblom, C. (1960) The science of 'muddling through'. *Public Administration Review*, **19**: 79–88.

Lindblom, C. (1968) *The Policy-Making Process*. Englewood Cliffs, N.J.: Prentice-Hall.

Lindblom, C. (1977) *Politics and Markets*. New York: Basic Books.

Linder, S. and Peters, B. Guy (1990) An institutional approach to the theory of policy-making: the role of guidance mechanisms in policy formulation. *Journal of Theoretical Politics*, **2**: 59–83.

Lipietz, A. (1988) *Choisir l'audace: une alternative pour le vingt et unième siècle*. Paris: La Découverte.

Lipietz, A. (1992) *Towards a New Economic Order: Post-Fordism, Democracy and Ecology*. Cambridge: Polity.

Lipsky, M. (1971) Street level bureaucracy and the analysis of urban reform. *Urban Affairs Quarterly*, **6**: 391– 409.

Lipsky, M. and Olson, D. (1977) *Commission Politics: The Processing of the Racial Crisis in America*. New Brunswick: Transaction Books.

Lowi, T. (1964) American business, public policy, case studies and political theory. *World Politics*, **16**: 677– 715.

Lowi, T. (1972) Four systems of policy, politics and choice. *Public Administration Review*, **32**: 298–310.

Maass, A. (1951) *Muddy Waters*. Cambridge, Mass.: Harvard University Press.

Mabileau, A. (1991) *Le Système local en France*. Paris: Montchrestien.

Madison, J., Hamilton, A. and Jay, J. (1788) *The Federalist Papers*. London: Penguin, 1987 edn.

Majone, G. (1989) *Evidence, Argument and Persuasion in the Policy Process*. New Haven: Yale University Press.

Malpass, P. and Murie, A. (1994) *Housing Policy and Practice*, 4th edn. Basingstoke: Macmillan.

March, J. and J. Olsen (1989) *Rediscovering Institutions.* New York: Free Press.

Marsh, D. (1995) Explaining Thatcherite policies: beyond uni-dimensional explanation. *Political Studies,* **43**: 595–613.

Marsh, D. and Rhodes, R. (eds) (1992a) *Policy Networks in British Government.* Oxford: Clarendon.

Marsh, D. and Rhodes, R. (eds) (1992b) *Implementing Thatcherite Policies.* Buckingham: Open University Press.

Marshall, G. (1984) *Constitutional Conventions: The Rules and Forms of Political Accountability.* Oxford: Clarendon.

Marx, K. and Engels, F. (1848) *The Communist Manifesto.* Reprinted in H. J. Laski (ed.) (1954) *The Communist Manifesto: A New Appreciation.* London: Allen and Unwin.

Mayhew, D. R. (1991) *Divided We Govern.* New Haven, Conn.: Yale University Press.

Mazmanian, D. and Sabatier, P. (eds) (1981) *Effective Policy Implementation.* Lexington, Mass.: D. C. Heath.

Miliband, R. (1969) *The State in Capitalist Society.* London: Weidenfeld and Nicolson.

Milner, H. (1994) *Social Democracy and Rational Choice: The Scandinavian Experience and Beyond.* London: Routledge.

Moynihan, D. P. (1969) *Maximum Feasible Misunderstanding: Community Action in the War on Poverty.* New York: Free Press.

Mullard, M. (1995) *Policy-Making in Britain.* London: Routledge.

Neustadt, R. E. (1960) *Presidential Power.* New York: Wiley.

Niskanen, W. (1971) *Bureaucracy and Representative Government.* Chicago: Aldine.

Nordhaus, W. (1975) The political business cycle. *Review of Economic Studies,* **62**: 169–90.

Nordlinger, E. A. (1981) *On the Autonomy of the Democratic State.* Cambridge, Mass.: Harvard University Press.

Norton, P. (1975) *Dissension in the House of Commons: Intra Party Dissent in House of Commons Divisions Lobbies, 1945–1974.* London: Macmillan.

Norton, P. (1980) *Dissension in the House of Commons, 1974–1979.* Oxford: Oxford University Press.

O'Connor, J. R. (1973) *The Fiscal Crisis of the State.* New York: St Martin's Press.

Offe, C. (1985) *Disorganised Capitalism.* Cambridge: Polity Press.

Olson, M. (1965) *The Logic of Collective Action.* Cambridge, Mass.: Harvard University Press.

Ostrom, E. (1990) *Governing the Commons: The Evolution of Institutions for Collective Action.* Cambridge: Cambridge University Press.

Ostrom, E. (1994) Constituting social capital and collective action. *Journal of Theoretical Politics,* **6**: 527–62.

Parsons, W. (1995) *Public Policy.* Aldershot: Edward Elgar.

Peters, B. G. (1993) *American Public Policy.* New Jersey: Chatham House.

Peters, B. G., Doughtie, J. and McCulloch, M. (1977) Types of democratic systems and types of public policy. *Comparative Politics,* **9**: 327–55.

Peterson, J. (1995) Policy networks and European Union policy making: a reply to Kassim. *Western European Politics,* **18**: 389–407.

Peterson, P. (1981) *City Limits.* Chicago: University of Chicago Press.

Petracca, M. (ed.) (1992) *The Politics of Interests.* Boulder, Col.: Westview.

Philpott, D. (1996) The possibilities of ideas. *Security Studies,* **5**: 183–96.

Picciotto, S. and Radice, H. (1973) Capital and state in the world economy. *Kapitalstaten,* **1**: 56–68.

Piven, F. F. and Cloward, R. (1979) *Poor People's Movements: Why They Succeed, How They Fail.* New York: Vintage.

Pressman, J. and Wildavsky, A. (1973) *Implementation.* Berkeley: University of California Press.

Putnam, R. (1993) *Making Democracy Work.* Princeton: Princeton University Press.

Quattrone, G. and Tversky, A. (1988) Contrasting rational and psychological analyses of political choice. *American Political Science Review,* **82**: 719–36.

Reich, R. (1988) *The Power of Public Ideas.* Cambridge, Mass.: Harvard University Press.

Rhodes, E. (1994) Do bureaucratic politics matter? Some disconfirming findings from the case of the US Navy. *World Politics,* **47**: 1–41.

Rhodes, R. A. W. (1986) *The National World of Local Government.* London: Allen and Unwin.

Rhodes, R. A. W. (1988) *Beyond Westminster and Whitehall.* London: Unwin Hyman.

Rhodes, R. A. W. (1992) Local government finance. In D. Marsh and R. A. W. Rhodes, *Implementing Thatcherite Policies.* Buckingham: Open University Press.

Rhodes, R. A. W. (1995) From prime ministerial power to core executive. In R. A. W. Rhodes and P. Dunleavy, *Prime Minister, Cabinet and Core Executive.* Basingstoke: Macmillan.

Rhodes, R. A. W. and Dunleavy, P. (1995) *Prime Minister, Cabinet and Core Executive.* Basingstoke: Macmillan.

Rhodes, R. A. W. and Marsh, D. (1994) Policy networks: defensive comments, modest claims and plausible research strategies. Paper given at the PSA annual conference, University of Swansea, 29–31 March.

Richardson, J. (ed.) (1982) *Policy Styles in Western Europe.* London: Allen and Unwin.

Richardson, J. (1996) Policy-making in the EU: interests, ideas and garbage cans of primeval soup. In J. Richardson (ed.) *European Union Power and Policy-Making.* London: Routledge.

Richardson, J. and Jordan, G. (1979) *Governing Under Pressure*. Oxford: Martin Robertson.

Richardson, J., Maloney, W. and Rüdig, G. (1992) The dynamics of policy change: lobbying and water privatisation. *Public Administration*, **70**: 157–75.

Riker, W. (1980) Implications from the disequilibrium of majority rule for the study of institutions. *American Political Science Review*, **74**: 432–46.

Riker, W. (1982) *Liberalism Against Populism*. Prospect Heights: Waveland Press.

Robson, W. A. (1948) *The Development of Local Government*. London: Allen and Unwin.

Rosati, J. (1981) Developing a systematic decision-making framework: bureaucratic politics in perspective. *World Politics*, **81**: 234–52.

Rose, R. (1980) *Do Parties Make a Difference?* London: Macmillan.

Rose, R. (1993) *Lesson-Drawing in Public Policy*. New Jersey: Chatham House.

Rose, R. and Davies, P. (1994) *Inheritance in Public Policy: Change Without Choice in Britain*. New Haven: Yale University Press.

Sabatier, P. (1986) Top-down and bottom-up approaches to implementation research: a critical analysis and suggested synthesis. *Journal of Public Policy*, **6**: 21– 48.

Sabatier, P. (1988) An advocacy coalition framework of policy change and the role of policy-orientated learning therein. *Policy Sciences*, **21**: 129–68.

Sabatier, P. (1991) Towards better theories of the policy process. *Political Science and Politics*, **24**: 147–56.

Sabatier, P. and Brasher, A. (1993) From vague consensus to clearly differentiated coalitions: environmental policy at Lake Tahoe. In P. Sabatier and H. C. Jenkins-Smith (eds) *Policy Change and Learning*. Boulder, Col.: Westview.

Sabatier, P. and Jenkins-Smith, H. C. (eds) (1993) *Policy Change and Learning*. Boulder, Col.: Westview.

Sabatier, P. and Jenkins-Smith, H. (1996) The advocacy coalition framework: an assessment. Paper to the annual meeting of the American Political Science Association, San Francisco, August.

Sanderson, J. B. (1961) The national smoke abatement society and the clean air act (1956). *Political Studies*, **9**: 236–53.

Savage, S., Atkinson, R. and Robins, L. (eds) (1994) *Public Policy in Britain*. New York: St Martin's Press.

Schattschneider, E. E. (1960) *The Semi-Sovereign People*. New York: Holt.

Schultz, K. (1995) The politics of the political business cycle. *British Journal of Political Science*, **25**: 79–99.

Schumpeter, J. (1939) *Business Cycles: A Theoretical, Historical and Statistical Analysis*. New York: McGraw Hill.

Schumpeter, J. (1942) *Capitalism, Socialism and Democracy*. London: Unwin, 1976 edn.

Scott, J. and Hughes, M. (1980) *The Anatomy of Scottish Capital*. London: Croom Helm.

Segal, J. (1997) Separation-of-powers games in the positive theory of justice. *American Political Science Review*, **91**: 28–44.

Shapiro, M. (1978) The Supreme Court: from Warren to Burger. In A. King (ed.) *The New American Political System*. Washington: AEI.

Sharpe, L. J. (1985) Central coordination and the policy network. *Political Studies*, **33**: 361–81.

Sharpe, L. J. and Newton, K. (1984) *Does Politics Matter?* Oxford: Oxford University Press.

Shepsle, K. (1979) Institutional arrangements and equilibrium in multi-dimensional voting models. *American Political Science Review*, **23**: 27–59.

Shepsle, K. and Weingast, K. (1981) Structure-induced equilibrium and legislative choice. *Public Choice*, **37**: 503–19.

Simon, H. (1957) *Administrative Behavior*, 2nd edn. New York: Free Press.

Skocpol, T. and Finegold, K. (1982) Capitalists farmers and workers in the New Deal. *Political Science Quarterly*, **97**: 255–78.

Smith, M. (1990) *The Politics of Agricultural Support in Britain*. Aldershot: Dartmouth.

Smith, M. (1993) *Pressure Power and Policy*. Hemel Hempstead: Harvester Wheatsheaf.

Steinmo, S. (1989) Political institutions and tax policy in the United States, Sweden and Britain. *World Politics*, **41**: 500–35.

Steinmo, S. (1993) *Taxation and Democracy*. New Haven: Yale University Press.

Steinmo, S., Thelen, S. K. and Longstreth, F. (eds) (1992) *Structuring Politics*. Cambridge: Cambridge University Press.

Stoker, G. (1989) Creating a local government for a post-Fordist society. In J. Stewart and G. Stoker (eds) (1989) *The Future of Local Government*. Basingstoke: Macmillan.

Stoker, G. (1991) *The Politics of Local Government*. Basingstoke: Macmillan.

Stone, C. (1989) *Regime Politics: Governing Atlanta 1946–1988*. Lawrence: University Press of Kansas.

Stone, D. (1988) *Policy Paradox and Political Reason*. Glenview: Scott Foresman and Co.

Stone, D. (1989) Causal stories and the formation of policy agendas. *Political Science Quarterly*, **104**: 281–300.

Streek, W. and Schmitter, P. (1991) From national corporatism to transnational pluralism: organised interests in the single European market. *Politics and Society*, **19**: 133–64.

Taylor, M. (1987) *The Possibility of Cooperation*. Cambridge: Cambridge University Press.

Thatcher, M. (1994) Regulatory reform in Britain and France: organisational structure and the extension of competition. *Journal of European Public Policy*, **1**: 441–64.

Throgmorton, J. A. (1991) The rhetoric of policy analysis. *Policy Sciences*, **24**: 153–79.

Truman, D. (1962) *The Governmental Process*. New York: Alfred Knopf.

Vickers, G. (1965) *The Art of Judgment*. London: Sage, 1995 reprint.

Vile, M. J. C. (1967) *Constitutionalism and the Separation of Powers*. Oxford: Clarendon Press.

Walkland, S. A. (1968) *The Legislative Process in Britain*. London: Allen and Unwin.

Ward, H. (1993) State exploitation, capital accumulation and the evolution of modes of regulation: a defence of bottom-line economism. Paper given to UK Political Studies Association, annual conference, Leicester.

Ward, H. (1995) Rational choice theory. In D. Marsh and G. Stoker (eds) *Theory and Methods in Political Science*. Basingstoke: Macmillan.

Ward, H. (1996) Game theory and the politics of global warming: the state of play and beyond. *Political Studies*, **44**: 850–71.

Ward, H. (1997) The possibility of an evolutionary explanation of the state's role in modes of regulation. In J. Stanyer and G. Stoker (eds) *Contemporary Political Studies*. Nottingham: Political Studies Association.

Ward, H. and John, P. (1997) Targeting benefits for electoral gain: constituency marginality and the distribution of grants to English local authorities. *Political Studies*, forthcoming.

Weaver, R. K. and Rockman B. A. (1993) *Do Institutions Matter?* Washington D.C.: Brookings Institution.

Weber, M. (1948) The social psychology of the world religions. Reprinted in H. H. Gerth and C. Wright Mills (eds) *From Max Weber*. London: Routledge and Kegan Paul.

Wildavsky, A. (1979) *Speaking Truth to Power*. Boston: Little Brown.

Wildavsky, A. (1986) *Budgeting: A Comparative Theory of the Budgeting Processes*. New Brunswick, N.J.: Transaction Books.

Wilensky, H. (1975) *The Welfare State and Equality*. Berkeley: University of California Press.

Wilks, S. and Wright, M. (1987) *Comparative Government–Industry Relations*. Oxford: Clarendon.

Wilson, J. Q. (1980) *The Politics of Regulation*. New York: Basic Books.

Winkler, J. (1976) Corporatism. *Archives Européenes de Sociologie*, **17**: 100–36.

Wistow, G. (1992) The health service policy community: professionals preeminent or under challenge. In D. Marsh and R. Rhodes (eds) *Policy Networks in British Government*. Oxford: Clarendon.

Wood, B. Dan (1988) Principal, bureaucrats, and responsiveness in clean air enforcements. *American Political Science Review*, **82**: 213–34.

Wood, B. Dan and Waterman, R. (1993) The dynamics of political control of the bureaucracy. *American Political Science Review*, **85**: 801–28.

Worms, J.-P. (1966) Le préfet et ses notables. *Sociologie de Travail*, **8**: 249–75.

Wright, M. (1988) Policy community, policy network and comparative industrial policies. *Political Studies*, **36**: 593–612.

Yanow, D. (1996) *How Does a Policy Mean?* Washington: Georgetown University Press.

Yee, A. (1996) The causal effects of ideas on policies. *International Organisation*, **50**: 69–108.

Name Index

Subject Index